REDISCOVERING
SAINT PATRICK

Patrick's Place of Origins
And Royal Family

Marcus Losack

ISBN-13: 9781730759192

The Saint Patrick of Ancient Ages.

CONTENTS

Acknowledgements..*i*

Geographical References ....*iii*

1. REDISCOVERING PATRICE.. 1

2. A DOORWAY IN TIME.. 11

3. PATRICK'S CONFESSION... 22

4. THE UNKNOWN APOSTLE.. 41

5. OUR MAN IN ARMAGH.. 59

6. ILLUMINATING MANUSCRIPTS 80

7. THE WOOD OF FOCLUT.. 97

8. PIRATES OF THE MARE OCCIDENTALE.......................... 125

9. ISLES OF THE TYRRHENE SEA...................................... 135

10. MARTIN OF TOURS 152

11. BRITAIN OR BRITTANY?.. 175

12. SAINT PATRICK'S FAMILY 209

Conclusions...*232*

A Possible Chronology For Saint Patrick..............................*249*

Historical Background..*250*

Bibliography *254*

About The Author...*261*

Acknowledgements

The publishers are grateful for permission to use the following materials in the publication of this book: Translations of St Patrick's *Confession* and *Letter to Coroticus* are by John Luce (2009), revised by Marcus Losack (2011) incorporating elements from N. J. White (1905), Ludwig Bieler (1962), Daniel Conneely (1979), Pádraig McCarthy (2001), © John Luce and Marcus Losack, 2011. Passages from Dom Morice *Histoire de Bretagne* are translated by Francine Bernier; extracts from Joseph Viel *La Gouesnière et Bonaban* (Dinan, 1912) translated by Francine Bernier and Christophe Saint-Eloi. Maps of Roman Britain and the settlement in Brittany at the time of the rebellion of Magnus Maximus (385 CE) and the Bay of Mont St Michel including the ancient Forest of Quokelunde are by Kevin O'Kelly, Alan Oram and Marcus Losack, based on the work of L'Abbé Manet and René Henry. The map of La Forêt de Quokelunde and coastline before the inundation of the Bay of Mont St Michel by the sea in 709 CE is by René Henry, *Au Peril de la Mer*, © Éditions Découvrance, La Rochelle, 2006. The aerial photograph on page 250 is reproduced with the kind permission of Château de Bonaban. Genealogical tables for the early kings of Brittany are from Piérre Le Baude, Dom Morice and M. Daru. A number of other charts have been adapted from various genealogical tables compiled by Laurence Gardner and published in *The Bloodline of the Holy Grail* (New York, 2001). These have been greatly simplified, showing only the main lines of descent and succession that are relevant to the origins of St Patrick. If we have failed to acknowledge or trace any copyright material, we offer our sincere apologies.

Marcus Losack, 2018

Geographical References

Alba: An ancient name for Scotland.

Britannia: (Latin, singular) The Roman name for Britain.

Britanniis: (Latin, plural) The name given for St Patrick's homeland. Trans: 'in the Britains' 'among the Britons' or 'in Brittany'.

Bannavem Tiburniae: The place where Calpurnius (Patrick's father) owned the estate from which St Patrick was taken captive.

Caledonia: The Roman name for northern Britain, now Scotland.

Gaul: A region of Empire on the continent.

Silua Uoclut/Vocluti: (Latin) Known in Irish as 'Fochlad'. Wood of Foclut. A place that St Patrick remembered in a disturbing dream when he heard the 'Voice of the Irish' calling him to return to them.

Tyrrhene/Tyrrenian Sea: Refers to the Bay of St Malo between the Isles de Chaussey, Tombelaine and Mont St Michel.

Isles of the Tyrrhene Sea: Islands where there were early forms of monastic community in the Bay of Mont St Michel.

Nemthor (Naem Tor/Holy Tours: Recorded in later documents as the place where St Patrick was born.

Sabhall: (Gaelic) Trans: 'Barn'. The place where St Patrick founded his first church in Ireland. Now known as Saul, near Downpatrick, Co. Down.

Armorica: The name applied by the Romans to Brittany.

Armoric Letha: A coastal region of Armorica. Identified in some of the ancient sources as the place where Patrick was taken captive. Also known as 'Letha' or 'Lethania Britannia'.

La Forêt de Quokelunde: (French) An ancient forest in Brittany. Local traditions record that Irish pirates crept up through this forest before they attacked the Calpurnius estate at Bannavem Tiburniae and took St Patrick captive.

The personality, birthplace and mission of St Patrick constitute a link between ourselves and our sister island, appealing to the deepest sympathies of religion and consanguinity, which I should be loath to see dissevered, and which I hope, therefore, may resist the rudest assaults of sceptical criticism, although this and every other consideration must give way to the voice of truth.

It is impossible that all of which has been handed down to us as to the existence and actions of such a personage should be a mere fiction – that a nation should have been deceived as to the most important event of its history – the introduction of Christianity – and the man who was the principal instrument in the work; or that it should have made itself, either voluntarily or involuntarily, the agent of deception.

St Patrick has an abiding presence whose memory is in the hearts of millions; with his spirit we may still hold communion through the literary remains, scanty as they are, which he has bequeathed to us.

J. H. TUKNER, M.A.
SCOTLAND, 1872

CHAPTER ONE

REDISCOVERING PATRICE

Sometimes the meaning of a journey
Is unknown to the traveller. [1]

As we drove through old wrought-iron gates along a tree-lined avenue towards the front entrance of the hotel there was a moment of sudden anxiety and disappointment. We expect a French château to be luxurious, extravagant and well-kept but this one at first sight seemed neglected. First impressions are notoriously unreliable. I had travelled to France with a friend to research some of the sacred sites associated with the Celtic Tradition in Brittany, in preparation for a pilgrimage planned for the following year.

The hotel had been booked online at the last minute, simply to provide a break from work and celebrate a jubilee birthday. All the tower rooms at the château have high ceilings and spectacular views of the grounds and surrounding forest. I noticed a coat of arms at the

---

[1] Dietrich Bonhoeffer, *Letters and Papers from Prison* (Minneapolis, 2010).

1

top of a sheet of headed note paper which had been left on the table. Written in French with an English translation, it provided basic information for guests about the château's history and local significance. What I read next came as a complete and total surprise that would change my image and understanding of St Patrick forever.

> The first castle or rather fortress that was built here dates from the Roman period, during the fourth century. At that time, this place was called Bonavenna (or Bonabes) de Tiberio. It belonged to a Scottish prince, Calpurnius, who had come here to avoid Saxon forces who were invading Britain... One night, Irish pirates arrived in nearby Cancale.
>
> They spread through the Wood of Quokelunde, which stretched under Gouesnière-Bonaban as far as Plerguèr. Armed with pikes and axes, they slaughtered the prince and all his family. His property was looted and the castle burned to the ground ... Only his youngest son, Patrice, survived from this slaughter. He was taken captive to Ireland.
>
> There he looked after sheep and learned the language of the country of which he became the oracle and the disciple.[2]

I have read a lot of books about the Irish saints and have visited many of the ancient, sacred sites associated with St Patrick in Ireland, but before arriving at this hotel I had no idea whatsoever that Patrick had any connections with Brittany. I had to read this information several times to process the enormity of what was being said, as the significance of these claims began to sink in. Could this really be the place where St Patrick once lived, before he was taken captive and sold as a slave in Ireland?

The only reliable historical information we have about St Patrick is contained in his own writings. Patrick wrote two letters, which scholars have dated to the fifth century.[3] No 'autographed' originals

---

[2] Historical information provided for guests at Château de Bonaban, 35350 St Malo, Brittany (2013).

[3] For a full description and history of the texts, see The Royal Irish Academy website *Confessio.ie*. Also Ludwig Bieler, *Libri Epistolarum Sancti Patricii Episcopi* (Dublin, 1993), p. 7 ff. Various other English translations of St Patrick's writings can be found in Ludwig Bieler, *The Works of St Patrick* (New York, 1952) and Daniel Conneely, *The Letters of St Patrick* (Maynooth, 1993), edited posthumously by Patrick Bastible. For a new translation rendering 'Britanniis' as Brittany: John Luce

have survived, but these manuscripts are acknowledged as authentic copies of the two original letters written by St Patrick. The arguments for authenticity and dating to the fifth century include the mention of Decurion (an employee in the Roman administration) use of the words 'Britanniis' or 'Britanniae', quotes from biblical texts that existed before Jerome's Vulgate edition and St Patrick's reference to the practice of Christians in Roman Gaul, sending ransom money to the pagan Franks to free Christians held captive as slaves (LC:10).

This must have been written after they crossed the Rhine and settled in Gaul in 428 CE but while the Franks were still pagan before 496 CE when they followed their king, Clovis, into the Church.[4]

In his *Confession*, St Patrick mentions the name of a place where his father owned an estate, which he called 'Bannavem Tiburniae' in Latin. One day, when he was only sixteen years old, the estate was attacked by pirates.

Patrick was taken captive to Ireland, where he was sold as a slave. These are St Patrick's words, based on the oldest surviving copy of his *Confession* found in the *Book of Armagh*, a tenth-century Irish manuscript now preserved in Trinity College, Dublin:

My name is Patrick, a sinner without a formal education, the least of all the faithful and greatly despised in the eyes of many. My father was Calpurnius (a Decurion) the son of Potitus, an elder in the village of Bannavem Tiburniae; he had a small estate nearby from where I was taken captive. I was about sixteen years of age.[5]

Early Irish and Breton sources say his father and mother, Calpurnius and Conchessa (who is said to have been 'French' and a close relative of St Martin of Tours), were both killed during the attack, together with many others. The place where this happened has never been identified, its precise location lost to historical memory in the years after St Patrick's death.

---

and Marcus Losack, *The Letters of Saint Patrick* (2015).

[4] N. J. White, *A Translation of the Latin Writings of St Patrick* (London, 1918).

[5] Confession 1 (C:1).

Countless books have been written about St Patrick over the centuries but we still don't know where he came from and, therefore, who he really was. Most scholars insist he came from somewhere in Britain, either Strathclyde in Scotland, Wales, Cumbria, the Bristol Channel or even Glastonbury in England. The uncertainty about St Patrick's place of origin has never been resolved. It is one of the great unsolved mysteries surrounding his life and the unknown origins of the early Irish church. This is what made the information provided for guests at Château de Bonaban so intriguing.

I felt that we had stumbled across a significant, local tradition about St Patrick in Brittany, but which for some reason had never found its way into the any of the countless books on St Patrick that had been written by English and Irish speaking scholars. The names mentioned in the information provided by the Château were fascinating to me. 'Bonaban' and 'Bonabes de Tiberio' were clearly recognisable as another form of the name for Patrick's home which he called 'Bannavem Tiburniae' in Latin but there was something even more intriguing about the information provided by the hotel.

Could the Breton Forest of Quokelunde be the same as the Irish Wood of Foclut that St Patrick remembered in his dream when he heard the 'Voice of the Irish' calling him to return? This is how Patrick described the dream he had about this wood:

> One night in a dream, I saw a man whose name was Victor, dressed as if coming from Ireland and carrying many letters. He gave me one of them to read and as I did, I heard the *Voice of the Irish*. In that same moment as I was reading I thought I could hear the voice of those around the Wood of Foclut, which is close beside the Western Sea. It was as if they were crying out to me with one voice, 'We beg you, O holy youth, to come and walk once more among us.' I woke up suddenly feeling that my heart was broken and I could read no further.[6]

I spent a few moments contemplating the possible implications, if these claims about St Patrick and his family were true. There was a feeling of being drawn into a tangled web of history and touched by

---

[6] C:23

the hidden hand of destiny. Could it be possible that both these places that were mentioned by St Patrick in his Confession - Bannavem Tiburniae and The Wood of Foclut - were right here under our feet, in the grounds of the château?

Local geography is consistent with the story preserved at Château Bonaban when it describes how Patrick was taken captive. The pirates are said to have landed at nearby Cancale and crept up through the wood called Quokelunde before they attacked the estate where Patrick and his family were living. The Château is built on a very ancient site close to the sea where remains from the late Roman period have already been discovered. It would have been accessible and vulnerable to attacks by Irish pirates.

If the local tradition provided for guests staying at Château de Bonaban was true, this would have enormous implications for our traditional understanding of St Patrick and the origins of the early Irish Church. Any plans made for the next day now had to be cancelled. Local research was required in the hope of finding some historical evidence to support the château's claim to fame.

After breakfast the next morning we decided to visit St Malo, the nearest large town, hoping to find a book or perhaps an old map to verify the names. Imagine the feeling of surprise when we saw a large sign on the roadside.

The name 'Quokelunde' appeared again, not as a forest this time but as part of an advertisement for local tourist accommodation.

In *Macbeth*, Shakespeare asks the question, 'What's in a name?'

It was as if someone had just dropped a billboard from the skies saying: 'TRUST THIS SIGN – THE QUEST IS ON'. 'Quokelunde' was obviously a name with local significance in Brittany. In Ireland, historical sites can often be identified from the original Irish or Gaelic name, usually included on maps but also on local road signs. For example, the name 'Kildare' comes from the Irish *Cill Dara* which means 'the church of oak' (*cill* = church and *dar* = oak). The village called Saul, near Downpatrick, County Down in Northern Ireland comes from the Gaelic *Sabhall* which means 'a barn'.

According to an ancient tradition, when St Patrick returned to Ireland as an apostle the first church he founded was in a barn given to him by a local chieftain. This is preserved in the ancient Irish

(Gaelic) name of the village. Place names can sometimes provide the oldest reliable evidence, preserving the location of an ancient, historical site. It would be important to try and find out whether the forest called 'Quokelunde' also had an ancient pedigree.

As we followed the coast road towards St Malo, the ocean was visible most of the way, stretching out beyond the horizon to the west. Ireland was out there somewhere, buried in the mist. Passing through one of the gates that lead into the old, walled city we knew it was like looking for a needle in a haystack.

Just as we were about to leave empty-handed from a shop that specialised in old maps, the owner recommended a bookshop called Bibliothèque Le Môle, which we discovered a few minutes later, tucked neatly away among old alleyways and narrow, cobbled streets. This shop was dark inside, like Aladdin's cave. Books were strewn all over tables and floors.

Having explained in very inadequate French what we were looking for, the owner, M. Duquesnoy, immediately checked his computer for titles. Then he made a telephone call and beckoned us to follow him outside before leading us through a labyrinth of back alleys to the local municipal library, Bibliothèque Municipale de St Malo, on the Rue D'Alsace. He whisked us upstairs to meet the assistant librarian, Mme Sophie Ellvard. After some brave attempts at conversation in French she disappeared but then returned a few minutes later with five or six old books saying, 'I think you might find what you need in here.' We sat down at a reading desk and started taking notes.

It did not take long to find what we were looking for.

St Malo had been almost completely destroyed by bombs during the Second World War but the town and surrounding countryside has an ancient history. In Roman times it was called 'Aleth', the strategic site of a military base or *tiburnia* for the Legion of Mars.[7] This might explain why St Patrick linked the two words *Bannavem* and *Tiburniae*. In Celtic languages the word *Bannavem* or *Bonaban* can be interpreted etymologically as the 'foot' (or 'mouth') of a river. In Gaelic, *bun* (*ban*,

---

[7] Bertrand Robidue, *Histoire et Panorama d'un Beau Pays* (Rennes, 1953), p. 60. See also *Cambridge Ancient History, XII: The Crisis of Empire, AD 193–337* (Cambridge, 2005), p. 259.

bon, bonn) means 'sole' of a shoe or 'foot' and *am, aven* or *avon* is a river. [8] At the time of St Patrick, a tributary of the River Rance flowed from Aleth towards the present site of the Château.

It could, therefore, be correctly understood as existing near 'the foot' of this river, accessible by ship from the coast, vulnerable to an attack by pirates. Such etymological derivations have been used to support the claims of Strathclyde, the Bristol Channel and even Boulogne as the place St Patrick came from, but it can also be applied to the ancient site of Château de Bonaban as Aleth or St Malo stand at the 'mouth' of the River Rance where there was an important naval base and a military camp or 'tiburnia' for the Legion of Mars in the late Roman period, towards the end of the fourth century.

Tiburnia is a Latin name applied by the Romans to a military base in Gaul.

Etymology can be intriguing. In Greek, for example, the name 'Aleth' means 'true, nothing concealed, real'. In classical mythology, Lethe was a river in Hades whose water caused forgetfulness of the past for those who drank from it. In Greek, *lethe* means forgetfulness, oblivion, morbid drowsiness or a continued and profound sleep, from which a person finds it difficult to be awakened; a state of inaction or indifference. What a great omen and such an appropriate one for the quest to recover the truth about St Patrick!

The next discovery suggested that local traditions about St Patrick presented to guests at Château de Bonaban could have more than a shamrock of truth. In Roman times a large oak forest that was sacred to the Druids and early Christian monastic communities stretched along the coast from St Malo to Mont St Michel. An ancient forest called 'Quokelunde' definitely existed here in the fifth century. It was part of a more extensive and well-known forest called the 'Desert of Scissy', taking its name from the large number of hermits who lived there. One French writer described it as a *Thébaid Celtique* or 'Celtic Desert', referring to a place in Egypt where desert monasticism originated in the fourth century. [9] Then we found the source which

---

[8] Irish/English online Dictionary and Buillet, *Dictionary Celtique*.

[9] Robidue, *Histoire et Panorama d'un Beau Pays* (Rennes, 1953), ch. 1, pp. 14–22. Robidue quotes other sources for the information about Patrick and Calpurnius including P. H. Morice, *Histoire de Bretagne* (Paris, 1742), i, pp. 284–386, n. 30.

had been used to inform guests at the château. It was tucked away on page fifty-five of a wonderful book called *Histoire et Panorama d'un Beau Pays* (The History and Panorama of a Beautiful Country), by the French historian Robidue.

The author gives credit to a Breton antiquarian for being the first to identify Bonaban as the place from which St Patrick was taken captive.[10]

> Scottish historians hold Dumbarton to be the birthplace of St Patrick. M. de Gerville identified Bannavem Tiburniae, the geographical designation given in Latin in St Patrick's *Confession*, as Bonaban, and the place of his birth. He believed this to be so without doubt, a view which is shared with unanimity by all the local Breton historians, except Lobineau.[11]

Having given credit to M. de Gerville, Robidue continues his account. The following passage has been translated and paraphrased from the original French. This text provides more detailed information about St Patrick's family and their connections with Brittany, providing an historical context for the local tradition discovered at Château de Bonaban.

> It was in 388 AD, when the Roman general Magnus Maximus withdrew his legions from Britain, that St Patrick's family moved here from Scotland. Maximus was hoping to become Emperor and came to Brittany with many soldiers under his command …
>
> As Britain was left without protection, St Patrick's father, Calpurnius, who was a Scottish Prince, also came here with his family. He was cousin to Conan-Meriadec, the legendary king of Wales, who gave him a

---

[10] Robidue, *Histoire*, p. 54, n. 1. See Charles de Gerville, *Lettres sur la communication entre les Deux Bretagnes* (Valognes, 1844). Charles de Gerville 1769–1854) was a Breton antiquarian, famous for being the first to apply the name 'Roman' or 'Romanesque' as an architectural term. M. de Gerville not only identified the site of Château de Bonaban as Patrick's 'Bannavem Tiburniae', he claims St Patrick was born there.

[11] Robidue, *Histoire*, p. 54 ff. See also *Les Memoires de Gallet*, ch. 1, n. 15 and M. Trebutien, *Le Mont St Michel: au Peril de la Mer* (Caen, 1841).

large fertile estate on lands next to the sea. Local tradition claims it was from here St Patrick was taken captive to Ireland, when pirates attacked the family estate at Bonaban.[12]

We thanked the librarian for her helpfulness and walked outside to the busy streets, knowing that enough had been achieved for one day. It was definitely time for coffee and a visit to the local crêperie! We needed some time to reflect on the strange experiences which had occurred over the previous twenty-four hours. The situation we found ourselves in was impossible to explain rationally. Surely, these events could not have happened by chance? Having found the historical source for a local tradition that St Patrick was taken captive from Brittany, there was a strong sense of what can only be described as 'historical intuition' that an even greater story was going to be revealed.

As experienced pilgrimage leaders familiar with many other sacred sites, we knew it was important not to leave without giving thanks and honouring the stories associated with this place and memories sacred to its past; so the following morning, after loading suitcases into the car in preparation for an early departure, we took a short walk through the grounds of the château, past the beautiful lake, into the forest, looking for an appropriate place simply to pray. We lit two small votive candles, then gathered some wild flowers and placed them under the boughs of an inviting old oak tree.

Among all the trees of the forest, the oak was especially sacred to the Celts, who believed it contained memories of the past. Had these particular oak trees grown from the seeds of others, the ancestors of older trees that existed in this forest at the time of St Patrick?

The thought that St Patrick had been here before had touched our hearts deeply, not least because of what he may have suffered in this forest as a teenager if this really was the place where he was taken captive.

We gave thanks for the *Lives of St Patrick* and his family and prayed for the healing of memories. There was an almost tangible, mystical sense of God's presence as if St Patrick had appeared through the

---

[12] Robidue, *Histoire*, p. 54 ff.

trees and was standing beside us as we savoured these moments in deep, peaceful silence.

As we walked back through the forest the sun broke through in majesty with golden rays, illuminating the path with bright light and the trees with halos of amber. Having been reserved online at the last minute without prior knowledge of what was to be expected, the short stay at Château de Bonaban had certainly provided some very unexpected surprises.

Driving back along the tree-lined avenue and through those old wrought-iron gates, feeling a mixture of joy and yet sorrow for having to leave this sacred and mysterious place, we talked philosophically about the dangers of jumping to conclusions, making rash judgements and how first impressions can be so notoriously unreliable.

As St Patrick knew so well from his own experience, sometimes we never can tell where destiny and the hand of providence may be leading us.

CHAPTER TWO

A DOORWAY IN TIME

Sometimes the present creates the future by
Breaking the shackles of the past; but it is equally
True that sometimes the past creates the future by
Breaking the shackles of the present. [13]

After the strange and unexpected events that took place in Brittany the search for evidence to verify the Château's claim to fame quickly turned into a sacred and determined quest. There was a feeling of compulsion to investigate this matter further and try to establish the truth. Could evidence be found elsewhere to support the local traditions about St Patrick preserved at Château de Bonaban? What could never have been imagined back home in Ireland is how challenging the quest would be and how many more intriguing surprises would slowly but surely be revealed.

---

[13] Fred Turner, Professor of Arts and Humanities, Texas University.

In his own writings, St Patrick provides very little information about his place of origins or family background. Those places he does mention have never been securely identified. Despite the huge number of books written about him – enough to fill a whole library – we still did not know where he came from and, therefore, who he really was, until now. The fifth century has been called 'the lost century' because there are very few historical records for this period.

This has always presented great difficulties for enquiring scholars.

Serious historical uncertainties surround most of the traditional claims made about St Patrick.

At the same time, this is what makes the study so challenging.

If Patrick came from Britain as most writers insist, or from Brittany as many of the early Breton historians and some Irish writers claimed, then the first step is to find out what was happening in those regions at that time. What were the historical circumstances that may have shaped Patrick's life? Only by entering St Patrick's world can we begin to appreciate the context in which his letters were written, which in turn might help to disentangle the threads of legend and tradition which have been woven together in so many of the claims that have been made about him.

The dates of St Patrick's birth and death are uncertain. Patrick does not mention specific dates. 385 CE is the approximate date for his birth. 461 CE is traditionally given as the year of his death. The ancient Irish Annals mention various dates, with inherent contradictions and uncertainties. If we can understand the historical context into which he was born and lived his life, this will help shed light on aspects of his biography.

To further this inquiry, it is necessary to step back through a doorway in time and explore some of the key historical events that were taking place around the time of St Patrick. This beckons a return to the late fourth century and the Roman world into which St Patrick was born. A series of events were about to unfold that must have had a dramatic impact on St Patrick's life and destiny; they would change the whole future course of European history.

Europe and the fall of Rome

In the closing decades of the fourth century, the Roman Empire was on the brink of collapse. From the time of St Patrick's birth and for several decades afterwards, the coastal regions of Britain and north-west Gaul descended into military chaos through local rebellions, barbarian invasions, political instability and piracy. Military and economic resources were stretched beyond their limits and security was deteriorating rapidly. Ireland stood on the margins of Europe and therefore was not subject to such attacks, apart from occasional raids from Britain. For the seven years St Patrick was held captive as a slave in Ireland, this was probably a safer place to be than his homeland.

Around the middle of the fourth century, when Patrick's parents were probably still teenagers, Germanic tribes had intensified attacks on the northern frontier of the Empire. Incursions were frequent. National security was undermined by local rebellions. Roman generals hungry for power plotted with their enemies, the Barbarians.

Regional uprisings were common, especially in Britain and Gaul.

In 350 CE, Julian was appointed by the Emperor Constantius II as Caesar over the Western Provinces in efforts by the imperial authorities to restore security. Known as Julian 'the Apostate', he reigned as Emperor from 361–363 CE and was a member of the Constantine dynasty.[14]

Magnus Maximus (340–388 CE) was commander of the Roman legions in Britain. He must have been concerned about the rapidly deteriorating military situation and the soldiers under his command observed with increasing alarm, various developments taking place on the continent, including security issues and Julian's support for a return to 'pagan' traditions.

Magnus was related to the Imperial House of Constantine, a powerful dynasty which had ruled the Empire only a few years before when the Empire was more secure and prosperous. This family had already produced several Emperors including Constantius Chlorus (306 CE) and Constantine the Great (312–337 CE), whose official recognition and acceptance of Christianity generated great wealth and

---

[14] W. F. Skene, *Celtic Scotland: A History of Ancient Alban* (Edinburgh, 1886).

prestige for the Church. Constantine was succeeded by his son Constans (337–350 CE), followed by two more Emperors carrying the same name.[4] Under Constantine, the Empire was divided into four 'dioceses', to correspond with two Emperors and two Caesars. Each was placed under a senior officer, called the Praetorian Prefect.[15]

As Barbarian attacks became more frequent and severe, memories of those 'golden days' of Constantine the Great must have been forefront in many minds, not least those in Britain who held to an ancient belief that members of this particular family had a divine right to imperial rule. When security deteriorated even further, the legions in Britain decided the Empire would be better served under the leadership of Magnus Maximus and acted swiftly to secure their ambitions. Britain was one of the strongest, wealthiest regions of the Roman Empire. Perhaps the British felt they alone could save it from impending disaster? Other factors may also have been significant.

According to a Welsh legend known as the 'Dream of Macsen Wledig', a deliberate plan to further the claims of Britain to imperial rule had been orchestrated when Maximus was invited by the British aristocracy to marry Helen or Ellen, daughter of the high king of Britain, Eudes (Eudaf Hen). This is said to have been an arranged marriage through which Britain hoped to provide an Emperor in the west. Macsen Wledig is the Welsh name given for Magnus Maximus. The title 'Wledig' means a ruling leader.[16]

Helen's identity is controversial. Carrying the same name as Helena, the mother of Constantine the Great, she was related to the House of Constantine. It is not unreasonable to think of this as a sacred or 'holy' bloodline. Roman Emperors were considered divine, even when they were Christians. Through this marriage, Maximus inherited a place within a British royal family, related to the House of Constantine.

Such actions would not have been viewed as abnormal. There had been a long history of rebellion and 'usurpation' in Britain and Gaul against the ruling Emperors. Magnus was only the latest in a long line

---

[15] Skene, *Celtic Scotland*, p. 92 ff.

[16] David Nash Ford, *Early British Kingdoms* [website] <www.earlybritishkingdoms.com/bios/maximus.html>.

of Roman commanders encouraged by supporters in Britain to challenge the established authorities.[17]

In 383 CE, Maximus was clothed with imperial purple by the soldiers under his command before they crossed the Channel into Gaul, determined to seize power. His name alone carried power.

In Latin, Magnus Maximus means 'the greatest of the great'. In the context of these imperial ambitions Magnus had much to live up to because of this name and the noble blood that flowed through his veins.

The British appear to have believed they had God on their side. This can be confirmed from a reliable contemporary source, the *Life of St Martin of Tours* by Sulpitius Severus. According to Severus, Maximus told St Martin that 'he had not of his own accord assumed the sovereignty'. He had simply 'defended by arms the sovereign necessities of the Empire'.[18]

The Latin phrase used by Severus – *regni necessitatem* – is significant. It implies a tradition of sacred kingship in Britain linked, at least in part, to the House of Constantine. It can be translated as the sovereign necessities (or requirements for divine rule) within the Empire. Severus confirms this when he tells us that Maximus had to pay regard to this expectation which had been imposed on him by the soldiers 'according to the divine appointment'.

Maximus is often referred to as a 'usurper' just as rivals in a disputed Papacy are called 'antipopes'. The reality of political, military and religious life within the Empire at this time was far too complex for stereotypes. The rebellion was viewed as a usurpation and gross act of treason by Imperial families ruling on the content and Maximus has been demonised in most historical records. Hence the significance of his rebellion has been overlooked or neglected, not least in terms of its significance for providing an historical context for St Patrick's biography and the life of St Patrick's family.

Gibbon acknowledged how complex the political situation was at this time, especially the conflict and rivalry between Maximus and

---

[17] Peter Heather, *The Fall of the Roman Empire: A New History* (London, 2005).

[18] Sulpicius Severus, 'Life of St Martin' in *The Nicene and Post Nicene Fathers*, eds Philip Schaff and Henry Wace (New York, 1894), xi, p. 13, n. 1.

Theodosius, the Emperor in the East who had been appointed by Gratian and Valentinian. Gratian was only twenty years old and caused public scandal and great offence to the army because he dressed as a barbarian. He 'frequently showed himself to the soldiers and people with the dress and arms, the long bow, sounding quiver and the fur garments of a Scythian warrior.'[19]

The rebellion came to a head when Gratian, one of the incumbent Emperors in the west, was executed by soldiers loyal to Maximus. Gratian's brother, Valentinian, had to flee for his life but managed to return with the support of Theodosius, Emperor in the East. In an effort to make peace, Theodosius brokered a treaty with Maximus from 383–388 CE.

The British had set their sights on imperial rule and through rapid, successful military advances they had now achieved it. As the newly installed Emperor of the West, Magnus Maximus quickly established his centre of command at the royal palace in Trier, the former residence of the Emperors Gratian and Valentinian. In many ways, Trier was more important than Rome at this time. Strategically, it was the capitol for imperial administration. From there, the Romans monitored operations along the Rhine, guarding the northern frontiers against the Barbarians.

Maximus had gained a reputation for ruthlessness, which gave Theodosius no reason to trust him. The decisive moment came at Aquileia in Italy, in September 389 CE. Maximus was marching towards Rome with his British and Gallic supporters. If he had gained victory in this battle he would have been crowned Emperor of Rome. As the 'First Lady' of Empire, his wife, Ellen, would have become one of the richest and most powerful women on the planet. But this particular period of British imperialism was to be short lived.

Less than five years after crossing from Britain to initiate this rebellion, the British were defeated. Magnus was arrested and executed immediately by soldiers loyal to Theodosius, beheaded at the third milestone from Aquileia. In the same year his son Victor was killed in Gaul. This marked the end of an era for the House of Constantine.

---

[19] Gibbon, E., *Decline and Fall of the Roman Empire*, 8 vols (London, 1862), iii, p. 358.

Imperial rulers would think twice before ever trusting the British again.

When the rebellion was launched, forces loyal to Maximus appear to have attacked on two fronts. Some British forces landed at the mouth of the Rhine. According to several early Breton historians, others landed in Brittany at the mouth of the River Rance, using the strategic and fortified Roman port at Aleth (St Malo) where they enlisted local support and consolidated the rebellion. This is a significant issue for Patrick's biography, to which we will return.

The political and religious situation which existed from 385–432 CE in the north and western coastal regions of the Empire created a series of events which probably had a significant influence on Patrick's life and destiny. After the legions crossed into Gaul with Maximus, Britain was left without military defence, vulnerable to attacks from the Picts in the north and Irish to the west.

Rebellions had been taking place in Britain and Gaul for a long time before Magnus Maximus came to power and they did not end with his death. Gibbon records that, after Maximus, Marcus was placed on the throne as lawful Emperor of Britain and the West although 'the Latins' were ignorant of this fact.[20] This is not surprising; Nennius describes the situation which existed between Britain and Rome at this time as a war.[21]

The breakdown in communications also resulted in a lack of reliable historical records. After the execution of Maximus, chaos ruled throughout the western Empire. Britain was left in a vulnerable state for the next forty years, denuded of its soldiers and military defences. This is confirmed by Gildas, who speaks of those left in Britain as a 'wretched remnant' who made a desperate appeal to the Roman Consul, Aetius, for support.[22]

From 390–405 CE Rome had tried to bolster its defences in Britain and Gaul but the Roman navy was struggling to contain piracy in the

---

[20] Gibbon, *DFRE*, iv, p. 54, n. 95.

[21] Nennius, 'History of the Britons' in *Six Old English Chronicles*, ed. J. A. Giles (London, 1858), p. 29.

[22] 'The Works of Gildas' in *Six Old English Chronicles*, ed. J. A. Giles (London, 1868) p. 307.

Iccian Sea, the name given to the stretch of water between what is now Ireland, the south-west coast of England and France. In 405 CE the situation was so serious that the Roman legions in Gaul were withdrawn to defend Italy, the heartland of the Empire. The legions in Britain, strengthened after the execution of Maximus, were also withdrawn in 406 CE in a final effort to save Rome.

This left Britain and Gaul with no defence. Constantine took control of power in 407 CE and subdued Spain in 408 CE but the military situation was very unstable and security deteriorated rapidly. Britain and Brittany became more 'independent' at this time. Gibbon mentions another revolt in 409 CE and says 'the independence of Britain and Armorica was soon confirmed by Honorious, the lawful Emperor of the West'. Unrest continued from 409–413 CE.

Both regions took responsibility for their own security in the face of increasing attacks from the Barbarians. Whether St Patrick came from Britain or Brittany, both places were dramatically affected by these historical events.

The period between Magnus's push to become Emperor from 383–388 CE, the Barbarian invasions of 405 CE and the fall of Rome in 409 must have been a critical time for St Patrick and his family.[23] For some, it must have seemed as though the end of the world was nigh. That which could never have been imagined now became reality.

In his book, *How the Irish Saved Civilization*, Thomas Cahill describes very dramatically how events unfolded on the night of 31 December 406 CE when the River Rhine froze in Germany. It was not the first time this great river had frozen. Attacks from Germanic tribes had been taking place for years.

The Rhine provided a natural barrier between the Roman Empire to the south and Barbarians to the north and west, bordered by Roman forts along the Limas line. Several legions had been stationed along the river at the northern frontiers of the Empire around what is now Frankfurt and Mainz, in the region of Hessen.[24] In the winter of

---

[23] For details of Maximus in Brittany, see P. H. Morice, *Histoire de Bretagne* (Paris, 1707); also *Memoires Pour Server de Preuves a l'histoire de Bretagne*, 3 vols (in folio) (Paris, 1742–6). Morice was drawing on earlier sources including Bertrand d'Argentré, *Abrégé de l'Histoire de Bretagne* (Paris, 1695).

[24] Thomas Cahill, *How the Irish Saved Civilization* (New York, 1995).

406 CE the Rhine froze at Mainz. After an extended period with sub-zero temperatures, it turned into an autobahn of ice.

Roman defences along the northern frontier were breached by hordes of Barbarians desperate for food and hungry for land. Various tribes including Huns, Vandals, Arans and Sueves poured across the bridge that nature herself had built. It has been estimated that as many as one hundred thousand Barbarians crossed the river at this time. For the next three years the Empire would be plundered by marauding tribes. When Alaric and his warriors entered the Salesian Gates in Rome on 24 August 409 CE, Rome's defences were breached for the first time in a thousand years. The 'eternal city' had fallen into the hands of the enemy. Germanic tribes rampaged through Gaul and Spain and did not stop before crossing into North Africa.

North Americans in general and New Yorkers in particular will understand what it must have felt like to be Roman on that day. As O'Driscoll remarks, in many ways this was Rome's 9/11.[25] The unthinkable had become reality and the military and cultural power that had conquered and controlled most of the western world was suddenly struck to its own heart's core. The richest and most powerful Empire in the world was forced to submit and negotiate agreements previously intolerable. Nothing would ever be the same again.

Like the twin towers in New York, the Empire fell rapidly; within twenty years of Alaric's triumphal entry into Rome, the western Empire consisted essentially of the city of Rome and its original territories in Latium, central Italy.[26] What took place on land was mirrored on the high seas.

After Julius Caesar defeated uprisings in Gaul and the Romans had conquered the south of Britain in 47–50 CE, the Empire maintained a sophisticated and powerful naval force capable of defending incursions from various barbarian seafaring tribes including the Irish. The *Classis Britannica* was a major Roman military fleet stationed at the Port of Iccius in north-west Gaul, now Boulogne-Sur-Mer, in France. Roman military strength had been unequalled since then, although there were signs of weakness and

---

[25] Herb O'Driscoll, teachings given on pilgrimages with Céile Dé in Ireland.

[26] Peter Heather, *The Fall of the Roman Empire* (London, 2005).

impending decline.

Fiscal corruption and political decadence were apparent many years before the final crash. These are the kind of 'unforeseen' disasters we neglect to prepare for, ignoring signs which may be there but are never taken seriously, until it is too late. As Roman power collapsed in the early fifth century, so went the Roman navy.[27] In 429 CE, Vandals embarked on ships from southern Gaul and landed in North Africa, establishing their own dominion in the breadbasket of the Roman Empire. The Vandals were not just sword wielding horseback riders as we imagine Attila the Hun to have been. They had a powerful navy which contributed to the fall of the Western Empire when their pirate king, Gaiseric, eliminated Roman shipping on the Mediterranean.

By the middle of the fifth century, the Vandals were masters of the sea and by 476 CE 'Old Rome' had fallen completely from power in Western Europe. The Barbarian invasions in many ways marked the end of the classical civilisations of Greece and Rome. Europe entered the so-called 'Dark Ages' which would last for the next five hundred years, from 400–900 CE. The devastation is vividly described by Gildas, who could have been speaking about the situation in Britain or Brittany when he writes with dejection:

> The more we try to push Barbarians to the sea the more barbaric things we see. If we want to avoid having our throats cut, the rising flood tide swallows us. To whichever side of the coast we turn, we meet death.[28]

Before we start to imagine the whole world imploding, it is important to remember that only the western Empire fell to the Barbarians. The eastern Empire was not so radically affected and continued to thrive, based at the ancient crossroads between east and west in the Imperial City of Constantinople, now Istanbul in Turkey. When the west collapsed the east flowered as 'Nova Roma' or 'New Rome' – Byzantium.

In the west, things began to unfold in a different way.

---

[27] 'Roman Navy', *UNRV History* [website] <www.unrv.com/military/roman-navy.php.>

[28] Gildas, ch. 20.

As Barbarian tribes flooded into Gaul, massive changes were taking place in Britain, especially after the legions were recalled to defend Rome in 405 CE. Germanic tribes including Angles, Saxons and Jutes attacked Britain from the North Sea. The Picts (the name means 'painted ones' because of tattoos on their bodies and their use of war paint) invaded southwards from Caledonia (Scotland). Irish chieftains began raiding the coasts of Britain and Brittany.

After the fall of Rome security once provided by the Roman army was gone and the whole country was ripe for plunder. Britain was trapped by invasions on three sides. Around 450 CE, Germanic tribes invaded Britain in greater force. The ancient Britons became the victims of what is now called 'ethnic cleansing'. Part of the island the Romans had called 'Britannia' was renamed Angle-land or England. Before these invasions the Britons were a Celtic speaking people steeped in the cultural traditions of their Gallic ancestors.

Finding itself pushed towards the western margins of Britain, Celtic culture managed to survived only in Ireland, Scotland, Wales and parts of south west England, as well as Brittany. Celtic place names were eradicated from south-east England and as far north as the border with Scotland. Somewhere, either in Britain or on the north-east coast of Brittany, St Patrick was born into this cauldron of social instability and unrestrained, physical violence.

As we listen to St Patrick's words and try to understand his story, as recorded in his *Confession*, special attention will be given to the geographical references that are crucial to identify where he came from and who he really was. St Patrick wrote this letter when he was an older man, reflecting on some of the key events that shaped his life and destiny and conscious that death, his own death, was imminent. In the following chapter we shall explore some of the treasured memories St Patrick wanted to share with us.

CHAPTER THREE

PATRICK'S CONFESSION

My name is Patrick, a sinful person without any formal education, least among all the Christians and greatly despised in the eyes of many. I am the son of Calpurnius (a Decurion) as he was the son of an elder, Potitus, who belonged to the village of Bannavem Tiburniae. Near this village he had a small estate from where I was taken captive, when I was about sixteen years old. I was not aware of God's presence at that time and I was taken as a slave to Ireland, along with thousands of others.[29]

When St Patrick sat down to write about his life, he began by telling us his name; *Ego Patricius* in Latin, meaning 'I am Patrick' or 'My name is Patrick'. He also mentions the names of his father and grandfather, Calpurnius and Potitus. The family belonged as citizens to the Roman Empire as can be seen from the Latin form of their names. In his first letter, to the Soldiers of Coroticus, Patrick says his father was a Decurion. This title applied to a senior official in local government whose duty was to provide a cavalry of at least ten horsemen to support the Roman army. It was only possible for those

---

[29] C:1

who owned sufficient land and resources.[30]

Patrick tells us that his family owned a villa or small estate near a place called 'Bannavem Tiburniae'. The location is uncertain and was lost to historical memory in the years after St Patrick's death.

Despite the countless books written about him and extensive research by scholars, neither the location of St Patrick's homeland nor the village from which he was taken captive have ever been securely identified.

Frustrated by the lack of geographical detail given in St Patrick's own writings and confused by contradictory accounts in the ancient sources, most writers have given up the quest. Scholars assume that St Patrick came from Britain but there is no agreement as to the precise location. Despite the view taken by the majority, the identification of Patrick's homeland on the Island of Roman Britain, whether in the north at Strathclyde or anywhere else, has not been supported with any reliable evidence and therefore remains uncertain. Ludwig Bieler, one of the foremost authorities on St Patrick, said, 'The search for Bannavem Tiburniae is quite hopeless.'[31] Patrick's place of origins is one of the great unsolved mysteries surrounding his life and the origins of the Irish and early European church. This is what made the unexpected and surprising discovery of a local tradition in Brittany so exciting and challenging.

In his *Confession*, Patrick did not say he was born at Bannavem Tiburniae. Neither does he say how long he had lived there or been there before he was taken captive. He does not mention another home, which might suggest that he had grown up on his father's estate during those years before the age of sixteen, when he was taken captive.

There is not enough specific geographical detail to make any assumptions. All we can know for certain is that Bannavem Tiburniae

---

[30] Decurion (Latin: *decurione*) has been included because of St Patrick's statement in his Letter to Coroticus 10, *decurione patre nascor* – meaning 'I am the son of a Decurion'. The word deacon (Latin: *diaconum*), which can be found in the *Book of Armagh* copy of Patrick's *Confession*, appears to be an interpolation reflecting later ecclesiastical influences. See Eoin MacNeill, *Saint Patrick, Apostle of Ireland* (London, 1934), p. 6.

[31] For a summary of efforts to identify 'Bannavem Tiburniae' see Bieler, *The Life and Legend of St Patrick* (Dublin, 1949), pp. 51–3, 133 ff.

existed close to where his father, Calpurnius, owned an estate. Patrick remembered this place and what happened there when he was a teenager. This is where he was taken captive when Irish pirates attacked his family home before he was sold as a slave in Ireland. It was a traumatic experience and one that St Patrick would remember for the rest of his life.

Let's try and imagine what it may have been like for him.

The estate was attacked by pirates. Patrick may have witnessed friends or neighbours being killed. Wrenched away in the flower of his youth, he was dragged across the seas to a foreign country outside the territory of the Roman Empire. Ireland at that time had a fearful reputation as a pagan, barbaric nation located 'at the ends of the earth'. Slave trading and raiding was common practice amongst the Celts in Ireland, as it was across the whole of Europe and North Africa at the end of the fourth century.

Irish pirates in the fifth century did not operate with the ethics of the Salvation Army. Old Irish and Breton sources say Patrick's mother and father were both killed during the frenzy. Patrick may have witnessed their deaths.

Those who were taken with him from the village that day would have known each other and some must have been friends. Slave traders took only the girls and boys who were saleable. Adults were usually killed or had to flee. An orgy of rape, murder and gratuitous violence was probably the order of the day.

It was a case of kill or be killed. The Celts often severed the heads of their victims, which were then displayed either on their belts, bridles of horses and the masts of their ships or on poles outside their villages when they returned.

This horrific and traumatic event must have had a huge impact on Patrick as a young teenager. However painful it was, Patrick managed to triumph over adversity and find peace within himself and with God. Reflecting on these events as an older man, he tells us that he bore no grudge or malice about what happened even against those who had taken him captive. This is one of the most enduring qualities of his personality and shows a degree of spiritual and psychological maturity which provided the foundations for his teachings and legacy. Patrick had experienced God's forgiveness in his own heart and wished to extend that forgiveness and love towards others. His personal and profound faith in God deepened through these experiences. A sense of spiritual direction came to fruition in his life despite these events, perhaps even because of them.

St Patrick was held captive as a slave in Ireland for six or seven years.

He does not tell us where he was enslaved or the name of his slave master. Instead he chose to describe the personal transformation which began when he was suffering. In the midst of these difficulties between the ages of sixteen and twenty-three, Patrick began to have a series of mystical or religious experiences which changed the course of his life. It was during this time of exile from homeland and family that he came to embrace a deeper faith. Patrick sensed the presence of God through this spiritual awakening and left us an extraordinary account of his experience. He describes how his heart turned towards prayer and became more aware of God's presence in the midst of loneliness and the hardship of slavery, tending animals in all weathers on a remote and deserted hillside. In these moments when he had lost everything, he found God. We can let St Patrick's words speak for themselves:

> There the Lord opened my unbelieving mind so that at that late hour I should remember my sins and turn with all my heart to the Lord my God. He kept me safe as a father would comfort his son …
>
> After I came to Ireland I was herding cattle and I used to pray many times a day; more and more the love of God and awareness of God's presence came to me, my faith increased and my spirit was moved so that in one day I would pray as many as a hundred times and in the night nearly as often, even while I was staying in the woods and on the mountain …
>
> Before daylight I used to be stirred to prayer in snow, frost and rain and felt no ill effects from it because the spirit was fervent within me.[32]

Patrick escaped from Ireland during the seventh year of his captivity. In his *Confession* we hear nothing about the people he worked for or

---

[32] C:16

what relationships he may have had. He probably spent much of this time in isolation. He practised asceticism through a discipline of regular prayer and fasting. Asceticism derives from the Greek *askesis*, a self-imposed discipline of spiritual exercises involving some form of renunciation. It was during this time of renunciation, constantly exposed to the elements of nature that he began to hear voices and see 'visions'. Divine intervention and encouragement was about to turn the wheel of fortune in his favour.

This is the second time in his *Confession* that St Patrick provides a clue to his place of origins. Patrick describes how one night in a dream he heard a voice saying it was time to return to his homeland. It told Patrick that a ship was waiting and ready to take him there:

> And there, as it happens one night I heard in my sleep a voice saying to me; 'it is good that you fast, you are soon to go to back to your homeland'. And after a while again I heard a voice say to me, 'Look your ship is ready.' It was not nearby but at a distance of perhaps two hundred miles. And I had never been there nor did I know anybody there …Shortly after that I took flight, left the man with whom I had been for six years and journeyed by the power of God, who directed my way unto my good. And I feared nothing until I reached that ship.[33]

Patrick describes in detail how he escaped. He had to walk a long way from the place of his captivity to a ship that was waiting, which he boarded almost immediately. The captain was not sure about taking him at first but changed his mind suddenly, allowing Patrick to sail with them. The crew members were not Christian. They invited Patrick to 'suck their breasts' – an old Celtic ritual which was a form of male bonding as a sign of promised loyalty, friendship and commitment for the journey. The sucking of breasts was a pre-Christian rite of protection, well attested in ancient Ireland.[34] Patrick says he refused to do this because of his religious beliefs but they took him on board anyway.

---

[33] C:17

[34] M. A. O'Brien, *Miscellanea Hiburnica, Etudes Celtiques,* 3 (1938), p. 372 ff.

The ship sailed and they were three days at sea before they reached land. St Patrick does not tell us where the ship sailed from, which port it was sailing to or where it landed. The narrative suggests he was expecting to return home.

Scholars are divided in their opinions about where the ship landed. Those convinced that St Patrick was born in Britain and was taken captive from Britain usually accept that he was planning to return home after his escape and, therefore, sailed from Ireland to Britain. Others say the ship landed in Gaul. Wherever it sailed to, St Patrick was aware of God's guidance and support throughout this daring escape and bid for freedom. Patrick's account of this journey provides a few descriptive details which allow for speculation as to where he escaped from and where the ship may have landed.

If he was held captive in County Antrim in the north of Ireland as most of the ancient sources claim, such a long walk could have taken him to one of the ports on the south-east coast of Ireland, including Wicklow or Arklow. In the fifth century these ports were used for trading on the continent. The ship was probably a trading vessel large enough to carry cargo and a small crew. Where is the ship likely to have arrived after a three-day journey?

Members of Wicklow Sailing Club helped shed light on St Patrick's journey from a maritime perspective. The distance between Wicklow Harbour and St Malo in Brittany, the nearest port to Château de Bonaban, is about 365 nautical miles. This allows for some interesting calculations. In a vessel that would travel at 5 knots-per-hour (about average in those days for a medium sized boat carrying cargo) with light prevailing westerly winds, the journey would take three days (365/5 = 73 divided by 24 hrs = 3.04 days).

These calculations are based on a 24-hour clock, since the ship would have continued sailing through the day and night with no landings before the coast of Brittany. Another possibility is that it landed further down the coast.

The journey from Wicklow to Carantec would have been even shorter, only 340 nautical miles, and it would have taken less than three days sailing to reach this port. On the other hand, Ireland to Holyhead in Wales is about 70 nautical miles. Even at 3 knots-per-hour such a journey would have taken only about 18 hours (70/3 = 23.3 divided by 24) less than one day's sailing.

Journey times are ultimately dependent on weather conditions, prevailing winds and other crucial factors, such as the size of the boat and the experience of the crew. The reason for including these calculations is simply to show that from the evidence given in his own writings it is certainly possible that when St Patrick escaped from Ireland he could have travelled as far as Brittany.

If his intention was to return to his homeland, as seems clear from his *Confession*, then it is also possible that the home to which Patrick sought to return was in Brittany and not Wales, or northern Britain.

This allows for the possibility that the Calpurnius estate where Patrick was taken captive was not located in Britain but on the continent. Wherever the ship landed, the situation encountered there was very dangerous.

The ship's crew had to walk through a deserted landscape, wandering for twenty-eight days without seeing other human beings during which time they almost starved to death. This was not the place to be with a cargo of dogs.

These may have been Irish wolfhounds, large dogs that were prized by the Romans on the continent at that time. In desperation, the sailors asked Patrick for help. Even though they were Gentiles or 'pagans' and not Christians, they suggested he pray to 'his God' for them. The word pagan derives from the Latin *pagus*, which refers to a Celtic tribal area. The *pagani* were literally 'country people' outside the Roman urban centres or *civitas*. Paganism was originally, therefore, a reference to the old religious traditions, practised especially in the countryside, before the adoption of Christianity.

After miraculously finding food in a herd of wild pigs which kept the crew from starvation, St Patrick's reputation increased among the sailors but he refused to eat the wild honey when they invited him to share in a ritual of thanksgiving. The narrative suggests that Patrick was trying to return to his homeland but that he did not reach 'home' for many years.

Much depends on how we interpret the text, which could be taken to mean he was reunited with his extended family again after 'many years' in captivity.

Some accounts claim Patrick's mother and father were both killed during the attack that took place on the day St Patrick was taken captive. If so then when he returned to his homeland after escaping from slavery in Ireland, he would have met his closest surviving relatives.

This is the second passage of three in this letter, where the name 'Britanniis' is mentioned and again it is given as the name for his homeland. More than any other geographical reference in his writings, this name provides the key to knowing where St Patrick came from. As the meaning of 'Britanniis' is uncertain, the original Latin form from the *Book of Armagh* will be retained in the following passage, without committing to any specific translation:

> After many years [of captivity] I was '*in Britanniis*' again with my [extended] family who received me like a son and sincerely begged of me, that after all the troubles I endured, I should not leave them to go anywhere else.[35]

Most scholars have identified *Britanniis* exclusively with Britain but it is important to note, the original word in Latin is recorded in plural form.

The question is, does it refer to the island of Britain, to Brittany or perhaps to both? Some writers have suggested that when St Patrick spoke about his homeland, he was referring to a region on the continent that was also known as 'Britain'. It is possible that a coastal region in Armorica had adopted this name during or perhaps even before the rebellion of Magnus Maximus in 383 CE. Most of the early Breton historians insist that a British colony was established there at that time and called 'Britain' from which the name 'Bretagne' in French is derived. This is a very controversial subject with widely differing views among historians, but one which is crucial to understanding the truth about St Patrick.

Even though it appears in plural form in the earliest surviving manuscript, most English translations usually give the singular form 'in Britain' despite the fact that this is potentially misleading. Critical editions of St Patrick's *Confession* in Latin were published by N. J. White in 1905, followed by Ludwig Bieler in 1950. These are now

---

[35] C:23

two of the accepted texts for academic study. In their translations, White and Bieler both render the Latin name for St Patrick's homeland as 'Britain'. The implications of this situation in relation to St Patrick's biography cannot be underestimated. As a consequence of decisions made with regard to translation, widespread credibility was given to the established view which identifies St Patrick's homeland and place of origins, exclusively with the island of Britain. Almost the full weight of established and current academic opinion is strongly in favour of the theory of Britain.

After the unexpected discoveries made at Château de Bonaban, there appeared to be equally strong grounds for me to question this. M. de Gerville considered the established tradition to be a 'gross historical error'. Could the truth about where St Patrick came from have been lost simply because of the way one single Latin word has been interpreted and translated?

Following more extensive reading, it appeared to me that no substantial or compelling historical evidence had ever been provided to support the theory of Britain and therefore there were no sure grounds for giving it such categorical support. The arguments that were given in support seemed to me to be far from conclusive and possibly based on unsafe foundations. This matter is of such great importance it will be explored fully in due course. At this stage, we must simply focus on the evidence, as it appears in St Patrick's writings.

After finding his way back home, Patrick tells us that members of his extended family welcomed him back with love and affection 'as if' he was their son. This suggests that his mother and father were no longer alive. His closest relatives who were still there, begged him, after all the troubles he had endured, never to leave them again. At the very moment when he was reunited with his extended family after so many years of separation, St Patrick experienced another powerful dream in which he felt called to return to Ireland.

This is one of the most moving passages in St Patrick's Confession and one of the most impressive and evocative accounts of a spiritual calling in the whole of Christian literature. St Patrick's account of his dream has touched the hearts of millions, not least those who have recognised in these words a lasting testimony of God's call for Patrick to return to Ireland as an apostle and fulfil the command of Jesus to carry the gospel 'to the ends of the earth'.

And there, in a vision of the night, I saw a man coming as it were from Ireland, whose name was Victor, carrying many letters. He gave me one to read and as I did so, I heard the *Voice of the Irish*. In that same moment as I was reading from the beginning of the letter, I thought I could hear the voice of those around the Wood of Foclut – which is close beside the Western Sea. It was as if they spoke with one voice, 'we beg you, holy youth, to come and walk once more among us.' When I woke up my heart was broken and I had to stop reading. Thank God that after all these years the Lord has granted them what they cried out for.[36]

Patrick's account of this dream is not only great literature, that continues to hold deep religious and spiritual significance for others, it includes some very significant geographical references which have influenced our traditional understanding of his place of origins. Just as most books written about St Patrick claim that he came from Britain, so there has been a traditional assumption that the Wood of Foclut existed in Ireland.

The origins of this assumption date back to the seventh century. An influential Bishop in Ireland called Tirechán claimed that St Patrick's 'Wood of Foclut' existed in his own diocese near Killala, in County Mayo.

This claim became enshrined in one of Ireland's most ancient ecclesiastical records when Tirechán's narrative was included with other Patrician documents in the *Book of Armagh*, still preserved in Trinity College, Dublin. Since then, it has formed part of an established tradition that has never been seriously questioned. Ever since Tirechán made this claim, it has been widely accepted that the Wood of Foclut existed in the west of Ireland.[37]

If Tirechán was telling the truth, my thoughts about the Forest of Quokelunde in Brittany would have been misguided. One of Ireland's most respected historians, D.A. Binchy, consistently warned students of St Patrick not to trust anything Tirechán said, just because Tirechán had said it.[38] This has always been one of the greatest

---

[36] C:23

[37] Stokes, *Tripartite Life*, ii (London, 1887), p. 421.

[38] D. A. Binchy, 'Patrick and his Biographers', *Studia Hibernica*, 2 (1962).

challenges for those wishing to know the truth about Patrick's biography – how to separate the false claims of hagiography from facts that can be verified historically.

An interesting conversation that took place at a special St Patrick's Day celebration in Washington DC helped to address this question. I met someone there who said he worked for 'the intelligence communities' in the United States. His expertise involved analysing reports in the hope of teaching intelligence agents how to write better reports. The formula he advocates is this: 'Always remember that just because somebody tells you something is true does not mean it necessarily is true, unless sufficient and reliable evidence is given to support it.' The same principle can fruitfully be applied to any claims made about St Patrick, including those you may find on these pages.

Tirechán wrote his narrative more than two hundred years after St Patrick's death. He insisted that the Wood of Foclut existed in his own diocese in the west of Ireland. Understandably for a bishop of his time, he did not provide historical or geographical evidence to support this.

Medieval hagiographers were not constrained by the same standards which are supposed to apply to modern historical analysis.

Despite these uncertainties, Tirechán's claim has always been given a high degree of historical credibility. It has been suggested that 'Foclut' or 'Foclud' is the only genuine Irish name in the whole of St Patrick's *Confession*. This too is based on an assumption that Tirechán was telling the truth and that 'Caille Foclaid' was the name of an Irish wood that could be identified with the place St Patrick recalled in a dream. The existence of a forest called 'Quokelunde' in Brittany and a local tradition that claims that this wood is the place from which Patrick was taken captive, gave me a reason to question the Tirechán tradition. Could the name of the wood recalled by Patrick in his dream have had Breton or Gallic rather than Irish origin and that both the Latin, Irish and English forms are derived from an original Gallic/Breton name, a forest called 'Quokelunde' that existed close to the present site of Château de Bonaban?

When St Patrick recalled this powerful dream, he said a man called 'Victor' appeared before him carrying many letters and looking 'as if' he came from Ireland. There is no justification on the basis of a particular interpretation of this dream to assume that the Wood of

Foclut must have existed in Ireland. This assumption has often been made on the grounds that because Patrick heard the 'Voice of the Irish' calling from the Wood of Foclut for him to return to them, these voices must have been voices coming from Ireland and from people he must have known, perhaps from a place near where he was held captive or somewhere in Ireland with which he was familiar.[39]

As with other geographical references in St Patrick's *Confession*, however, it is possible that the true location of the Wood of Foclut may have been lost to historical memory in the years after St Patrick's death, disappearing in the twilight zone between the claims of Irish hagiography and an imaginative but mistaken form of dream analysis.

Jeremy Taylor, a Jungian analyst and expert in group spiritual direction through dreams, identifies issues which must be taken into account when trying to understand or interpret the images and symbols we experience in dreams. He warns against the dangers of 'mistaken literalism'. This can happen when we try to interpret a dream in a specific way and he advises caution because 'only the dreamer knows the meaning of a dream'.[40]

St Patrick's description sounds more like a nightmare than a dream. When he heard these voices calling him, Patrick says he woke up suddenly, feeling heartbroken. He was so disturbed that he could 'read no more'. If we heed Taylor's advice, we should not make any historical or geographical assumptions based on what was experienced in a dream or nightmare. However significant it may be, his dream should not be interpreted to support a particular geographical location, unless there is real evidence elsewhere to make an alternative interpretation impossible.

Having said that, because St Patrick left so few geographical references concerning his place of origins, it is important to consider the possibility as most writers have always done, that even though Patrick remembered this wood in the context of a dream, it was a real place with a historical and geographical reality and was not simply

---

[39] 'Silua Focluti', *Proceedings of the Royal Irish Academy, Section C: Archaeology, Celtic Studies, History, Linguistics, Literature*, 36 (1923), pp. 249–55. See also Patrick O'Neill, 'The Identification of Foclut', *Journal of the Galway Archaeological and Historical Society*, 22/4 (1947).

[40] Jeremy Taylor, *Dreamwork* (New York, 1983).

part of his subconscious dream world. When historical facts are uncertain, sometimes speculation or 'historical intuition' is the only resource left. So what was it about those voices and what may have happened in the Wood of Foclut to cause St Patrick such sorrow and heartbreak? One possibility is that his distress can be understood in the context of the traumatic experience of being taken captive.

This thought had first occurred to me during a walk through what is probably a remnant of the old forest that surrounds Château de Bonaban, the day our prayers were offered under those old oak trees. For whatever reason, there was a sense that St Patrick may have suffered there.

If Patrick's 'Wood of Foclut' could be identified with the Forest of Quokelunde, which existed close beside the location of the family's home on the north-east coast of Brittany, then could it also be possible that St Patrick may have been experiencing in his dream the memory of the traumatic events which took place in that forest the day he was taken captive? Perhaps the voices that he associated with this wood were the cries of friends and family who had been killed or taken captive to Ireland, including those who were still being held in Ireland as they had not yet managed to escape from slavery as Patrick had recently done? Perhaps those cries had continued to haunt him; it was as a direct result of this dream that Patrick felt strongly a calling from God to go back to them. In other words, an alternative understanding of Patrick's dream would suggest 'The Voice of the Irish' that St Patrick heard calling to him from the Wood of Foclut could have been associated in his mind not with people he knew and remembered in the place where he was held captive in Ireland, but the place where he was taken captive – in Brittany.

What makes St Patrick's account doubly significant is that it is the first occasion in his writings where he mentions two place names in conjunction which is a rare coupling of geographical references. He describes the Wood of Foclut as being 'close beside the Western Sea'. Those who accept Tirechán's claim, that Foclut existed in the west of Ireland, have usually gone one stage further in a form of speculative dream interpretation, claiming that when St Patrick mentions the 'Western Sea' ('Mare Occidentale' in Latin) he must have been referring to the Atlantic Ocean off the west coast of Ireland.

Again there is no evidence to support such an exclusive interpretation. The 'Mare Occidentale' was a name given by the Romans to the ocean which existed to the west of the Roman Empire. It could have referred to the west coast of Spain or France, including the coast of Brittany.

Despite this traumatic and powerful dream, Patrick tells us that he did not return to Ireland immediately. He ends his account by simply saying, 'Thanks to God, after so many years their cries have been heard by the Lord.' Perhaps he was referring to the 'many years' his friends and neighbours were held in captivity in Ireland, before he could return again to care for them?

The Missing Years

St Patrick tells us nothing about what happened next, from the time of his escape from Ireland at the age of twenty-three to his return as an apostle, traditionally dated 432 CE. These are sometimes called the 'missing years', a period clouded with more legend and uncertainty than any other part of his biography. Most accounts of what happened during this time are contained in later sources providing an abundance of fascinating detail much of which is spurious but including some traditions that are authentic. The question as to where Patrick went for religious training and formation will be discussed later.

Wherever it was, Patrick eventually returned to Ireland as a self-proclaimed apostle. He went back to the land of his captivity, this time not as a slave but as a servant of God and a hostage to Christ.

As Patrick draws towards the end of his *Confession*, some final geographical clues are given which may help us to identify his homeland. These are contained in a few short passages in which Patrick describes difficulties he experienced with his 'seniors'. We are left wondering what exactly may have caused or motivated him to write his *Confession*. It appears to have been prompted by a situation of difficulty. The religious community which may have initially supported his mission in Ireland had turned against him.

Unidentified Church leaders (Patrick calls them his seniors) were seeking his removal. This is the first time readers are made aware of an issue that would have a significant influence on St Patrick's biography in the centuries after his death – Church politics. St Patrick wrote the *Confession* not only as a thanksgiving to God for all the gifts received in this life, but also in response to accusations of personal misconduct. A *Confessio* was an autobiography written to justify a spiritual calling and as a defence against possible charges of grave misconduct or even heresy.[41] Patrick had been in Ireland for some time before his suitability for this ministry was questioned. It appears from the description given of these events that he was rejected by leaders in the Church, possibly clerics or Church elders who held a position of authority over him.

They challenged his suitability for the Irish mission and had convened a meeting or tribunal to discuss his case. St Patrick does not name these shadowy figures who were resident in a country outside Ireland. Neither does he tell us which church or religious group they represented. When he describes his rejection by these 'seniors', Patrick provides further clues as to where he came from and where members of his religious community were based.

Patrick explains how the attack made on his own character and integrity had arisen because of the public report of a 'sin' which he admitted committing when he was about fifteen years old, before he was taken captive to Ireland. There has been much speculation as to what this sin might have been. It was probably at the higher end of the scale such as participating in pagan worship, or some form of perceived sexual misconduct. Patrick had found himself in a situation of grave difficulty because of these charges: Before he became a deacon, Patrick had confessed this 'sin' to a close friend, who had betrayed him by disclosing it to others. Patrick tells us that he had been 'corrected by the Lord' before he went to Ireland and therefore had a clear conscience about the work he was doing and that the past should not be held against him. As Patrick tries to explain the situation, he provides more clues about where he came from and where these 'seniors' were based:

---

[41] Nora Chadwick, *Age of the Saints in the Celtic Church* (Durham, 1960; facs., Llanerch, 2006), p. 24 ff.

I feel very sad to talk about one of my closest friends, with whom I had trusted the secrets of my soul. I found out from some of the brethren at the gathering that was held about me; *I was not present at it nor was I 'in Britanniis'* – nor did it originate from me – that he would stand up for me in my absence ... he even told me to my face with his own words 'Look, you are going to be recognised as a bishop' – something for which I was completely unworthy.[42]

The familiar phrase *'in Britanniis'* which occurs in this passage, is again usually translated as *'in Britain'*, but could Patrick have been referring to Brittany? If so, the meeting held to discuss his position might have been held not far from Brittany, perhaps in neighbouring Gaul. If so, an appropriate translation of the text would be:

'And I had learned from some of the brothers before that gathering at which my defence came up – I was not present at it nor was I in Brittany nor did the matter originate from me – that he would argue for my defence'.

A clue which might reveal the truth can be found shortly afterward. Having dealt with his defence, St Patrick switches attention away from his problems with Church leaders to focus on his ministry in Ireland. After describing the success of his work, as well as the difficulties he experienced, Patrick explains how attached and committed he was to the Irish mission, which as far as he was concerned was not negotiable. It had been ordained and supported by God.

It appears there may have been a complete breakdown in relations between Patrick and those who had been seeking his dismissal. In response to criticisms and attempts to remove him from office he does not mention being absolved, at least not by his seniors. Patrick gives the impression he decided to 'go it alone' and stay where he was, without bowing to these external pressures.

He describes how, even though he might have wished to leave Ireland to make a journey back to his homeland and family *'in*

---

[42] C:32. * Emphasis added.

Britanniis' he could not do so because he had made a vow to God that he would remain in Ireland for the rest of his life, to serve the flock entrusted to him:

> The Lord has given grace to many of his female disciples, because even though they are forbidden they continue steadfast in their following of him ... As a result, even if I would wish to leave them and make a journey *in Britanniis* – and I would most dearly love to make that journey, so as to see my homeland and family; not only that but also to proceed further in to the Gauls to visit the brethren and see the faces of the saints of my Lord. [43]

St Patrick's description of his longing to make this journey is very significant from a geographical point of view. Most scholars insist the word 'Britanniis' should again be translated as Britain. This would make sense if St Patrick's family was in Britain and his church or religious community was based in Gaul. Exactly the same could be said about Brittany, however, if St Patrick's homeland was located there this passage would still have a sense of geographical integrity, perhaps even more so. A revised translation can be offered to see whether it makes geographical and literary sense. If St Patrick was actually referring to Brittany, then the geographical references in the passage above could be translated as follows:

> As a result, even if I would wish to leave them and make a journey to Brittany and I would most dearly love to make that journey to see my homeland and family not only that but also to proceed further into the Gauls to visit the brethren and see the faces of the saints of my Lord. [44]

The journey St Patrick was contemplating would make perfect sense from a geographical point of view, if it can be shown that Brittany and 'the Gauls' were considered separate regions on the continent at the time of St Patrick, in terms of local, ethnic geography. If so, this passage reflects a genuine consistency in Patrick's mental geography.

---

[43] C:42

[44] C:43

This would be the case, for example, if Patrick's homeland was on the coast of north-east Brittany, but the religious friends he longed to see were based at St Martin's Monastery on the banks of the River Loire, which was in Gaul. This is a controversial matter of great importance to Patrick's biography, and to which we shall return in due course.

As St Patrick draws his *Confession* to a close, he reflects deeply on the significance of his life, the good and bad, the light and dark and the many blessings he had received despite all the dangers and difficulties experienced. Patrick had found peace within himself despite countless adversities. His strong faith and trust in God led him to experience a profound sense of intimacy with Christ, the gift of wisdom and a truly loving and compassionate heart which had carried him to the threshold of a deeper, steadfast joy.

Patrick was now ready to face death, in gratitude for everything that had happened and the many gifts from God he had received. Even though he was as an older man when he wrote this letter, St Patrick was obviously sound of mind. As he draws his *Confession* to a close, he does so with thanksgiving to God for all that he had experienced during his life, the good and the bad. St Patrick had fulfilled the commandment of Christ in the Gospels, 'to preach the Gospel to the ends of the earth'.[45] For whatever reason, he sensed that death was close at hand:

I give un-wearying thanks to my God who delivered me from all my troubles and so helped my work with such divine power. I steadfastly exalt and glorify your name where ever I am, not only when circumstances favour me but when I am afflicted, so that whatever happens to me, good or bad I must accept with an even mind and thank God always. God showed me that I should believe and that God is endlessly to be trusted. And who so helped me, that I, a man ignorant of God's ways, in the last days should dare to undertake this work so holy and so wonderful. And as we have seen it written so we have now seen it fulfilled, we are the witnesses that the gospel has been preached to the limit beyond which no one dwells.

None shall ever assert that the credit is due to my own uneducated self, but regard it rather as a true fact to be firmly believed, that it was all the

---

[45] Mark 16:15

gift of God. And this is my Confession before I die.[46]

There is no record of what happened to Patrick after this letter was written. From the way the *Confession* ends, he appears to have sensed that death was imminent. It is possible that Patrick may have died or been killed shortly after this letter was published and that he remained *persona non grata*, rejected as unwelcome by the ecclesiastical authorities that refused to recognise him.

This alone explains what happened next.

Patrick disappeared from the Church's radar after his death, like a ship gone down in the Bermuda Triangle. He simply vanishes from all known ecclesiastical or historical records in Ireland, Britain and the continent, for the next two hundred years. Patrick's writings seem to have disappeared with him as if they went out of print or were deliberately taken off the shelves in the ecclesiastical bookshops of that time. It was not only Patrick's place of origins that became lost to historical memory in the centuries after his death. Any clear record of his mission to Ireland was also forgotten.

His complete disappearance from all surviving official documents for the next two centuries is astonishing. In the historical and ecclesiastical records for this period, it appears that as far as Church leaders, writers and the most respected chronicles were concerned, St Patrick never existed.

---

[46] C:62

CHAPTER FOUR

THE UNKNOWN APOSTLE

Mark (about to receive the injection): '*Is this going to hurt?*'
Therapist (moving towards him): '*Truth always does, a little.*'[47]

In the two hundred years following St Patrick's death in 461 CE, until the closing decades of the seventh century, it is impossible to find any clear historical references to him or his writings. The St Patrick we know today fails to appear in any surviving historical records from this period. This remains an enigma and one of the great unsolved mysteries of his life and legacy.

After St Patrick's death, Ireland developed a sophisticated and creative monastic culture. Christianity was embraced by increasing numbers. From the beginning of the sixth century, the Irish church entered a 'Golden Age' which would last for another five hundred years. Celtic Christianity blossomed in Ireland, Wales and other regions on the margins of Western Europe, where indigenous

---

[47] From *Flash Forward*, a television series.

religious and cultural traditions were strong.[48]

The Irish tradition became rooted in Scotland through St Columba's foundation on Iona, then spread to Northumbria and as far south as Glastonbury in England before being carried even further into France, Belgium, Germany and the heartlands of Europe.

Before the arrival of Augustine in Canterbury in 597 CE, the influence of Irish and Welsh monastic traditions in Britain was pervasive and stronger than anything Rome had to offer in these regions at this time. Irish monastic foundations developed on many of the sites where hermitages had been established by early Irish saints. The largest monasteries became centres of learning and some acted as proto-universities.

The Monastic City at Glendalough is a perfect example. A large monastery developed in 'Gleann dá loch', the 'valley of two lakes', where St Kevin lived as a hermit in the sixth century.[49] With a dynamic combination of education and spiritual formation, students flocked to Ireland's 'monastic cities' from across Ireland, Britain and the continent.

An early form of Christian monasticism, following the example of the Egyptian Desert Tradition, was developed by the pioneering efforts of John Cassian and Martin of Tours in Gaul, David in Wales, Declan of Ardmore, St Brigid of Kildare and St Enda of Aran in Ireland, among many others.

Irish monastic teachers including St Finnian of Clonard and St Finnian of Moville, attracted thousands of students, as did the famous monasteries at Bangor in County Down, Northern Ireland and Bangor, North Wales.

Much to our surprise, there are no references to St Patrick within the literature that emerged from any of these monasteries during this period.

In the sixth century, a large monastic federation developed around St Columba, who left Derry in 563 CE to found a monastery on the island of Iona. The Irish form of his name, Colm Cille, means 'dove

---

[48] T. M. Charles-Edwards, *Early Christian Ireland* (Cambridge, 2000).

[49] Michael Rodgers and Marcus Losack, *Glendalough: A Celtic Pilgrimage* (Dublin, 1996; Revised 2011).

of the church' or perhaps 'Messenger of the church' (*colum*: dove, or messenger (hence *columbarium*, a name given by the Romans to 'dovecots' for homing pigeons, used for carrying messages) *cill*: a foundation church or monastic cell.

Columba was born in Donegal in 521 CE, only fifty years after St Patrick's death. Tradition closely associates St Patrick's mission with Columba's native stronghold in the north of Ireland. Slieve Mis (Mount Slemish) in County Antrim is said to be the place where St Patrick was held captive as a slave and County Down was the location of Patrick's first church in the Barn at Saul, not far from Downpatrick. Strangely, there is no record of St Patrick in any of the writings which emerged from St Columba's monasteries, or from the monasteries in Down or Armagh before the seventh century.

The Book of Durrow, preserved in Trinity College Dublin, is one of the earliest ecclesiastical documents to have survived in Ireland, dated to the sixth century. It has a brief entry for *sancta praesbiter Patrici* (a holy elder called Patrick) which is somewhat vague and could be a reference to anyone.

The title presbyter or elder was an early form of Christian leadership before the development of diocesan organisation with its characteristic order of deacons, priests and bishops.

Likewise, there is a brief mention of 'Abba Patrick' in Adamnán's *Life of St Columba* which was first published in 688 CE but as scholars have noted, this is an isolated reference, too vague again to justify any claim that St Patrick was remembered with any special form of veneration within the early Irish church. Adamnán was closely related to Columba's family as were all the abbots of Iona and he helped convene the Synod of Birr in 697 CE, which introduced Roman reforms in the Irish church.

It is certainly surprising that Adamnán fails to mention the contribution of St Patrick and the reference to Patrick which has been included in his work appears to have been added later to his *Life of Columba* in a second preface written after the Synod of Birr.

It is also very strange and more than surprising that St Patrick is not mentioned in the earliest hagiography of an Irish saint, Cogitosus's seventh-century *Life of St Brigid*, and not a word of significance about him can be found in any of the important

Hiberno-Latin manuscripts written during this period, including the Penitentials of Finnian, Cummian and Fota. When the lack of recorded information is compared with claims that he makes in his own writings and the prominence given to him in later documents and Church traditions, this silence is not simply astonishing, it is completely bewildering.[50]

Cummian's letter *De Controversia Paschali* (Concerning the Easter Controversy) is dated around 630 CE. It was addressed to Segene, fifth abbot of Iona (632–652 CE). Cummian cites ten Easter cycles which he says were known in Ireland, beginning with 'that which holy Patrick, our bishop, brought and followed' (II: 208–209).[51] Cummian states that all of these ten disagreed with the eighty-four-year cycle practised on Iona.

He says St Patrick brought and composed the first Easter Cycle 'with Easter on moon 15 to 21, and equinox March 21'.

This was not true. St Patrick could not have used this cycle, known as the Dionysian Cycle, which was not introduced even in Rome until the sixth century. It therefore appears that even Cummian (who was one of the most highly educated and best informed scholars of his day) was possibly unsure concerning the real identity and truth about St Patrick.

If St Patrick was the founder of Irish Christianity and the apostle of Ireland as he is acknowledged today, why was he not mentioned by the saints who came after him, especially in the sixth and seventh centuries when Irish Christianity must have gained some inspiration from his mission and legacy? If the seeds of the gospel had been planted by Patrick in Ireland and those he converted to the faith, why was his presence not recorded or his achievements honoured?

Most alarming of all, there are no references to St Patrick in the writings of St Columbanus (540–615 CE), who left Bangor in 595 CE, and established several Irish monasteries on the continent, including Luxeil in France and Bobbio in Italy. He is one of the most highly educated and probably best informed monks in the early Irish Church, many of whose writings have survived, yet Columbanus

---

[50] Heinrich Zimmer, *The Celtic Church in Britain and Ireland* (London, 1902), p. 81

[51] Liam de Paor, *St Patrick's World* (Dublin, 1993), pp. 151–3.

appears to be unaware of Patrick's existence and shows no knowledge of his writings. He appears never to have read or even heard of St Patrick's *Confession* or *Letter to Coroticus* and makes no reference to them.

In one of his own letters, written to Pope Boniface IV in 613 CE, Columbanus refers to the origins of the Church in Ireland, about which he claims to speak with authority. There is no mention of St Patrick, as if Patrick had no part to play.[52] In this letter, Columbanus acknowledges to the Pope that Ireland had received Christianity from Rome, saying, 'Our possession of the Catholic faith is unshaken: we hold it just as it was first handed to us by you.'

But he makes no reference to Patrick. St Columbanus may have been referring either to the mission of Palladius, who was sent to Ireland by Pope Celestine in 431 CE according to the *Chronicle of Prosper of Aquitaine*, or perhaps to the monasticism of St Martin of Tours, who is often associated with the origins of Irish, Welsh, Scots and Breton monasticism.

St Ninian is alleged to have visited St Martin and named his first church 'Candida Casa' or the 'The White House', following Martin's foundation at Tours. When he was about to be deported from France, St Columbanus went to Tours for an all-night vigil at St Martin's tomb. This suggests there was an established veneration of St Martin in the early Irish Church. A copy of Severus's *Life of St Martin* was preserved alongside other important Patrician documents in the *Book of Armagh*, suggesting there was a significant link between St Martin and St Patrick. If so, Columbanus appears not to have known about it or perhaps for some reason, he chose not to mention it.

Why does St Columbanus not mention him, especially if St Patrick had been ordained in Rome by Pope Celestine or if St Germanus of Auxerre and the Roman authorities had supported St Patrick's mission and were responsible for the form of Christianity introduced to Ireland, as many later sources claim?

St Patrick's absence from ecclesiastical records in Ireland is compounded by a similar omission from historical documents of Britain and the continent from the fifth, sixth and seventh centuries.

---

[52] Liam de Paor, *St Patrick's World*, pp. 141–3.

Patrick fails to make an appearance in Bede's *Ecclesiastical History*, even though the most famous saints trained in the Irish tradition, including Columba, Colman, Aidan, Cuthbert and Hilda, are given extensive coverage.

Some writers have suggested this silence is because Bede was dealing specifically with the history of the Church in England and Britain but if his mission had been commissioned by the Papacy and St Patrick had introduced the ecclesiastical customs and traditions of Rome to Ireland, as later tradition claims, we would have expected Bede to mention this somewhere in his prolific writings. No excuse is credible in relation to Prosper of Aquitaine, the most reliable and best informed Roman Chronicler of his day.

Prosper never mentions St Patrick or his ministry in Ireland, even though they were contemporaries. Neither does Sulpitius Severus, another well informed, very influential writer at the turn of the fourth century who was a contemporary of St Patrick. Severus records detailed information which is very significant in relation to claims found in several ancient documents that St Patrick was trained in the community of St Martin at Tours, but he never mentions St Patrick by name in any of his writings.

If Patrick's mother, Conchessa was a close relative of St Martin of Tours and Patrick spent four years in spiritual formation with his community and was tonsured there, as later documents claim, it is strange that Severus also fails to mention him. Some scholars have taken all this deafening silence to even question St Patrick's existence.

The reality is, a person called Patrick wrote two significant letters and definitely existed. His writings are not forgeries. They are genuine historical documents from the fifth century, proven to be so from internal evidence. So what happened to any information that did survive during the two centuries after his death? What caused his contribution to the origins of early Irish Christianity to be so neglected for these first two centuries and go unrecognised? This is certainly fertile ground for conspiracy theorists.

Later traditions associate St Patrick very closely with St Germanus of Auxerre, an influential Church leader in Gaul who was well connected to the authorities in Rome. If Patrick had prepared for his mission to Ireland with St Germanus, we would expect Prosper and Bede to have known about it. This suggests we may not have been told the truth about St Patrick.

The best source we have for information about Germanus can be found in a *Life of St Germanus* written by Constantius of Lyon in 480 CE, only a few years after Patrick's death. This document does not mention anyone called Patrick as a student of St Germanus in Auxerre.

In fact, it does not mention St Patrick at all.

When J. H. Todd published his book *St Patrick, Apostle of Ireland* in 1864, it caused great controversy because Todd suggested this lack of historical record raises serious doubts as to whether St Patrick's mission to Ireland was ever commissioned or sponsored by the Papacy. Similar concerns apply to the notion that St Patrick had any close or positive relationship with Roman ecclesiastical authorities in Britain or Gaul.

Whatever was happening in the church of the fifth century, St Patrick's place within that church remains a mystery.

In the most reliable Chronicle for this period, Prosper of Aquitaine tells us that in 431 CE, Palladius was ordained by Pope Celestine and sent as the first bishop 'to the Irish believing in Christ'.[53] Prosper appears not to have heard of Patrick, who according to Irish ecclesiastical traditions is supposed to have been appointed by Rome the following year, in 432 CE, after Palladius's sudden and unexpected death. We know that Palladius was a confident of St Germanus and had close relations with the Church in Auxerre, where he worked before being appointed to a senior position in Rome. This makes Prosper's silence about St Patrick even more remarkable and suspicious.

The one place we would expect to find some record of St Patrick's life and mission is within the ancient annals of Ireland. Conspiracy theorists will be disappointed to discover that at last we can find some references to St Patrick in entries for the fifth century but these are still very unclear and contradictory. For example, in the entry given for the year 4357 (335 CE) the *Annals of Ulster* record, 'According to some, Patrick was born here ... but this is incorrect.' Then, for the year 4395 (352 CE): 'Patrick was brought as a captive to Ireland, but this is incorrect.' Again for the year 4416 (358 CE):

---

[53] Liam de Paor, *St Patrick's World*, pp. 70–87.

'Patrick was released from captivity, but this is incorrect.' These dates contradict other entries recorded for St Patrick in the Irish annals.

The fact that another scribe felt it necessary to comment 'this is incorrect' on all three occasions, shows how uncertain the information was.[54]

The annals of Ireland are rightly venerated as a priceless national archive but within them even the identity of the person we know as St Patrick is very unclear. They contain references to various ecclesiastical figures called Patrick whose lives cannot easily be distinguished.

The *Annals of Ulster*, for example, were compiled in the north of Ireland where St Patrick is said to have founded many churches. The Irish annals include the following entries which make very interesting reading:

431: St Patrick was ordained bishop by the Holy Pope, Celestine, who ordered him to go to Ireland to preach and teach faith and piety to the Gaeidhil (Irish) and baptise them. (A4M)

432: Patrick came to Ireland this year, and proceeded to baptise and bless the Irish. (A4M)

432: Bishop Patrick holds Ireland - begins to baptise the Scotti (Irish) (AI)

441: The testing of Holy Patrick in the Christian faith. (AI)

442: Bishop Patrick was approved in the Catholic faith. (AU)

443: Bishop Patrick flourishing in the fervour of the faith and in the doctrine of Christ in our Province. (AU)

457: Repose of Old Patrick, as some books state. (AU) 461: Here some read the repose of Patrick.

492: The Irish state here that Patrick the Archbishop died.

493: Patrick, son of Calpurn, first primate and chief apostle of Ireland whom Pope Celestine had sent to preach the gospel and disseminate religion and piety among the Irish ... resigned his spirit to heaven.

---

[54] *Annals of Ulster (AU)*, trans. Sean Mac Airt and Gearoid Mac Niocaill, Dublin Institute for Advanced Studies (Dublin, 1983).

In an entry for the year 441 CE, nine years after St Patrick arrived in Ireland and began his mission, the *Annals of Ulster* state that he was 'confirmed in the Catholic faith'. This is an intriguing entry, not easy to explain. It implies that for the nine years before 441 CE, St Patrick was not confirmed or 'approved' in the Catholic faith, or that for some reason he still needed to be confirmed in that faith. This completely contradicts the claim in the *Annals of the Four Masters* that he had been ordained in Rome by Pope Celestine in 431 CE before he was sent to Ireland.

The *Annals of Inisfallen* record 'the testing of Holy Patrick in the Christian faith'. These are strange remarks, yet to be fully understood or satisfactorily explained. Perhaps St Patrick did something wrong to lose his credentials in the eyes of the authorities, and then did something right to retrieve them. Statements about St Patrick's close relationship with Papal authorities must be viewed with extreme caution. The claim that Patrick was trained and sent to Ireland by Pope Celestine is impressive but it is most likely the result of later hagiographical interpolation.

All that can be gleaned from what is recorded in the annals, is that if St Patrick was ordained by Pope Celestine in 431 CE and came to Ireland in 432 CE, was not confirmed in the Catholic faith until ten years later in 441 CE but was 'flourishing in the faith and doctrine of Christ' within a year in 442 CE, then everyone else in the Irish church, in Britain, on the continent and in Rome was completely clueless about what was going on because no one else appears to have heard about him. Was St Patrick's presence not important enough to record? Considering all these uncertainties, the only reasonable inference is that any reliable information which may have existed was lost or greatly obscured in the centuries after St Patrick's death.

The uncertainties which surround St Patrick may have been compounded by the fact that there were several figures called Patrick whose lives may have been confused or woven together. Tirechán tells us that Palladius was also called 'Patrick'.[55] One of Ireland's most rigorous historians, D. A. Binchy, said that when no trustworthy historical information is available it is legitimate even for historians to

---

[55] Thomas O'Rahilly, *The Two Patricks* (Dublin, 1942; repr. 1981).

engage in speculation, since this is the only resource left. What follows is pure speculation. What was going on at that time which might help to explain the anomalies and the deafening silence?

There has to be a rational explanation for Patrick's absence from records which survived from the fifth and sixth century.

St Patrick tells us in his own writings that attempts were made by unnamed Church leaders to remove him from office and his mission to Ireland. Patrick was already working in Ireland when a conflict arose with those he calls his 'seniors'. Had St Patrick become *persona non grata* as a result of these disputes, to the extent that his position was not recognised or sanctioned by emerging leaders in the Church who were becoming influential in Britain and Gaul? The Latin phrase *persona non grata* refers to 'an unwelcome person'.

This was a legal term used in diplomacy that indicates a proscription against a person entering a country. In non-diplomatic usage, when someone was *persona non grata* it suggests that he or she had for some reason been ostracised, so as to be figuratively non-existent. This appears to have happened to Patrick. Speculation centres on issues of concern raging within the western Church at that time and events which must have affected St Patrick's life and ministry, either directly or indirectly.

In his *Chronicle*, which is known to be reliable, Prosper of Aquitaine informs us that St Germanus had been sent to Britain by Pope Celestine in 429 CE as part of an official mission by Rome to combat the Pelagian heresy, said to be rampant in Britain and Ireland at that time.

These visits were part of an initiative undertaken by diocesan Church authorities in Gaul on behalf of Pope Celestine to bring the British and Irish churches in line with the teachings of Rome.

Prosper states that Pope Celestine regarded Britain as the stronghold of Pelagianism and ordered those who shared such views to be banished from Italy. Prosper says Celestine 'was at no less pains to free Britain from the same plague. For certain men who were the enemies of Grace had taken possession of the land of their birth'. Pelagius had been condemned as a heretic, largely through the influence of Augustine and Jerome, whose stance against him was ill-tempered, vitriolic and racist. Jerome called Pelagius a 'fat dog weighed down with Irish porridge'.[56] Shortly afterwards, Pelagius disappeared and was never seen again. Whether he went to the desert, as some traditions claim, or was killed by the champions of orthodoxy, we will probably never know.

Patrick must have been aware of these controversies, since he was probably just beginning some form of biblical study and spiritual formation in preparation for the mission to Ireland, at the time that St Augustine's *Confessions*, which had been completed in 397 CE, was beginning to circulate.

These issues dominated the Church's agenda on the continent and in Britain, throughout the time of St Patrick's mission in Ireland. St Augustine died in 430 CE, which is probably around the time Patrick returned to Ireland. From the evidence available it is difficult to know which side he may have leaned to in this dispute, if any.[57]

James Kenney says St Patrick's writings show 'the unconscious influence of the Anti-Pelagian controversy and his declaration of faith resembles that of Pelagius'. Some scholars suggest that Patrick's way of thinking shows a strong leaning towards Pelagius, while others say his letters reflect the teachings of Augustine.[58] Let's simply acknowledge the silence that surrounds St Patrick in all historical records from this period, which has yet to be explained.

In relation to the Pelagian controversy, we frequently find references to this as an 'arch heresy'. Writers speak of 'the evil poison of Pelagianism' and Pelagius is demonised as a 'heresiarch'. In the midst of serious theological and ecclesiastical controversy, it might be helpful to ask, who exactly were these dastardly Pelagians? Where was the ecclesiastical stronghold from which their 'devilish poison' threatened the life of the western Church?

After being castigated in St Augustine's influential book *Contra Pelagius* (Against Pelagius), Pelagianism was condemned as a heresy, especially by influential bishops in Gaul who were in conflict with the

---

[56] *Contra Collatorem*, XXI; Nora Chadwick, *Age of the Saints in the Celtic Church* (Llanerch, 2006), p. 15.

[57] Gerald Bonner, *St Augustine of Hippo: Life and Controversies* (Norwich, 2002), ch. 8, pp. 313 ff.

[58] Daniel Conneely, *The Letters of St Patrick*, ed. Patrick Bastible (Maynooth, 1993)

type of monasticism pioneered by St Martin. They initially lobbied and then supported Augustine on this issue in efforts to combat the influence of early forms of Gallic monasticism that were unwelcome to many diocesan clergy.

In a letter written to the Irish church in 638 CE Pope John says, 'We have learned that the poison of the Pelagian heresy has revived among you and so we urge you to put out of your minds completely this poisonous crime of superstition ... this detestable heresy.' [59]

Pelagianism never existed as an organised, separatist religious movement. It became a convenient and powerful stereotype, used by the authorities in Rome and North Africa and their supporters in Gaul to counter what was essentially an alternative way of thinking within the Church. Augustine and Jerome, then Pope Celestine, Prosper of Aquitaine and St Germanus of Auxerre were all at the forefront of efforts to combat the teachings of Pelagius. When we meet references to the 'evil poison' of Pelagianism it can be helpful to read between the lines to 'Early Irish, Welsh and Breton Christianity'.

Prosper records that Pope Celestine freed Britain from 'the disease' of Pelagius by sending Germanus of Auxerre to Britain in 428 CE. He describes how Celestine had challenged 'the enemies of grace' also by 'ordaining a bishop (Palladius) for the Irish' (in 431 CE). Prosper remarks that by these actions 'he (Pope Celestine) made the Barbarian island (Ireland) Christian while taking care to keep to the Roman island (Britain) Catholic'. There is no mention of St Patrick having taken a part in it. [60]

St Germanus, Pope Celestine, Prosper of Aquitaine and St Augustine were of the same party. Prosper records, 'Augustine was always in communion with us ... people in Gaul who rejected (his) writings were deprived of the liberty to speak evil.' This confirms that the Church in Britain, Ireland and parts of Gaul was seen to be 'Pelagian' by the Papal authorities and influential diocesan bishops who supported the teachings of Augustine.

---

[59] See Liam de Paor, *St Patrick's World*, p. 149.

[60] Prosper of Aquitaine on Pope Celestine and Pelagius in de Paor, *St Patrick's World*, p. 70 ff.

In a challenging recent study, the Irish author Dara Molloy has argued strongly that the early Irish church (which had developed indigenously before the arrival of more direct Roman influence towards the end of the sixth century) was strongly sympathetic to the teachings of Pelagius and that Rome sought to 'rectify' this. This suggests that efforts made by Rome at this time to challenge and undermine the teachings of Pelagius formed part of a deliberate strategy to confront and control the British and Irish churches and the growing influence of indigenous spiritual traditions, wherever they existed.

Papal letters that survive describe how Celestine launched a strong crusade against Pelagianism at this time. His appointment of Palladius to Ireland must have been designed to support this strategy, hoping to bring the Irish church into line with Rome's official teachings.

The key question is, where did St Patrick stand in relation to all this?

These events all took place at exactly the same time Patrick was being prepared for his mission to Ireland. We tend to forget that Augustine, Jerome, Martin of Tours, Pelagius and Patrick were all basically contemporaries. So was the Emperor Magnus Maximus who was executed and reviled by the Imperial authorities in the aftermath of the rebellion in 383-389 CE. Can the silence which greets us in usually reliable sources be explained because Patrick may have been associated with a religious group accused of being Pelagian, or some other marginal group classified as heretical? This would certainly help to explain St Patrick's absence from existing historical records.

At the beginning of the fifth century, such groups were in conflict with the diocesan bishops who had given their full support to St Augustine's teachings. Some of these bishops had been appointed to the Church in Gaul, where they quickly acquired positions of great influence, wealth and responsibility, replacing 'Celtic' bishops who were sympathetic to Pelagius.

This was part of a deliberate strategy developed by the Church, directed by newly appointed bishops who once held positions of executive responsibility in the imperial administration. The Roman Empire may have collapsed early in the fifth century but its legacy survived and was rejuvenated in many ways by the Church. In a detailed study of the fall of Rome, Peter Heather says:

At the top end of Roman Society, the adoption of Christianity made no difference to the age-old custom that the Empire was God's vehicle in the world.[61]

By 438 CE, the Senate in Rome was a Christian body. The Church was able to rejuvenate a sense of Roman 'imperialism' through an influential and growing ecclesiastical organisation. It adapted many traditional customs and values of the Empire, including dioceses with a hierarchical structure based on the order of deacons, priests and bishops. The Pontiff, based in Rome, continued to dress in purple, the sacred colour of imperial rule.

This was a potent, traditional symbol of both secular and divine authority. These are only a few examples of the many customs, traditions and structures of administration adopted by the Church from its 'secular' forerunner.

After Rome had fallen to the Barbarians, rules and doctrines developed by the Church and administered by the Curia, offered new hope for the preservation of unity and order. A strategy was being developed for the 'Romanisation' of western Christendom. It would take another five hundred years before this policy finally came to absolute fruition with the Norman Invasion of Ireland but this strategic goal, which formed an essential component of St Augustine's teachings, was eventually achieved.

This process began during Patrick's lifetime and, together with Pelagius, St Patrick may have been one of its first victims.

As the fifth century progressed, the monastery of Lerins appears to have become a centre for the promotion of Catholic orthodoxy based on St Augustine's teachings, disseminated through supportive diocesan authorities. Churches in Britain, Ireland and parts of Gaul and Spain were caught in the midst of this influential political development.

The story of the struggle for pre-eminence between the sees of southern Gaul is a complicated one but before long, bishops were appointed from Rome and Lerins to replace the Celtic bishops in

---

61 Peter Heather, *The Fall of the Roman Empire: A New History* (London, 2005).

Gaul. Lupus of Troy, who accompanied St Germanus on the visit to Britain in 429 CE to combat the teachings of Pelagius, was a monk from Lerins. All these developments had a major impact in Brittany and disturbed Martin of Tours greatly. These issues must have had great significance also for St Patrick and his followers.[62]

We catch glimpses of tensions that existed at this time between early forms of Irish, Welsh and Gallic monasticism which were all strongly influenced by Egyptian traditions – and an emerging diocesan hierarchy strongly supportive of Rome. St Ambrose, a close friend and mentor of St Augustine, was afraid to visit Gaul in 392 CE because of the conflict that was raging there between monks and diocesan bishops.[63]These tensions between monasticism and an expansionist and increasingly powerful, Roman diocesan structure may help to shed light on those 'missing years' in the life of St Patrick.

Shortly after sending Palladius as a bishop to Ireland, Pope Celestine wrote to the bishops in Vienne and Narbonne condemning the practice of appointing 'wanderers and outsiders' over the heads of the appointed local clergy. He makes no secret of his dislike of 'monastic bishops' and says:

> It is not surprising they who have not grown up in the Church act contrary to the Church's usages, and that, coming from other customs, they have brought their traditional ways with them *into our church*. Clad in cloak, and with a girdle round the loins, they consider they will be fulfilling the letter rather than the spirit of the scriptures ... Such a practice may be followed as a matter of course rather than reason by those who dwell in remote places and live their lives far from their fellow men. But why should they dress in this way in the churches of God, changing the usage of so many years, of such great prelates, for another habit?[64]

---

[62] Kenney, *Sources*, pp. 163–5; Heinrich Zimmer, *The Celtic Church in Britain and Ireland*.

[63] Chadwick, *Age of the Saints*, p. 31.

[64] Epistle 4, Mansi, III, p. 264. *Emphasis added.

Pope Celestine's description of these 'wanderers and outsiders' who practiced an ascetic Christian lifestyle based on the need for 'purity of heart' through which they considered themselves to be fulfilling the biblical law is an appropriate description for the approach taken by St Martin and St Patrick.

According to an ancient tradition, St Patrick spent four years in spiritual formation with St Martin's community and was tonsured there. These groups had an uneasy relationship with diocesan authorities. Some were sympathetic to the Priscillians, as St Martin was.

St Columbanus never mentions St Patrick or Pelagius by name but he does make an intriguing and surprisingly defensive remark which may help shed light on issues of concern at the time he was writing. In his letter to Pope Boniface IV, written in 613 CE, Columbanus seeks to assure Rome, that the early Irish church was and always had been part of the one true Catholic and Apostolic Church and not a separate "Celtic" Church. What he actually says is: 'No Jews, schismatics or heretics can be found amongst us.' Is it possible that St Patrick had been forgotten and erased from history because he had been associated with one or more of these three groups? [65]

One of the most controversial claims found in many of the ancient sources is that St Patrick's ancestors were Jewish. [66]

This has always been dismissed as a 'legend' without historical foundation but if there is any truth in this claim then it would certainly help explain why the surviving records are so silent with regard to St Patrick. In the sixth century, when anti-Semitism was pervasive, this would have been a factor strong enough to guarantee a journey into historical oblivion.

Considering that St Patrick is such an anonymous figure in all the surviving records from the fifth and sixth centuries it is a miracle that his two letters survived. But survive they did, God bless them,

---

[65] Liam de Paor, *St Patrick's World*, pp 141–3.

[66] *Quidam sanctum Patricium ex Iudeis dicunt originem duxisse*: 'Some state that St Patrick's origins was of the Jews'. See 'Vita IV' in Ludwig Bieler, ed., *Four Latin Lives of St Patrick*, (Dublin, 2005), p. 50. For a detailed study of this possibility, see 'Was St Patrick Jewish?' in Marcus Losack, *St Patrick and the Bloodline of the Grail: The Untold Story of St Patrick's Royal Family* (Annamoe, 2012), p. 119 ff.

through all the great dangers and difficulties of this turbulent period in history that followed the collapse of the Roman Empire, fuelled by the Barbarian invasions in Europe and the Anglo-Saxon invasion of Britain. A cult of St Patrick must have existed somewhere, possibly in the north of Ireland where his writings were preserved by friends or followers. Suddenly, in the closing decades of the seventh century after more than two hundred years of historical and ecclesiastical silence, something happened to turn Patrick's 'biography' upside down. St Patrick was about to reappear from the historical oblivion with great fanfare and glory, in hagiographical documents published by the Church in Armagh.

Whatever may have happened in the previous two hundred years, around 685 CE someone decided it was time to open the file and prepare Ireland's apostle for an official resurrection.

Bishop Aed of Sletty, who was active in efforts to reform the Church in Ireland and encourage wider acceptance of Rome, commissioned an Irish scribe called Muirchú to write an official 'biography' of St Patrick. This has shaped our image and understanding of Patrick to the present day. By the time Muirchú put pen to paper, the world was a very different place to that which St Patrick had known when he first came to Ireland.

On the margins of Western Europe where indigenous and Celtic traditions were strong, Christianity was rapidly being Romanised and organised more effectively at an international level with diocesan structures capable of propagating official Church teachings and doctrines.

As part of a well-developed and deliberate strategy, ecclesiastical, political and military alliances had been formed between the Roman Church and the Franks in Gaul and with the Anglo-Saxons in Britain. Such alliances increased the Church's influence and authority and now gave it the secular muscle required to overcome opposition.

A new world order was emerging.

Christianity on the continent was becoming more homogenised and uniform. The Roman Church was now expanding westwards and growing stronger. Roman ecclesiastical traditions were not only becoming more popular – in some parts of Ireland and elsewhere they were becoming more desirable; and they could now be effectively imposed. Those who refused to conform to Rome's teachings and accept reforms were becoming increasingly isolated and marginalised. It is within this historical context that Ireland's 'unknown apostle', St Patrick, was about to come out of the invisible closet into which history had so far confined him.

Muirchú was a genius. His *Life of St Patrick* would quickly find its way onto the front page of the Irish ecclesiastical record and gain great influence. To meet the changing circumstances of the times, whatever may have happened before, Patrick's image and the ecclesiastical record now had to be acceptable. St Patrick was about to be presented to the Church and the world as a fully paid up, card carrying member of the Catholic Church, with a pristine behavioural record. Any talk of conflict with ecclesiastical authorities or the reason for his absence from historical records had to be discounted.

Whatever uncertainties had existed in the past, whatever might have been the truth about St Patrick's place of origins or his obscure and controversial religious and ethnic background, St Patrick's story was about to go public and this time, therefore, it had to be kosher. This was not the time to mention any possible association there may have been with those now seriously out of favour, such as the three groups branded by St Columbanus as schismatics, heretics and Jews or 'Judaizers'.

This term applied to Christians who decided to adopt Jewish customs and practices such as keeping Saturday as the Christian Sabbath, giving high priority to the Law of Moses and celebrating Easter with the Jewish Passover.

Greatly honoured and now to be remembered for all time, St Patrick was heralded as the sole founder of Irish Christianity, soon to be Ireland's patron saint and national apostle, founder and first archbishop of the Church in Armagh, blessed by Pope Celestine and in full communion with Rome.

It wasn't the truth, but for Ireland and the Irish Church at the end of the seventh century, it served far more than its purpose. That's how the 'Legend' of St Patrick was born.

CHAPTER FIVE

OUR MAN IN ARMAGH

One of the easiest and most effective ways to promote a deception is by the misspelling of words. Names can be distorted and misspelled to such an extent it requires long and patient effort to trace their true and proper form.[67]

A file labelled 'St Patrick' must have been tucked away somewhere, perhaps in the basement at the monastery of Armagh. It had gathered a lot of dust by the time Muirchú opened it and he knew that his task would not be easy. More than two hundred years had passed since St Patrick's death and the information which had survived about him was obscure. Muirchú began his narrative with surprising frankness and honesty. He says St Patrick's life was uncertain and controversial. Scribes had found 'discrepancies' and 'so many had expressed doubts, they had never arrived at a coherent narrative of events'. Muirchú complains of 'uncertain sources' and 'unreliable memories'.

He also expresses genuine anxiety bordering on fear about the responsibility he had been given, concerned that he was entering

---

[67] Conor MacDari, *The Bible: An Irish Book* (London, 2005).

what he describes as the 'deep and dangerous sea' of fifth-century church history.

The information about St Patrick was obviously complex and uncertain but what could possibly make an investigation into this subject so dangerous? This is how Muirchú described what he found when he opened the file at the end of the seventh century:

> My lord Aed: Many have tried to bring certainty to the order of this narrative according to what their fathers and those who were from the beginning servants of the Word have handed down to them, though because of this most difficult work of narration and the different opinions and very great suspicions of so very many persons, they have never managed to achieve consensus or certainty with regard to an agreed history.

> For that reason, unless I am deceived, according to this proverb of ours 'as boys are led out into an amphitheatre' [we have found ourselves] being led through this deep and dangerous sea of holy narration where there are very violent eddies and whirlpools, uncharted waters never tamed or brought to order by any previous craft except by my father Cogitosus.[68]

> I have taken this initiative now with something tried and appropriated, the infant sailing boat of my own little intellect but just in case I am accused of fashioning something great from something small, know that I am working without sufficient literary sources, authors who cannot be identified, dependent on unreliable memories and the bad language that characterises this controversial subject …

> I do this with pious affection and holy charity, obedient to the command of your holiness and authority, even though I may be feeling weighed down with great uncertainty, I shall now take steps to unfold a few of the many deeds of holy Patrick.[69]

---

[68] Cogitosus's *Life of St Brigid* is one of the earliest Irish hagiographies dated c.650 CE. For an English translation see Liam de Paor, *St Patrick's World* (Dublin, 1993), p. 207 ff.

[69] For Muirchú's original Latin text and an English translation see David Howlett, *Muirchú Moccu Mactheni's 'Vita Sancti Patricii'* (Dublin, 2006), p. 46. Also Ludwig Bieler, *Patrician Texts in the Book of Armagh* (Dublin, 2004), p. 62 ff., and Kenney, *Sources for the Early History of Ireland: Ecclesiastical* (Dublin, 1997), p. 332.

Muirchú had been commissioned by the Church in Armagh to write an official 'biography' of St Patrick. Regardless of any difficulties, this had to be detailed and specific. 'Time, place and person' were demanded. Failure and further controversy was not acceptable. Muirchú's warning about uncertainties is quickly left aside as he launches into the main body of his narrative. He makes explicit geographical statements, in which Muirchú claims to know 'without doubt' that Patrick came from Britain:

Patrick, also named Sochet –

A Briton by race [*Brito natione*]

Born in the Britains [*in Brittanniis natus*]

His father Calpurnius [a deacon] the son

[As Patrick says] of an elder, Potitus

Who hailed from Bannauem Thaburniae –

A place not far from our sea …

This place, I am informed beyond

hesitation or doubt, is Ventra.

His mother's name was Conchessa.

Muirchú had access to a copy of St Patrick's *Confession*. He follows it closely in the first part of his narrative. He tells us that Patrick's family came from 'Bannauem Thaburniae'. This is an alternative spelling to the way it appears in the *Book of Armagh* version of Patrick's *Confession*, but it is still clearly recognisable. According to author David Howlett, who has made a detailed study of his text, Muirchú used numerology or gematria when composing his narrative. Gematria is based on numeric values given to Hebrew letters. Muirchú must have had access to a manual of the Hebrew alphabet designating these values although such a manual has never been discovered in Europe; individual words, sentences and paragraphs were constructed using alphanumeric values, based on letters in the Hebrew alphabet.[70] This might help explain a

---

[70] Howlett, '*Vita Sancti Patricii*', pp. 180–6.

difference in spelling in this case.

Muirchú is the first person we know to claim that he could identify the location of Bannavem Tiburniae. He said he knew without doubt it was called 'Ventra'. Unfortunately, 'Ventra' has never been identified. We don't know whether it was a town or village or even if it existed. It is possible that 'Ventra' could be Muirchú's rendering of 'Nemthor' which is mentioned in *St Fiacc's Hymn* as the birth place of St Patrick.

Muirchú states clearly, that it was in Britain and his narrative is one of the earliest sources used to support the view that St Patrick came from Britain. Muirchú identifies St Patrick's place of origins exclusively with Britain. He provides detailed geographical descriptions using names which appear to refer to Britain and have always been translated as Britain.

Let's take a closer look at the words he used in Latin, to see whether his geography is clear enough to be trustworthy.

Muirchú tells us St Patrick was 'a Briton' by nationality (*Brito natione*) born 'in the Britains' (*in Brittanniis*). When Patrick escaped from Ireland the ship took him back to 'the Britains' (*ad Brittanias nauigauit*). When Patrick left his homeland 'in the Britains' (*in Brittanniis*), he went to study in Gaul with St Germanus. Muirchú describes how St Patrick crossed the sea 'to the south of Britain' to get there. While Patrick was in Gaul news reached the continent that Palladius had died 'in the Britains' (*in Brittanniis*). After Patrick had finished his religious training in Gaul and was ready to embark on his mission to Ireland he 'came through to the Britains'.

Muirchú tells us that at that time 'the whole of Britain' (*tota Brittannia*) was frozen in the cold of unbelief, a statement which is reminiscent of how Gildas described the wretched state of Britain after the fall of the Roman Empire. Patrick crossed the Irish Sea (*Mari nostra* means 'our sea' presumably from somewhere on the west coast of Britain) before he landed at Wicklow Harbour (Inver Dee) on the south-east coast of Ireland. This was a port at the mouth of what is now the Vartry River, once called the Dee. It was an important port for trade between Ireland and the continent in the late

Roman period.[71]

Muirchú really goes overboard in a geographical sense, by including so much detailed, descriptive geography in his narrative. He uses several names which as far as Muirchú is concerned, all clearly refer to the island of Britain and are applied exclusively to Britain. Muirchú's use of different names for 'Britain' is suspicious and appears contrived. He may have included some of the names found in his sources, assuming these all referred to Britain and/or presenting them as referring to Britain. These geographical descriptions are cleverly designed to emphasise the 'fact' that St Patrick came from Britain and remove any lingering doubt about that. His narrative is impressively well constructed but is it trustworthy?

Hagiography is a particular genre of medieval literature, designed with one objective in mind, to publicise the life of a saint and emphasise their holy and miraculous deeds. Hagiographers cannot be viewed as reliable historical witnesses. Medieval hagiographers were professional spin doctors.

We cannot treat this information as trustworthy in the way we should be able to trust history, geography or biography, even though what Muirchú writes sounds very convincing. As Binchy once said, with Irish hagiography, nothing is impossible. Let's try to step inside Muirchú's shoes for a moment and appreciate his genius. When Muirchú described St Patrick's place of origins and episodes that took place in his life, he did this by creating a geographical picture. In other words, Muirchú created a 'map'.

Through the use of creative and pseudo-historical narrative, he uses this 'map' to explain and convince his readers as to where St Patrick came from, where he received his religious training and the various journeys St Patrick is alleged to have undertaken. Some of these journeys can be identified from St Patrick's writings but others cannot.

Muirchú's 'map' was carefully designed and deliberately crafted to locate St Patrick's origins in Britain. To understand his work, we have to be able to 'read' his map. Authors Ward Kaiser and Denis Wood have written a fascinating study of maps called *Seeing through Maps: The*

---

[71] Muirchú, XI:44, Howlett *'Vita Sancti Patricii'*, p. 61.

Power of Images to Shape our World View.[72] When asked if there is any such thing as a true and accurate map, they say, 'Maps are merely descriptions of the world or part of it, from a particular perspective or bias.' To understand what this bias is, they suggest we look first at what stands at the centre of the map, because this reflects a certain world view. This is true of all maps, but especially those from the medieval period. A good example is a twelfth-century map of the world called the *Mappa Mundi*, preserved at Hereford Cathedral, England. In this map, Jerusalem stands at the centre of the world. This reflects a religious world view held by some at that time, from a Jewish-Christian perspective.

Muirchú's 'map' was designed to explain key episodes in St Patrick's life and locate those events for the reader. His genius as a hagiographer is that he appears to speak with authority, to the extent that his narrative has shaped our image of St Patrick's biography for more than a thousand years. Most writers are still convinced that, in terms of his origins, Britain stood at the centre of St Patrick's world. Kaiser and Wood invite us to reflect more deeply on what we can learn from maps, saying that every map reflects an agenda and we can detect that agenda by observing what has been included and what has been excluded from the map. This is a sign of any map maker's priorities and defines their 'mental geography'. A map of Ireland designed to advertise cathedrals or sites of historical and archaeological interest, for example, would be very different to one designed to show golf courses. Can we detect any form of bias or hidden agenda in the 'map' Muirchú created for us?

Muirchú was commissioned by the church in Armagh to write the Church's first official 'biography' of St Patrick and he was expected to provide clear and specific information. He admits in his prologue 'time, place and person' were demanded. Those who funded his work had a strong political and ecclesiastical agenda which may have influenced the choices he made about what to include or leave out. This is where maps become really interesting. What Muirchú left out or excluded from his map is just as significant as what he included.

---

[72] Ward Kaiser and Denis Wood, *Seeing, through Maps: The Power of Images to Shape our World View* (Massachusetts, 2001).

We know Muirchú had access to a copy of St Patrick's *Confession*, so we can compare both documents and see what he included and what he excluded from Patrick's own writings. For example, any reference to St Patrick's difficulties with 'seniors' in the Church, those who were seeking to discredit Patrick's reputation and remove him from office, are excluded.

A conflict with (and estrangement from) certain figures who represented the ecclesiastical authorities stands at the centre of St Patrick's *Confession*, but Muirchú makes no reference to it.

Muirchú also excluded any reference to another tradition which said that Patrick was taken captive from a place on the continent, in Brittany.

We do not know what stories Muirchú had found in the files, or what sources he used, apart from St Patrick's *Confession*, but he was probably aware that Patrick's family had some 'French' connections. This is a reasonable assumption to make because Muirchú tells us that St Patrick's mother was called Conchessa, but he does not include the second part of that tradition, as it is passed down through most of the other sources, that she was 'of the Franks' and a close relative of St Martin of Tours.

In all the other ancient *Lives of St Patrick* which mention Conchessa by name, these extra details are always included, even in Jocelyn. Why did Muirchú choose not to mention it? One possible explanation is that it did not suit his objective as a hagiographer, which was to emphasise the pureness of Patrick's pedigree as an apostle who came to Ireland from Britain.

Muirchú's real genius can be appreciated when we understand the context in which he was writing. This was a critical time in Irish, British and European history. Recent developments in Britain had serious implications for Ireland and for the church in Armagh.

Muirchú's narrative cannot be understood in isolation from these events which probably influenced much of what Muirchú wrote about St Patrick and perhaps ultimately determined the whole design of his 'map'.

The Synod of Whitby, 664 CE

At the end of the year in which St Columba had died, 597 CE, Pope Gregory sent St Augustine to Canterbury, England, as part of a Roman mission. This began as a fairly small undertaking, centred on the church in Kent. Things changed dramatically when a new alliance was forged between the Roman Church and senior members of the Anglo-Saxon royal family. This was brought into effect through decisions taken at the Synod of Whitby in 664 CE.

At this Synod, the king of Northumbria, who was concerned about the practical implications of differences between the Roman Church and the Irish tradition with regard to the date for Easter, decided to accept the need for uniformity and submit the English Church to the authority of Rome.

After Whitby, the Irish Church also came under pressure to reform. The Catholic Church in Britain had begun to establish a very close alliance with the Anglo-Saxons and now benefited from English military expansion. By the time Muirchú started writing his *Life of St Patrick* the Anglo-Saxons had occupied coastal areas of north-west Britain and reached as far north as Carlisle and Dumbarton in Scotland. The Irish Church was watching these developments with grave concern especially when news came through that the English had taken the Kingdom of Strathclyde, an ancient and symbolic stronghold for the Irish. From an Irish perspective, the threat of an English invasion was not only real, it was imminent. The invasion of Brega in 684 CE shows how the ambitions of the Northumbrians now extended to Ireland. From Strathclyde or the Isle of Man, which had been occupied by the Northumbrians for fifty years, it was only a short distance across the sea to Armagh.[73]

For the first time in her history, Ireland faced the military might of the English, allied to the ecclesiastical authority of Rome. Threats concerning the use of force had been made clear to the Britons, a Celtic-speaking people who inhabited the island of Britain before the Anglo-Saxon invasions in the fifth century. It was implicit in 603 CE when Bede records that St Augustine of Canterbury 'urged the British bishops to cement Catholic unity' and backed this with a threat that

---

[73] T. M. Charles-Edwards, *Early Christian Ireland* (Cambridge, 2000), p. 438.

'if they refused to unite with their fellow Christians, they would be attacked by their enemies (the English) and if they refused to preach the faith of Christ to them, they would eventually be punished by meeting death at their hands'. [74] Bede said that St Augustine's threat proved itself to be a prophecy, soon to be fulfilled, when around one thousand two hundred British (Celtic) monks from the Monastery at Bangor in North Wales were killed by Anglo-Saxon forces at the Battle of Chester in 612 CE.

Anglo-Saxon military advances during the closing decades of the seventh century created a potentially serious situation for the Irish who were deeply divided. Some favoured Roman reform, while others wished to remain faithful to indigenous traditions of Irish monasticism, in many ways autonomous and independent from Rome. Meanwhile, Ireland was also in the midst of a civil war. A secular power struggle was taking place between rival chieftains, most notably the northern and southern O'Neills.

The church in Armagh had a pivotal role in this conflict. Catholic reform was top of the ecclesiastical, political and civil agenda. A religious component underscored the secular conflict. A violent struggle was taking place between two opposing religious factions. On one side, a group called the Romani had already adopted Roman customs for the celebration of Easter, and was seeking to bring the whole Irish Church under the authority of Rome. Standing against them, the Hibernensi held fast to Irish monastic traditions and resisted Roman reforms. Hibernia was the Roman name for Ireland. Carney writes:

> Armagh set out to claim jurisdiction over the whole island from about the mid-sixth century. The claim *legatus totus Hiberniae* implies a claim to jurisdiction over all Ireland and Papal authority for such jurisdiction.[75]

In the closing decades of the seventh century, Armagh became the headquarters of the Romani movement. It was also the mother house

---

[74] Bede, *Ecclesiastical History*, ii: 2, 3.

[75] James Carney, *Studies in Irish Literature and History* (Dublin, 1979), p. 399

for the *Paruchia Patricii* – 'Patrick's Fraternity' – a growing federation of monasteries and churches claiming jurisdiction over the whole of Ireland on the basis that St Patrick was their founder. There were important financial aspects to these arrangements. Membership of such monastic federations required loyalty to the founding saint with financial obligations. Armagh would receive gifts of land, rentals and tithes in return for the blessings and privileges of coming under the banner of St Patrick, the federation's patron saint.[76]

The church in Armagh was developing a strong federation in the name of St Patrick. It was in direct conflict with monasteries established by St Columba, which had suffered setbacks as a direct result of decisions taken in Northumbria at the Synod of Whitby.

The secular and religious landscape in Ireland was changing rapidly. It is no coincidence that Bishop Aed commissioned Muirchú to write an official 'biography' of St Patrick at this time, as a means of strengthening public support for Armagh's growing ecclesiastical ambitions. His *Life of St Patrick* would influence the outcome of this dispute in ways that St Patrick could never have imagined. Bishop Aed had recently allowed his own congregation at Sletty to be incorporated into the *Paruchia Patricii* after visiting Bishop Segene, who was Abbot of Armagh from 662–688 CE.[77]

Muirchú was a member of this new federation and had a vested interest in the outcome of these events. In fact, the church in Armagh was politically involved at the highest level in its desire to reform the Irish Church and bring it more closely under the authority of Rome. Cummian, a leading activist, had recently written a threatening letter to Segene, Abbot of Iona, about the Easter controversy. In this letter he strongly advised Iona to accept Roman reform, so there could be uniformity within the Irish Church.

Aed, Muirchú and Cummian were all members of the Romanising party. They were well educated and highly motivated political and ecclesiastical activists whose objective was to introduce reforms whilst at the same time enhancing the claims of Armagh. Events taking place in Ireland were beginning to mirror those in

---

[76] D. A. Binchy, 'Patrick and his Biographers', *Studia Hibernica*, 2 (1962) pp. 60–4.

[77] Kenney, *The Sources for the Early History of Ireland: Ecclesiastical* (Dublin, 1997), p. 340.

Northumbria. We sense how divisive the situation was from Bishop Tirechán, another key member of the federation, whose notes are preserved alongside Muirchú's narrative in the *Book of Armagh*. Tirechán was an influential figure in Connacht and the west of Ireland. He appears to speak with genuine concern and compassion, when he says:

> My heart is troubled within me for love of Patrick, since I see renegades and robbers and warriors of Ireland who hate Patrick's *Paruchia*; they have stolen from him what was his. And now they are afraid since, if the heirs of Patrick were to reclaim their territory, they could recover the whole island. God gave the whole island (to Patrick) with its people. All the primitive churches of Ireland are his.[78]

The 'renegades and robbers' were the so-called 'dissidents' that Tirechán despised, members of the Columban Church or those who still supported the older, Irish monastic foundations and refused to accept either the legitimacy of the claims of Armagh or the customs and reforms now being required of the Irish Church, by Rome. The position of Armagh is made very clear when Tirechán says, 'To Patrick belongs the church although the community of Columcille has encroached upon it.' [79]

The Synod of Birr, 697 CE

Aed and Muirchú are listed among clergy who attended the Synod of Birr in 697 CE, where the famous 'Law of Adamnán' was agreed. This was the Irish Church's response to developments which had taken place at Whitby, in Britain. The Synod of Birr had been convened in Ireland to secure an agreement between the southern and northern Irish churches, to introduce certain reforms and accept the authority of Rome. Author David Howlett has argued strongly

---

[78] Liam de Paor, *St. Patrick's World*, p.160.

[79] Liam de Paor, *St Patrick's World*, p. 160; 'Armagh and the Patrick of Legend' in Kenney, *Sources*, p 319 and Stokes, *Tripartite Life of St Patrick* (London, 1887), p. 97.

that as part of this agreement, the new Roman cycle for calculating the date of Easter and other Roman ecclesiastical customs were accepted in the north of Ireland while St Patrick was recognised as Ireland's national apostle in the south. Howlett is convinced that claims about St Patrick being the founder of Irish Christianity and patron saint of all Ireland were formulated in a more precise fashion at this time.[80]

The conflict taking place within the Irish Church and between the chieftains cannot be viewed in isolation from the ecclesiastical and military pressures being applied externally from Rome and Britain. Changes which took place in the aftermath of the Synod of Whitby were having a huge impact on the independence and safety of the Irish tradition. That is why it is incorrect to describe the Synod of Whitby as an insignificant event in the context of the wider affairs of the Church and for the British and Irish churches in particular.

St Wilfrid was a young and ambitious cleric who had acted as spokesperson for the Roman party at Whitby. The Irish were greatly concerned about his role in Church affairs and tried on several occasions to have him removed. They were especially concerned about Wilfrid's ambitions towards Ireland. Having tasted the fruits of success at Whitby, Wilfrid appears to have set his sights on becoming Metropolitan Archbishop not only of the whole of northern Britain but also Ireland. This is confirmed by ecclesiastical records.

Much of what follows is drawn from David Howlett's study, in which he identifies key issues surrounding the compilation of Muirchú's narrative.[81]

In 669 CE, five years after the Synod of Whitby, Theodore of Tarsus had been sent to Britain by Pope Gregory, as head of the Roman mission. Theodore was Greek and may have appreciated the orthodoxy of the Irish Tradition. At the Synod of Hertford in 672 CE, Theodore was designated 'Archbishop of Canterbury' but at the Synod of Hatfield a few years later (679 CE) he was entitled 'Archbishop of All Britain'. His attempt to divide dioceses led to a conflict with Wilfrid, who travelled to Rome from November 679

---

[80] David Howlett, 'Vita Sancti Patricii', p. 180 ff.

[81] David Howlett, Muirchú Moccu Mactheni's 'Vita Sancti Patricii' (Dublin, 2006), but also T. M. Charles-Edwards, Early Christian Ireland (Cambridge, 2000) p. 429 ff.

CE to March 680 CE to protest the diminution of his authority.

The Papal authorities approved his petition but when he returned to Britain, their opinion was rejected and Wilfrid was imprisoned for a short time by the secular and religious authorities in Northumbria, who appear to have briefly returned to their traditional loyalties.

After his release, Wilfrid moved to the south of England where he lived from 681–686 CE. Wilfrid's ambitions may have posed a threat to the church in Ireland. In 704 CE he returned to Rome to continue his personal 'crusade'. Speaking as if he was the Archbishop of York (which at that time he was not) Wilfrid vouched for the Catholic orthodoxy not only of the Anglo-Saxons in Northumbria but also 'all the inhabitants of northern Britain and Ireland and adjacent lands'.[82]

> For all the northern part of Britain and Ireland and the islands which are inhabited by the people of the English and the Britons, also the Scots [Irish] and the Picts he [Wilfrid] confessed the true and Catholic faith.[83]

Wilfrid's restoration in 687 CE probably sparked concerns in Armagh about who was going to be the future Metropolitan Archbishop in Ireland. During at least two visits to Rome, Wilfrid appears to have tried to persuade the Papal authorities that he was the right person for the job. If Wilfrid (who was English) had been granted authority in Ireland, this would have presented difficulties for the Irish and may have resulted in a greater loss of 'independence' for the Irish tradition.

Despite their serious differences, the Romani and Hibernensi shared nationalist Irish sympathies. Both groups must have been anxious to find a compromise and resolve domestic difficulties. Wilfrid's reputation would have suggested they guard themselves against him. This would have been even more the case if the Irish Church was aware of events taking place in Gaul, where Ebroin, one of the Dukes of Theodoric, king of the Franks, offered 'a full bushel of gold solidi' if the king of Friesland would 'send Wilfrid to him

---

[82] Howlett, 'Vita Sancti Patricii', p. 181–2 and B. Cosgrave, ed., *The Life of Bishop Wilfrid by Eddius Stephanus* (Cambridge, 1985).

[83] Howlett, p. 182. See also 'Life of Wilfrid', trans. J. F. Webb, *Lives of Saints* (London, 1986), p. 188.

alive, or slay him and send his head'.[84]

Wilfrid's political and ecclesiastical ambitions were not restricted to Britain and Ireland. For some reason, a price had been put on his head on the continent. Some of Wilfrid's clerical friends in Gaul appear to have been involved with activities which had already led to several deaths.

Eddius Stephanos, his close friend and biographer, describes how Wilfrid gave support to the exiled Merovingian king, Dagobert II, who was being protected at the Monastery of Slane in Ireland where he had been educated since he was a young child.

Immediately following the Synod of Whitby in 664 CE, Wilfrid became deeply involved with arrangements for Dagobert to return to Gaul to reclaim his right to the throne. Before leaving Ireland, Dagobert had married an Irish princess called Mathilde. They travelled to England in 668 CE to meet Wilfrid in York. Two years later, Mathilde died in childbirth before the royal couple left England. Dagobert was only twenty years old at the time.

Wilfrid now arranged for Dagobert to marry Gizelle de Razés, daughter of the Count of Razés, who was niece of the king of the Visigoths. Returning to France, Gizelle and Dagobert II were married in the Church of St Mary Magdalene at Rennes-le-Château, in 670 CE. It was through the agency of Wilfrid who was now appointed Archbishop of York, that Dagobert was restored to his kingdom, after the death and disposition of Childeric II.

These events place Wilfrid at the centre of what has been called 'The Merovingian Conspiracy'. This is a controversial subject but with significant implications for the study of St Patrick.[85]

Dagobert was crowned around 674 CE but his reign was to be short lived. After returning to France, he appears to have reneged on promises made to Wilfrid by not cooperating with the authorities of the Roman Church, much to the dismay of local diocesan clergy. Dagobert was assassinated shortly afterwards, an event linked to Wilfrid and efforts to influence the Merovingian succession. The

---

[84] Eddius Stephanus, *Life of Wilfrid*, trans. J. F. Webb (London, 1986).

[85] See Marcus Losack, *St Patrick and the Bloodline of the Grail – the Untold Story of Saint Patrick's Royal Family*, (Annamoe, Wicklow, 2012).

circumstances that surround Wilfrid's contact with clergy in Gaul, which led to the murder of Dagobert II, are very suspicious.

Whatever political and ecclesiastical intrigues may have been taking place, great pressures appear to have been placed on the Irish Church during the last thirteen or fourteen years of the seventh century from the restoration of Wilfrid in 686 or 687 CE to the death of Bishop Aed in 700 CE.

Muirchú's *Life of St Patrick* can only be fully understood in the context of these complex political and ecclesiastical realities. According to author David Howlett, this was a period in Ireland when Cogitosus and Muirchú both used hagiography as a medium to support ideas as to which saint would be accepted as the national apostle of Ireland and which church should become the Metropolitan See. Cogitosus had argued for St Brigid and Kildare. Armagh argued for Patrick. In simple terms, Armagh won and St Patrick instead of St Brigid became the national apostle and patron saint of Ireland.

The church in Armagh benefited greatly from Reforms but an ability to compromise and avoid further internal division, which opened the doors to 'Romanisation', also allowed the Irish Church to retain a certain degree of freedom and independence. Muirchú's 'biography' of St Patrick ensured an ecclesiastical triumph for Armagh, presenting St Patrick as the apostle and patron saint of Irish Christianity as founder of the Church in Armagh.

This probably helped keep Wilfrid out of Ireland, reducing tensions and threats of an English invasion. Muirchú may have invented stories to include senior figures from Anglo-Saxon royal families who were related to strategic places such as the Isle of Man, Wales and Strathclyde, perhaps to create the impression that St Patrick's religious authority was already well established with these people and, therefore, within the regions over which they had influence in Britain. Howlett says, Muirchú's *Life of Patrick* is a sophisticated work of hagiography which implements a national, political and ecclesiastical agenda. This shaped and determined what Muirchú said about St Patrick, much of which is fictitious. This relates also to St Patrick's place of origins.

Howlett argues that Muirchú's objective was to bring Patrick into relationship with powerful figures in Ireland and Britain, to establish an ecclesiastical pedigree for St Patrick and a line of protection for

the Irish Church. This line extended through the western coast of
Britain southwards from Strathclyde to Anglesey, northwards to the
Picts and east towards the Saxons, the region in which Wilfrid was
claiming authority:

> Muirchú is with an implicit geographical argument turning the tables,
> not only denying that Wilfrid is or can be Metropolitan of Ireland but
> suggesting that *the Briton* Patrick is the rightful metropolitan not only of
> Ireland but the entire archipelago on the western and north western side
> of the British Isles, the same islands and peoples mentioned by Wilfrid
> in Rome.[86]

Muirchú's *Life of St Patrick* was created as part of a strategic effort to
secure the claims of Armagh and perhaps even to safeguard Ireland's
national interest through the medium of hagiography. This required
an impressive but essentially fictional reinvention of St Patrick's
'biography'.

Professor Binchy speaks with authority on this subject when he
describes how the secular claims and ascendency of the Northern Uí
Neill which was one of the most powerful clans in Ireland at this time,
went hand in hand with the religious claims and ascendency of
Armagh:

> The Armagh canon is merely one of the numerous forgeries by means
> of which, in the course of the seventh century, the community of
> Armagh sought to buttress its claim to supremacy over the other
> monastic federations.[87]

Muirchú may have expressed doubts and misgivings about having to
'create big things out of something small' but thanks to his efforts, St
Patrick provided the church in Armagh and perhaps even the nation
of Ireland herself with what was needed to resolve current difficulties

---

[86] Howlett, '*Vita Sancti Patricii*', p. 182 ff.* Emphasis added.

[87] Binchy, '*Patrick and his Biographers*', p. 52

and avoid more serious conflicts. The information about St Patrick that had been available to Muirchú may have been uncertain and controversial but that kind of image was not helpful for the Irish Church at the end of the seventh century. If Muirchú was aware of uncertainty as to where St Patrick came from, he tries to correct that.

His task was to remove any doubt or confusion, which he did by creating a 'map' deliberately designed and crafted to emphasise St Patrick's close connections with Britain. We should not underestimate his ability to shape the map the way he and the church in Armagh wanted it to be shaped. In terms of St Patrick's place of origins, Muirchú is the first person to claim not only that it was in Britain, but he deals very cleverly with the contradictions and confusion that must have existed, concerning the location of St Patrick's *Britanniis*, by removing any claims which may have suggested a French connection. Muirchú places Britain at the centre of St Patrick's world but he was writing hagiography and not history or biography and we must always remember that. Those who support the claims of hagiography – however convincing they may appear to be – do so at great peril to themselves and to the demands of historical integrity. Muirchú's description of various journeys allegedly undertaken by St Patrick appears at first sight to be very convincing, but the template he uses is essentially hagiographical.

The result was an outstanding success from Armagh's point of view. Muirchú convinced most readers that he was speaking with authority – that he had dealt with any remaining doubts or potential conflicts and revealed everything of substance that could be found in the file. His narrative was so influential that it has completely defined many people's image and understanding of St Patrick for more than a thousand years.

But can we trust Muirchú's statement that St Patrick was British?

Writers may be sceptical about the claims of hagiography but most have accepted Muirchú's statement that St Patrick came from Britain, as if this is historically reliable and no longer in dispute. If so, the local tradition preserved at Château de Bonaban claiming St Patrick was taken captive from Brittany, cannot be trusted. Who is telling the truth? As our friend in Washington DC advises intelligence agents when he is teaching them how to write better reports – just because someone says something is true does not mean it necessarily is true, unless some real evidence is provided in support.

Muirchú provides no historical evidence to support his claim that St Patrick came from Britain. What he does provide is an impressive 'map' which dominated the front page of the ecclesiastical press in Ireland at the end of the seventh century. Muirchú had rescued St Patrick from historical oblivion and created a new ecclesiastical authority for Ireland's national apostle.

To make this transition possible, he presented Ireland's new patron saint with all the required credentials. This included a personal portfolio of his holy and miraculous deeds, a list of powerful and aristocratic English associates, an original 'British' passport and some pristine ecclesiastical qualifications that were well documented and now clearly and officially stamped 'Roman', 'British', 'orthodox' and 'Catholic'.

Muirchú was faithful to his sources in one very important respect. If he had found the name 'Britanniis' as a description of St Patrick's homeland in the copy of Patrick's *Confession* available to him, he retained this name with exactly the same spelling. He used this name to good effect in his narrative. When he designed his 'map' to locate St Patrick's homeland, Muirchú made sure this name applied to Britain.

If the claims recorded by local Breton historians and preserved at Château de Bonaban are authentic, for St Patrick this phrase may not have referred to the island of Britain but a region on the continent we now call Brittany.

If it can be shown that St Patrick was taken captive from Brittany and not Britain, then Muirchú had applied this name to the wrong country.

This may have been an innocent error due to a continuing confusion in surviving records. Muirchú may not have known the true location of Patrick's homeland but was determined to resolve contradictory claims he found in the existing sources. He admits the information that had survived was uncertain and he was expected to bring certainty to St Patrick's biography.

On the other hand, could Muirchú have been responsible for some kind of deliberate 'fraud' or deception, falsifying the evidence to suit a particular domestic or political purpose? Fraud and deception were not issues of concern to medieval hagiographers.

Their primary objective was to bring glory to the saint whose life was being documented and the church with which he or she was associated. The more miraculous, extravagant tales that could be told the better! Fabrication was the lifeblood of hagiography and the ends always justified the means.

From a historical point of view, it would be helpful to know if Muirchú 'tampered with the truth', especially in relation to St Patrick's place of origins.

In the quotation chosen to head this chapter, Conor MacDari remarks on how names can be misspelled or distorted to such an extent that great effort is sometimes required to establish their original and true meaning.

One thing is certain: Muirchú cannot be accused of bad spelling. In fact, he used the same basic form of spelling for St Patrick's homeland *in Britanniis* as it appears in the earliest surviving copy of St Patrick's *Confession* and in so doing, may have remained faithful to his source. The question is, did Muirchú introduce anything to distort the original meaning of this name as St Patrick would have understood it? Muirchú was a master of words and as Dan Brown has said, 'Language can sometimes be very adept at hiding the truth.' [88] It is possible that Muirchú may have made a confession of his own related to this issue towards the close of his narrative.

Every good writer knows that beginnings and endings are important.

At the very beginning, Muirchú was honest about the uncertainties which surrounded St Patrick, saying there was no clear record of events. Minds were confused; sources which had survived were unreliable and contradictory. Muirchú hints at more sinister controversy when he describes 'this deep and dangerous sea of church history'. Then, at the very end of his narrative, he makes another intriguing statement which is potentially the most controversial of all. Muirchú brings closure to his narrative with a reflection on illusions or 'delusions'. First he mentions stories related to 'illusions' that can be found in the bible, then concludes by saying, *'so also this delusion was arranged to secure concord between the people.'* The Latin word he uses is *seductio*, which can mean 'leading astray',

---

[88] Dan Brown, *The Lost Symbol* (New York, 2009), p. 196.

'delusion' or 'deception'.

Was Muirchú trying to tell us something?

Could this be a subtle reference to some of the claims about St Patrick which had been made in his narrative? Did he decide to end with one final flourish – the good old scribe that he was – with an intellectual honesty that has never been fully understood or appreciated? Was Muirchú admitting 'between the lines', so to speak, that his presentation of St Patrick was 'a delusion arranged to secure concord between the people'?

If Muirchú was being intellectually forthright about the 'illusion' or 'delusion' he had created, then he deserves to be remembered as one of the most honest hagiographers ever to have emerged from the murky waters of the medieval world.

Muirchú's influence cannot be underestimated because his narrative gave birth to the 'Legend' of St Patrick. If he created a deliberate illusion, however, Muirchú is admitting something far more serious. He may have been trying to tell us that he 'cast a spell' over St Patrick's story. This 'spell' was so powerful it has shaped our image and understanding of St Patrick's biography for more than a thousand years.

The Druids and Irish religious leaders of the Celts had been masters at casting spells by magic in the pre-Christian period and now the scribes and hagiographers of the Irish Church showed themselves to be equally adept in crafts they had inherited.

The "spell" that Muirchú cast has convinced almost everyone that St Patrick came from Britain. Most scholars who have written about St Patrick and those who have read and accepted their works, have more or less accepted the authority and reliability of Muirchú's 'map' and have continued to be bound and blinded by the 'spell' of Britain, even to the present day.

Was the truth about St Patrick's origins and therefore his real identity, suppressed when his file was tidied up by Muirchú at the end of the seventh century? Muirchú may have been the first, but fortunately he was not the last to write a 'Life of St Patrick'.

Information about Patrick must have survived elsewhere, perhaps in Irish monasteries on the continent. Other documents survived which included accounts not found in Muirchú. Some of these present a very different record of St Patrick's origins and where he was trained and ordained for the mission to Ireland. A unique sequence of events was about to unfold that would allow uncertainties to come back to the surface.

A thousand years had to pass, before certain developments would take place through which a very different account of St Patrick's story could come to light.

In 1640 CE, on the brink of Oliver Cromwell's invasion of Ireland, an Irish Franciscan called Fr. John Colgan and some close friends were determined to collect and preserve as many ancient documents as they could, related to the origins of Christianity in Ireland and the lives of the early Irish saints.

As a direct result of these efforts, several important old manuscripts written in Latin and Old Irish were about to enter the public domain for the first time.

Colgan published seven of these manuscripts in 1647, together with extensive notes and a commentary. These were priceless ancient manuscripts dated from the eighth to the twelfth century, containing snippets of older material.

Some had built on Muirchú's account and repeated his claim that St Patrick came from Britain. Others included stories and traditions which cannot be found in Muirchú and completely contradict what Muirchú had said. Many of these documents record that St Patrick was taken captive from Brittany.

The survival of these ancient *Lives of St Patrick* was a miracle. If they had fallen into the hands of Cromwell's army, they might have been lost forever. Instead, they were smuggled out of Ireland and taken to Louvain in Belgium saved from destruction just in the nick of time. These documents hold a number of clues that can help us to identify the truth about St Patrick's origins and the true location of his homeland.

Protected by providence for almost a thousand years, they had been waiting for someone, somewhere in the unforeseen future to get down on their knees and dig deeply into the ashes of the hearth fire of history. Let's see what treasure can be found there.

CHAPTER SIX

ILLUMINATING MANUSCRIPTS

Sometimes a legend that endures
For centuries, endures for a reason.[89]

A suppression of all things Irish by the British in Ulster following the Nine Years War in 1603 and the Flight of the Earls in 1607 was a disaster for Ireland and the Catholic Church. The violent nature of English oppression created huge sympathy towards Ireland especially within Catholic nations on the continent. St Anthony's College, Louvain, was founded in Belgium in 1607 to provide support. It quickly became a centre for Irish intellectual, spiritual and missionary activities. This college was established specifically for the propagation and preservation of Catholic faith in Ireland and Scotland, driven by concern to preserve information about Ireland's ecclesiastical and historical past. Following the Reformation, there had been a Scots-British interpretation of Irish history which was offensive to the scholars at Louvain.

---

[89] Dan Brown, *The Lost Symbol* (New York, 2009), p. 23.

This led to the preservation of several old manuscripts that contained ancient traditions about St Patrick, St Brigid and St Columba.

John Colgan was born in Ireland and joined the Franciscans in 1620 before moving to Louvain. He visited libraries on the continent, searching for information about the early Irish saints. At the same time, Michael O'Clery, one of an intrepid band of native Irish antiquarians who compiled the famous *Annals of the Four Masters*, was sent to Ireland in 1626.

He combed the countryside in efforts to discover and preserve as many ancient documents as possible. Several old manuscripts collected by these scholars were published by Colgan in 1647. His book *Trias Thaumaturga* is one of the great treasures of the seventeenth century and an essential resource for the study of St Patrick. It contains seven, ancient *Lives of St Patrick* written in Latin and Old Irish together with a commentary by Colgan himself, concerning the homeland and family of St Patrick.[90]

Without these documents, the clues required to locate Patrick's place of origins may have been lost forever. These manuscripts are classified as 'secondary sources' which means that, unlike St Patrick's own writings, they cannot be treated as reliable historical evidence. Nevertheless, they contain threads of truth passed down from earlier generations and copied from ancient records, woven into the complex fabric of hagiographical legends. The challenge is to disentangle those threads and see if they point in a particular direction.

These documents will now be examined, focusing first on those manuscripts which identify St Patrick's birthplace and homeland in Britain, since this is currently the accepted and established tradition. Where St Patrick was born appears to have been more important to seventeenth-century writers than where he was taken captive. It is important to recognize these as two separate issues. In his own writings, St Patrick does not tell us where he was born. He only gives

---

[90] John Colgan, *Trias Thaumaturga* (*Trias Thau.*), first published in Louvain, 1647. Facsimile edition published by Edmund Burke, Dublin, 1993 for De Burca Rare Books. See Appendix V, 'Concerning the Homeland and Family of St Patrick', p. 219 ff. Four of Colgan's Lives of St Patrick were published by Ludwig Bieler with a commentary in *Four Latin Lives of St Patrick* (Dublin, 1971).

the name of the place where he was taken captive.

St Fiacc's Hymn is the first 'Life' in Colgan's collection and is regarded as one of the most ancient documents. Fiacc or Fiecc is said to have been one of Patrick's first converts who became Bishop of Sletty, or Slebte in County Leix; a church incorporated into the *Paruchia* of Patrick in the seventh century.

This ancient hymn is written as a poem in Old Irish with a Latin version transcribed by Colgan. The earliest surviving copy was probably not compiled in its present form before about 800 CE but it contains information copied from a much earlier date. Fiacc says St Patrick was born in a place called 'Nemthor'. This is the earliest recording of 'Nemthor' or 'Nemthur' as Patrick's birthplace. This name was not given by St Patrick in his own writings but its value soon becomes apparent. Colgan published notes attached to *Fiacc's Hymn*, compiled by a person we call the Scholiast or 'the Scholar'. These notes cannot be dated earlier than the ninth century and could even be as late as the eleventh or twelfth century but they contain specific claims about St Patrick which are very significant and have always been taken seriously. The Scholiast identifies Nemthor with 'Alcluid', which according to the Venerable Bede was the ancient name of the fortress of the Britons at Dumbarton, near Strathclyde. This is the earliest record we have, claiming that St Patrick was born in Scotland.

That St Patrick's family was connected with this part of Scotland forms part of an ancient tradition that still forms part of the Scottish historical record but the true location of Nemthor must have been uncertain at the time these notes were written. The Scholiast had to clarify its location and did so by identifying it with Alcluid. Whether these notes were added in the ninth or twelfth century, it shows there was still uncertainty about where St Patrick came from.

'Nemthor' is an old and mysterious name. A clue to its meaning and possible location comes through etymology. It has Gaelic or Celtic and Latin roots. The prefix *Nem* possibly derives from the Gaelic *noem* meaning 'holy' or *neam*, a name for heaven. According to Colgan and other ancient writers, the suffix *thor* or *tor* comes from the Latin word *turris*, which denotes a tower or lighthouse. The Romans used lighthouses in most of the fortified coastal ports of the Empire, to assist the navy. Wood fires kindled at the top of these towers provided a beacon for ships entering a harbour at night.

Colgan used this argument to support the view that Patrick was born in Strathclyde although there is no evidence to confirm that a lighthouse existed there at the time of St Patrick.

From an etymological point of view other interpretations are possible.

The suffix *thor* could be the Gaelic *tor*, which designates a sacred high place or pointed hill as with Glastonbury Tor in England or Tor Abb (Hill of the Abbot) on the Island of Iona.

In the early days of Christianity in Europe during the fourth and fifth century, within monastic communities, to claim a person was 'born' in a particular place could mean two very different things. It might not refer to the place of actual physical birth but to the place where they were spiritually 'born' to a religious life of discipleship. The claim that St Patrick was born in Nemthor could have preserved a memory of the place he received spiritual formation and was spiritually nurtured as a Christian. It could have been the place where St Patrick accepted the religious life, perhaps where he was tonsured.

Some scholars have identified Nemthor with the city of Tours on the River Loire, where St Martin's monastery was established towards the end of the fourth century. The argument in favour of identifying Patrick's birth place at Nemthor with Tours again stems from etymology. *Nem* or *naem* is a Celtic word meaning 'holy' and *Thor* or *Tor* may be related to Tours, hence Nemthor could be a reference to 'Holy Tours'. If so, this leaves open the possibility that Patrick could have been born on the continent, rather than Strathclyde. This seems to be confirmed from accounts that describe St Patrick's mother, Conchessa, as being 'of the Franks' which is recorded in Old Irish as *di Frangeaib di* (of the Franks was she) with the additional comment 'through a sister of St Martin of Tours' (*ocus suir do Martin hi Hin Nemthur*). This description supports the view that Nemthor could be a name associated with Tours.[91]

The significance of this interpretation will become more apparent later, when we consider evidence that suggests that Patrick was trained and tonsured in St Martin's community and that his mother, Conchessa was St Martin's sister (or possibly niece).

---

[91] Stokes, *Tripartite Life*, n. 2, p. 8.

The *Second, Third* and *Fourth Lives of St Patrick* published by Colgan repeat the claim that Patrick was born or 'nurtured' in Nemthor, adding extra details in saying this was a town in the district or region of 'Taburne' where there was a military base in which the Romans pitched their tents for shelter during the winter months. Colgan was convinced that Strathclyde was the place of Patrick's birth and the location of the Calpurnius estate from which he was taken captive. The Rock of Clyde is a prominent feature of the landscape with an ancient history, but there is no historical or archaeological evidence for the existence of a lighthouse or Roman military base.

Like Muirchú's and Tirechan narratives, which were both written at the end of the seventh century, these documents greatly influenced other writers. They added fuel to the fire of a growing tradition that identified St Patrick's birthplace in Scotland. This is reflected in Colgan's *Sixth Life*, written in the twelfth century by a monk called Jocelyn, a monk who came to Ireland with a religious community that John de Courcy had brought from England and established at Downpatrick after the Norman invasion of Ireland in the twelfth century.[92] Jocelyn identifies Nemthor as the place where St Patrick was born and raised as a child, adjacent to a fortress located on the Rock of Dumbarton, near Strathclyde. He locates Nemthor and Bannavem Tiburniae in Britain, following Muirchú. Jocelyn follows Muirchú again by saying that Patrick returned to Britain after his escape from slavery in Ireland. [93]

Other manuscripts published by Colgan in 1647 include various claims which present us with a very different understanding of the location of these places. When considering these accounts, St Patrick's association with Strathclyde becomes less exclusive.

These documents challenge and sometimes completely contradict the notion that St Patrick was taken captive from Britain. Some claim that St Patrick was born in Strathclyde but was taken captive from Brittany (Armorica) when he was visiting with his family on the continent. One of the ancient authors goes further, claiming to know 'without doubt' that St Patrick was born in Brittany and that he grew

---

[92] O'Hanlon, *Lives*, iii, p. 461, n. 317.

[93] Jocelyn, The Life and Acts of St Patrick in *Ancient Lives of St Patrick*, ed. James O'Leary (NY, 1880)

up there as a child.

Colgan's *Fifth Life* of St Patrick is an intriguing document written by a monk called Probus. The text has been dated to the ninth century in its present form and can be considered one of the most reliable of all the ancient *Lives of St Patrick*, especially in relation to material found in Book I which appears to be the most archaic and original. Other parts were written later by a secondary author and show signs of interpolation. The name 'Probus' is intriguing. It comes from the Latin word 'probo' which means, to probe. Someone had obviously probed into the uncertainties which surrounded St Patrick.

This author presents an account radically different to all the others. Probus claims that St Patrick was a 'Briton' by nationality or ethnic background but that he came from the village or town called 'Bannaue' in the province of Neustria. The reference to Neustria is very significant.

Unlike Britanniis, Bannavem Tiburniae or Nemthor, the geographical location of Neustria is historically well documented and can be clearly identified without controversy. Neustria was the name applied by the Franks to a region in north-west Gaul between the Meuse and the Loire. The Province of Neustria formed part of the Merovingian kingdom in Gaul which included coastal regions of north-east Brittany.

Neustria was the 'new' land of the Franks (*neu* = new) as Austria was the 'south land' (*aust* = south). Neustria means the newly conquered land, a name which dated from the time of Clovis who was born in 465 CE about the time of St Patrick's death. He was of Merovingian descent and reigned as king of the Franks from 481–511 CE. Clovis invaded Brittany and, as a result, the north-east coast of Brittany between Aleth and Mont St Michel became part of the province of Neustria. In the tenth century, Normandy replaced Neustria as the name for this region but in Latin, the province of Neustria always referred to that part of Roman Gaul which is now divided between Normandy and Brittany. The significance of the account given by Probus cannot be underestimated. It correctly refers to Neustria a province. For the first time in the ancient documents we have discovered an alternative record in which St Patrick's birthplace is not located in mainland Britain but on the continent. This is how Probus writes about St Patrick's place of origins:

St Patrick, who was also called Sochet, was a Briton by nationality [*Brito fuit natione*] in which nation also having suffered many misfortunes in his youth he was fashioned for the salvation of his whole tribe and fatherland ...

This man was born in Brittany [*in Britanniis*] from his father Calpurnius who was the son of Potitus the Elder; his mother's name was Conchessa; from the village of Bannaue in the region of Tiburniae, not far from the Western Sea [Mare Occidentale]. We have established beyond doubt that this village belonged to the province of Neustria in which giants are said to have lived.[94]

The phrase *in Britanniis natus est* could mean St Patrick was born 'amongst the Britons' or more specifically, 'he was born in Brittany' accepting that a region called 'Britanniis' existed on the continent at the time of St Patrick and that this was certainly the location Probus was referring to, as can be confirmed from his later remarks. Brittany is, therefore, a more accurate and authentic translation, since Probus locates St Patrick's homeland on the continent, in Neustria and not on the island of Britain. Probus claimed to know without doubt that Bannavem Tiburniae was a village 'not far from the Western Sea' which belonged to the province of Neustria.

The Latin name he gives for this sea (Mare Occidentale) applied to the whole ocean to the west of the Roman Empire. For Probus, it clearly refers to the ocean off the coast of Brittany. This document is unique because it describes St Patrick's home from a continental perspective. It is also possible that some of the geographical material found in Probus pre-dates Muirchú and the Armagh Movement of the seventh century. Probus uses the same phrase to describe Bannavem Tiburniae as St Patrick did for the Wood of Foclut. Both are described as 'close beside the Western Sea'. If this is deliberate and authentic, it allows for the possibility that both places existed in the same geographical area. The significance of this document has never been fully appreciated.

---

[94] Probus, Life of Saint Patrick, in Bieler, ed., *Four Latin Lives of St Patrick* (Dublin, 1971), p. 192.

Probus is telling us very clearly that Patrick's parental home, the place from which he was taken captive, was in a region called 'Britanniis' that was definitely not located in Britain but on the continent. He says St Patrick was from the nation (or stock) of the Britons (*Brito fuit natione*) but this may not necessarily have been a reference to the island of Britain, exclusively.

The ancient Britons were associated with both Britain and Gaul, especially the coastal region of Armorica. If Patrick's origins were identified by Probus with these ethnic Britons on the continent, this would explain his claim St Patrick was British or from 'the stock of the Britons'. Alternatively, if Calpurnius came from Strathclyde and Probus was accounting for St Patrick's nationality on his father's side of the family, this could also explain how St Patrick was of the same 'nation' as the Britons.

Probus adds more detail when he says St Patrick was of the nation of the Britons 'in which nation he suffered the misfortunes of his youth'. If this is a reference to St Patrick being taken into captivity when he was sixteen years of age, which seems likely, then it confirms that as far as Probus was concerned, the place where St Patrick was taken captive was located in this 'nation of the Britons', which is described as being on the continent, close beside the Western Sea, in Brittany (*in Britanniis*) in the Province of Neustria.

The information given by Probus has geographical integrity and reveals a genuine consistency. He provides the most direct and impressive reference so far in all the ancient Lives, which identifies St Patrick's homeland as a specific region on the continent. Compared with Muirchú's account, which is geographically and ecclesiastically contrived, the information given by Probus is much more concise and has profound implications for our traditional understanding of St Patrick. Probus is not simply claiming that Patrick was taken captive from this region; he is claiming emphatically that St Patrick was born and grew up there, until the time he was taken captive.

This is radically different to any other account in the ancient Lives but it is not incompatible with what St Patrick says in his own writings, if Patrick's homeland was located on the continent.

In another passage, Probus speaks of the circumstances in which St Patrick was taken into captivity. In case anyone still has misgivings, there can be no doubt about what is being said. Probus states clearly that Bannavem Tiburniae was located in Armorica, the Roman name for the coastal province in western Gaul. He also states emphatically that this was St Patrick's homeland:

> While he was still in his homeland [*patria*] with his father Calpurnius and his mother Conchessa, also with his brother Ructhi and sister Mila, in their city Armuric [Armorica] great strife broke out in those parts …

In a devastating attack on Armuric [Armorica] and other places round about it, the sons of Rethmitus, king of Britannia [Britain?] slaughtered Calpurnius and his wife Conchessa; they led away captive their sons Patrick and his brother Ructi, together with their sister, Mila.

Several versions of this story survived in various ancient manuscripts but the account given by Probus again differs significantly from others. In most accounts, St Patrick's family travelled by sea from Strathclyde to Brittany to visit relatives, when St Patrick was taken captive. Probus is saying something very different. There is no mention of Strathclyde. Patrick was already resident in his homeland in Armorica, when the attack took place.

Probus is credited by some scholars as being one of the most reliable of the ancient authors. Others have dismissed his work as inconsistent and contradictory, claiming that Probus begins by saying Patrick was British (*Brito fuit natione*) and born in Britain (*in Britanniis*) then immediately contradicts this when he locates Patrick's birth in the Province of Neustria, on the continent. This reflects a misunderstanding and misrepresentation of his geographical descriptions. Probus is clearly referring to Brittany and not the island of Britain, so any apparent contradictions cease to exist.

In fact, contradiction only exists in the minds of those who are convinced that St Patrick came from Britain and who take the view that these names refer exclusively to Britain. By interpreting his work in this way, we are misrepresenting what Probus says. If by saying St Patrick was born as a Briton (*Brito fuit natione*) Probus meant St Patrick came from the nation or ethnic stock of the Britons and that he was born in Brittany (*in Britanniis*) in a village called 'Bannau' in the region of 'Tiburnia' (Bannavem Tiburniae) which was close beside the Western Sea (Mare Occidentale) in the province of Neustria (ancient Normandy including parts of Armorica) Probus was being exceptionally consistent from a geographical point of view. He is the first to be so clear and consistent using terms we can understand and clearly identify.

Probus provides reliable geographical information to support his claims, more than any of the other ancient authors. He locates St Patrick's homeland in Brittany and he claims that St Patrick was taken captive from this region. If the information given is accurate, the estate owned by St Patrick's father, Calpurnius, must have been located in Brittany.

In relation to our visit to Château de Bonaban what is most significant of all perhaps is that what Probus says matches perfectly the local tradition about St Patrick we discovered there and which is preserved in Brittany today.

One of the most controversial statements made about St Patrick in some of the ancient sources is that his ancestors were Jewish and had settled in Armorica, now Brittany. This claim has usually been dismissed as a legend. It is one of those stories passed down through the centuries which is impossible to verify but may have greater significance for understanding St Patrick than has so far been imagined. This claim can also be found in several of the ancient documents. For example, the *Fourth Life* of St Patrick, published as part of Colgan's collection in 1647, opens with a bold statement that Patrick's ancestors were Jewish, having been driven from the Holy Land following the destruction of the Temple in Jerusalem by the Roman Legions under Titus, in 70 CE. This document begins an account of St Patrick as follows:

> Some say that St Patrick was of Jewish origin. After our Lord had died on the cross for the sins of the human race, the Roman army, avenging His Passion, laid waste Judea, and Jews taken captive were dispersed amongst all the nations of the earth.
>
> Some of them settled among the Armoric Britons, and it is stated that it

was from them that St Patrick traced his origin.[95]

The author describes how Jewish families were dispersed from the Holy Land to Armoric Letha, where they settled and he says this land was beside the Tyrrhene Sea. The Armoric Britons were settled in Armoric Letha, on the north-east coast of Brittany, adjacent to the Bay of Mont St Michel in the same region where Château de Bonaban is now located.

Bury suggested this document contained some very old source material (he called it 'W') which could be dated from internal evidence to before the seventh century. The *Fourth Life* is the original document on which the second and third Lives depended, but they drew from it in different ways. The reference to Patrick's Jewish origins appears in a prominent position at the very beginning of the earliest document, but appears to have been removed by later copyists.

Beginnings and endings are always important for a writer, which suggests that the introduction to the *Fourth Life* was placed there for a reason. Why was this passage not included in the *Second* or *Third Life* in Colgan's collection?

When the manuscripts are compared, it suggests that this introduction may have been suppressed when the two later documents were compiled. This can clearly be seen because the *Second* and *Third Lives* begin in a very disjointed way, as if the statement which appears at the very beginning of the *Fourth Life* was deliberately excluded by the clumsy hands of an unsympathetic editor.

If Bury was right, the record of St Patrick's ancestors being Jewish must have formed part of the earliest material, which predated the Armagh Movement that took place in the seventh century. The reference to St Patrick's Jewish origins is probably the more original, archaic tradition, erased by later copyists. If it was erased intentionally, perhaps this was because of the reference to St Patrick's ancestors migrating from the Holy Land to Brittany, which contradicted other claims that he came from Britain. Another possible explanation is that it was erased because of the reference to St Patrick's ancestors being Jews, which would not have been looked

---

[95] 'Vita Quarta', 1:14, Bieler, *Four Latin Lives*, p. 51.

on with favour in some quarters of the Church at the time these later documents were written.[96]

In relation to the truth as to where St Patrick was taken captive, it is important to note that the *Fourth Life* directly associates St Patrick's family with Armorica, saying that Patrick's ancestors migrated there after their expulsion or dispersion from Jerusalem in 70 CE. If Bury is right, then this tradition belongs to archaic material that predates Muirchú. It accords with the archaic material found in Probus and both must, therefore, be considered significant and perhaps more trustworthy than Muirchú's narrative or the other ancient documents that depended on Muirchú.

Armoric Letha

The name 'Letha' or 'Armoric Letha' is not mentioned by St Patrick in his own writings but it appears in many of the ancient sources in a variety of different and unusual contexts. It provides one of the best clues available to help identify St Patrick's place of origins more precisely because it has a historical and geographical integrity not easily invented. This time there is reliable historical and geographical evidence to support a specific location. Armoric Letha must have been on the continent within the coastal region of Armorica.

The *Life of St Patrick* recorded by Probus was not the only manuscript published by Colgan to claim that Patrick was taken captive from Brittany. Fortunately, other references to Letha or Armoric Letha have survived in the ancient sources which help to identify its true location, removing further doubt or confusion. As we consider these, a more complex and intriguing picture of the life of St Patrick begins to emerge. In notes attached to *Fiacc's Hymn*, we find another version of the story given by Probus although there is a significant difference in the detail, concerning the circumstances in which St Patrick was taken into captivity. Probus said St Patrick was taken captive when he was resident in his 'homeland' in Armorica.

---

[96] For a more detailed exploration of St Patrick's Jewish origins, see *St Patrick and the Bloodline of the Grail: The Untold Story of St Patrick's Royal Family* (Annamoe, Wicklow, 2012).

The Scholiast also records that Patrick was taken captive from Brittany but he says the family were simply visiting Armorica at the time, having travelled by ship from Strathclyde to see relatives who lived on the continent. Consistent with Probus is the fact that Armorica is again identified as the place where Patrick was taken captive. The region in question is named as 'Letha' or 'Letavia'. Here is the account as it appears in the notes of the Scholiast, which were originally written in Old Irish and attached to Fiacc's Hymn. Patrick's family are said to have travelled to the 'Britons of Armorica, that is, to the Letavian Britons' (Britons of Letha):

This is the cause of his enslavement. Patrick and his father Calpurn, Concessa his mother, a daughter of Ocmus, and his five sisters, Lupait and Tigris and Liamain and Darerca and the name of the fifth Cinnemon, [and] his brother the deacon Sannan, all travelled from the Britons of Ail-Cluade [Strathclyde] over the Ictian Sea southwards on a journey to the Britons of Armorica that is, to the Letavian Britons, for there were relatives of theirs there at that time, and, besides, the mother of the children, namely Concessa, was of the Franks and she was a close female relation of [Saint] Martin ...

That was the time at which seven sons of Sectmaide, king of Britain, were in exile from Britain. So they made a fierce attack on the Britons of Armorica where St Patrick was with his family, and they slew Calpurn there, and they brought Patrick and Lupait with them to Ireland, and they sold Lupait in Conaille Muirthemne [County Meath] and Patrick in the north of Dalriada [County Antrim].[97]

Several versions of this story can be found in the manuscripts published by Colgan and other documents. All of them include an account of a journey allegedly made by Patrick's family, travelling from Scotland to 'Armoric Letha', where St Patrick was taken captive. These accounts differ only in details given about the family, the list of travellers and the names of the attackers. Some say Patrick had five sisters called Lupait, Tigris, Liamain, Darerca and Cinnemon, and one brother called Senan. Others mention only two sisters, Lupait and Tigris and no brothers. A similar list of names is recorded

---

[97] Notes on *Fiacc's Hymn*, trans. W. Stokes, *Tripartite Life of St Patrick* (London, 1887), ii, pp. 414–5.

in Breton historical sources. These stories are intriguing but to appreciate their significance, we must first identify the geographical location of "Letha" in documents related to St Patrick.

At an early stage of research for this book, having returned home to Ireland from Brittany and begun more extensive reading, I stumbled across a reference to Letha in one of my favourite old books, *Lives of the Saints from the Book of Lismore*, edited by Whitley Stokes, which helped to clarify its meaning and possible location. In some of the best books, the real treasures are found in the footnotes. This reference would have been meaningless to me, if I had not learned from a guidebook that Aleth was the ancient name for St Malo in Brittany, which is close to the site where we discovered a local tradition about St Patrick at Château de Bonaban.[98] Stokes mentioned that St Patrick was known by various names, including 'Patricius il Letha Luind'. He suggested that 'Letha' meant 'on the continent' without giving a specific geographical location.[99] When the connection with St Malo became apparent, this provided great encouragement to continue with further research.

In the late Roman period, Aleth was a place of considerable significance. At the time of St Patrick, it was an important military base for the Legion of Mars. The history and strategic significance of this port for the Roman navy is well documented.[100] A prefect of the Legion of Mars had a residence there and ships based at Aleth guarded both sides of what is now called the English Channel in efforts to combat piracy in the Iccian Sea, the name given to the stretch of water between Ireland, south-west Britain and the continent.

'Letha' may also be derived from *Laeti*, a Latin word used by the Romans for communities of barbarians (literally, babblers, those from outside the Empire who spoke in foreign tongues) who were given lands on which to settle within the Empire. This was granted on condition they provide recruits for the army. The son of the

---

[98] Philippe Barbour, *Cadogan Guide to Brittany* (London, 2008).

[99] *Anecdota Oxoniensia* (Oxford, 1890), facs. edn trans. Whitley Stokes, as *Lives of the Saints from the Book of Lismore* (Llanerch, 1990). See notes on p. 294 (p. 153).

[100] Jacques Doremet, *De Antiquité de la Ville et cité d'Aleth, ou Quidalet*, ed. Thomas de Querci (St Malo, 1894; Slatkine Reprints, 1971), p. 17; Jacques Doremet, *L'Antiquité d'Aleth* (La Cane de Montfort, 1628).

veteran was usually compelled to follow the profession of his father. Military service was an obligation because the *Laeti* considered themselves to be part of a military race. The soldiers not only held an estate distinct from the rest of the people, they formed an influential ruling caste from within which sovereign power was derived. Historical records mention the *Laeti* from the fourth century onwards, but these military alliances had been taking place for a long time.[101] Breton historians writing from an early period have claimed that a colony of the *Laeti* was established in Brittany at the time of the rebellion of Magnus Maximus in 383 CE and that St Patrick's family were part of this migration, having belonged to the Britons of Strathclyde.

Scholars have been aware for some time of the link between Letha and Armorica. Camden identified Letha as a coastal region in Brittany.[102] O'Hanlon understood that 'Armoric Britain' was called 'Letha' or 'Leatha' by the Irish and he refers to it as a 'maritime district of British Armorica'. It appears as 'Letha' or 'Lethania' in ancient Irish sources. Some writers called it 'Letavia'. In the ancient *Lives of St Gildas*, 'Letha' is clearly identified with Brittany.

Armorica, formerly a territory in Gaul, but was at that time called Letavia by the Bretons, in whose possession it was.[103]

This document states that 'in the Armorican region of Gaul there was another Britain called 'Letavia'. This suggests that 'Armoric Letha', 'Letavia' or 'Lethania Britannia' were all names applied to at least part of the region we now call Brittany. The identification of 'Armoric

---

[101] The *Notitia Dignitorum* is an official document compiled in the fourth and fifth centuries, which lists Roman civil and military posts. Title XLII contains a list from Gaul, *per tractum Rodunensem et Alanorum*. See M. Poslan, *Cambridge Economic History of Europe* (Cambridge, 1966), p. 187.

[102] Camden, *Britannica* (Abridged, London, 1701), col. cxxxii.

[103] 'In the Armorican region of Gaul there is another Britain called Letavia': See Hugh Williams, trans., *Two Lives of Gildas by a monk of Ruys and Caradoc of Llancarfan* (Cymmrodorion Series, 1899; facs. edn Llanerch, 1990), ch. 16. Also Bouquet, 3, p. 449: The MS Vita Caoci says, 'The province of Armorica known as Littau (Letavia) also called *Britannia Minor* (Little Britain)'. Cotton Library, Vesp. A. 14, p. 32.

Letha' as a region that included Aleth or St Malo, appears to be self-evident, although the importance of Aleth in relation to Patrick's place of origins has been overlooked and neglected by many writers. Apart from the early Breton historians, John O'Hanlon is one of only a few scholars who have recognised the significance of Aleth.[104]

Geoffrey of Monmouth gives an account of close contact between the ancient Britons in Britain and Brittany, in which the reference to the city of Aleth is so precise it must have come from a reliable source. This writer has often been maligned by scholars and accused of re-inventing history but Geoffrey's account in this case must have been based on some very accurate geographical information. He records how a delegation of Britons sailed from Britain to Armorica to appeal for help from King Salomon of Brittany. The ship docked at the port of Kidaleta. Breton historians date King Salomon's rule to 405 CE, around the time that St Patrick escaped from slavery in Ireland.

> Then the wind standing fair, he got ready his ship and hoisting sails they pursued their voyage, arriving at the city Kidaleta.[105]

Kidaleta or 'Quidalet' was another name for the city of Aleth.[106] Locals still refer to it by its ancient designation as *la cité*. This suggests that Aleth may have been the capital of Armoric Letha. According to Geoffrey, the king of Brittany was resident there and it was a centre for local government, where foreign delegations were welcomed. The location of Armoric Letha is critical to the study of St Patrick. Although this place is not named directly in Patrick's own writings, references in the ancient *Lives of St Patrick* are very significant and they point firmly not only to Brittany but to a specific local region on the coast of north-east Brittany between Aleth, Dol and Mont St Michel.

This becomes apparent when we consider a number of references to Letha in the ancient sources. One of the earliest can be found in

---

[104] O'Hanlon, *Lives of the Irish Saints* (Dublin, 1875), iii, p. 509, n. 67.

[105] Geoffrey of Monmouth, 'History of the Kings of Britain', in *Six Old English Chronicles*, trans. J. A. Giles and Aaron Thompson, (1848), p. 243.

[106] Jacques Doremet, *De Antiquité de la Ville et cité d'Aleth, ou Quidalet*, ed. Thomas de Querci (St Malo, 1894; Slatkine Reprints, 1971).

Cogitosus's *Life of St Brigid*, dated to c.650 CE. In this account a bishop called 'Conleath' had been invited to Kildare (the place where Brigid's monastery was located in Ireland) by St Brigid to share her ministry. Cogitosus writes:

> How many miracles she [St Brigid] wrought no man can fully tell. She blessed the vestments of Conleath which he had brought from Letha.[107]

Bishop Conleath may have come from Letha or was sent there to get vestments for St Brigid. The identification of Letha with lands adjacent to the Bay of Mont St Michel is apparent in the *Life of St Ailbe*. The following story appears in the context of Ailbe's visit to Brittany. The association with Dol-de-Bretagne is so direct it points to a specific geographical location.

> St Ailbe arrived at the city called Dolo Moir [literally 'Dol by the Sea' – now Dol de Bretagne] at *the farthest limits of Letha* where he and his people stayed in a hospice.[108]

Dol-de-Bretagne is one of the most ancient ecclesiastical sites in Brittany and is still close to the sea. This reference confirms that 'Letha' was the name of a specific local region within Armorica, close to Aleth and Dol de Bretagne.

In his *Confession*, Patrick tells us that he was taken captive from his father's estate at Bannavem Tiburniae. If the Armorican tradition is reliable, this home must have been located in the coastal area of north-east Brittany, between the Roman port at Aleth (St Malo) and Dol de Bretagne. Château de Bonaban is located at the centre of this region which suggests that the local traditions about St Patrick which have been preserved in Brittany, should be regarded as historically plausible and could therefore also be trustworthy.

---

[107] Cogitosus, 'Life of St Brigit the Virgin', in *Celtic Spirituality*, trans. Oliver Davies (NY, 1999), p 122.

[108] In the 'Life of St Ailbe', Dol de Bretagne is described as being at 'the farthest limits of Letha'.

CHAPTER SEVEN

THE WOOD OF FOCLUT

A dream that has not been interpreted
Is like a letter that has not been opened.[109]

The Wood of Foclut is one of the few geographical references that are recorded in St Patrick's *Confession*. Patrick remembered this wood in the context of a dream. His account of what happened is deeply moving and has strongly influenced our popular understanding of some of the events that shaped his life. In this 'vision of the night' St Patrick tells us that he saw a man who had come *as if* from Ireland. This person was carrying many letters and began reading them to Patrick. As he was opening the first letter, St Patrick describes how he heard the 'Voice of the Irish' and says in that same moment he could hear the voice of 'those who live beside the Wood of Foclut' calling him to 'come and walk once more among them'. He woke up suddenly, feeling 'heartbroken'.

---

[109] The Talmud

This was no ordinary dream, it was a nightmare. However traumatic it was, St Patrick understood this dream as a call from God to return to Ireland as an apostle. Here are St Patrick's words, as they are recorded in the earliest copy of his *Confession*, preserved in the *Book of Armagh*:

> And there, in a vision of the night I saw a man coming as it were from Ireland, whose name was Victor, carrying many letters. He gave me one of them to read and as I did so, I heard the *Voice of the Irish*. In that moment, as I was reading from the beginning of the letter, I thought I could hear the voice of those around the Wood of Foclut which is close beside the Western Sea. It was as if they spoke with one voice, saying 'We beg you, holy youth, to come and walk once more among us' …
>
> I woke up suddenly feeling my heart was broken and had to stop reading. Thank God that after all these years the Lord has granted them according to their cries.[110]

Something in this dream had disturbed St Patrick greatly. It seems to have brought back traumatic memories. His account of the dream has traditionally been interpreted as being a recollection of his experience as a slave in Ireland. The 'Voice of the Irish' must have come from those in Ireland who Patrick knew during captivity. He says he heard this 'voice' from those who lived near the Wood of Foclut, calling him to return to them.

Part of the difficulty with this particular interpretation is that we will never know the true meaning of St Patrick's dream. It would be foolish to take what St Patrick says in the context of a dream to support an argument in favour of one particular geographical location over another. Nevertheless, most writers have interpreted Patrick's dream as confirmation of the fact that the Wood of Foclut must have existed in Ireland. It is widely accepted that in this dream St Patrick experienced a calling to return to those he knew or met during the seven years when he was held as a slave there. There is nothing in St Patrick's account to justify making such an assumption.

As we have noted, Jeremy Taylor, who is a qualified Jungian,

---

[110] C:23.

expert in dream analysis, warns about the dangers of trying to interpret dreams and he strongly advises that we guard against what he calls 'mistaken literalism'.[111] In his opinion, 'only the dreamer knows the meaning of a dream'. We can benefit from Taylor's experience by approaching this subject with caution. At the same time, because St Patrick has left us with so few geographical references in his writings, the account of this dream is significant. The location of the Wood of Foclut is important for our enquiry. We will, therefore, assume, as most writers have always done, that when St Patrick wrote about this dream he was remembering a real wood or forest called 'Foclut' which was known to him from personal experience and had a definite geographical location. In other words, this wood existed somewhere and had a historical and geographical reality. It did not exist simply as part of St Patrick's experience of the 'dream world' arising from the depths of his subconscious mind.

There is nothing in St Patrick's dream which should lead us to assume that the wood must have existed in Ireland, even though this has been the traditional interpretation. St Patrick recalled the Wood of Foclut in the context of a dream he experienced many years before.

In his *Confession*, Patrick does not say the Wood of Foclut was located in Ireland. The only geographical reference given is when he describes this wood as being 'close beside the Western Sea'.[112]

Again, some writers have pushed a speculative form of dream interpretation even further by not only assuming the Wood of Foclut was in Ireland but also that when St Patrick describes this wood as being 'close beside the Western Sea', he must have been referring to the Atlantic Ocean off the west coast of Ireland. The temptation to draw such conclusions has been irresistible, especially since there has been an established tradition within the early Irish church claiming that the Wood of Foclut existed near Killala, in County Mayo, on the west coast of Ireland.

The earliest source claiming to know the true location of the Wood of Foclut is the work of an Irish Bishop called Tirechán, who published a narrative on St Patrick towards the end of the seventh

---

[111] Jeremy Taylor, *Dreamwork* (New York, 1983).

[112] C:23; Bieler, *Clavis Patricii II: Libri Epistolarum Sancti Patricii Episcopi* (Dublin, 1993), p. 71.

century. This is more than two hundred years after St Patrick's death. Bishop Tirechán said the Wood of Foclut existed in his own diocese near Killala, County Mayo. His claim was embraced by the Irish church in the seventh century and became enshrined in Ireland's ancient, ecclesiastical records in the *Book of Armagh*. Tirechán was writing about the same time as Muirchú (670 CE). He was very active in helping to expand the *Paruchia Patricii* in the west of Ireland as Muirchú did in Armagh.

Tirechán identifies this wood as the location for an important ecclesiastical centre in the west of Ireland, which he claims St Patrick founded. He calls it 'the Great Church of St Patrick'. Tirechán must have read or had access to a copy of St Patrick's *Confession* because he is aware of the significance of St Patrick's dream, which he builds upon in a very creative and skilful way to serve the purpose of his narrative.

He gives a detailed account of various journeys St Patrick is said to have undertaken around Ireland. In doing this he creates a hagiographical picture or 'map' just like Muirchú. He describes how St Patrick founded churches all over the country from Leinster, Munster and Connacht to Ulster. When describing these journeys, Tirechán lists a number of these churches and names the local chieftains who gave land to St Patrick for this purpose.

In the midst of these accounts we find several references to the Wood of Foclut. As we listen to these stories, we must bear in mind that they are designed to bolster the ecclesiastical claims of the church in Armagh to jurisdiction over these churches and the lands associated with them. In other words, however much these stories might convince us that Bishop Tirechán must have been telling the truth, it is also possible that he made the whole thing up. D.A. Binchy always urged his students to remember that with Irish hagiography nothing is impossible!

Nothing Tirechán says should be taken as true, simply because Tirechán has said it. Just as Muirchú may have created the legend or 'illusion' that St Patrick came from Britain, so Tirechán's narrative may have introduced another misleading claim that the Wood of Foclut was located in his own diocese, near Killala in the west of Ireland. Today, despite the strong voice of tradition, in the quest for knowledge and historical integrity we must try to search for the truth. What follows is a description of the main references to the Wood of

Foclut found in Tirechán's narrative, so that we can assess its historical credibility.

The family or tribe of the Amolngaids, were the traditional landowners and chieftains in a particular region of Connacht where Tirechán's diocese was located. They appear in reliable genealogies of the ancient Irish kings.[113] Tirechán describes in great detail how, after Easter, St Patrick went to Tara where he overheard a conversation between two nobles. One of them is introduced to us as Ende, son of Amolngaid:

> I am Ende, son of Amolngaid, son of Fiachae son of Echu, from the western district, Mag Domnon and the Wood of Foclut.[114]

According to Tirechán, when St Patrick heard the name 'Foclut', he felt great joy and said to Ende, 'I shall go out with you, if I am alive, because the Lord told me to go there.' St Patrick is said to have baptised Conall, Ende's son, and after blessing him, gave him to a bishop called Cathiacus for education and fostering. He was helped by Mucneus, the brother of Bishop Cathiacus, 'whose relics are in Patrick's great church in the Wood of Foclut'.

Tirechán describes how six of the sons of Amolngaid came before the high king in Tara, asking for judgement in a property dispute. Standing against them were St Patrick, Ende and Ende's young son (the seventh son) as the king proceeded to examine their case of inheritance. Patrick and King Loiguire passed judgement that they should divide their inheritance into seven parts and Tirechán says that 'Ende offered his part to Patrick's God and to Patrick'. This implies that it was given to the church in Armagh and the Patrician *Paruchia*. Tirechán explains, 'It is for this reason, some say, we are servants of Patrick to the present day.' St Patrick and the sons of Amolngaid are said to have concluded a treaty with King Loiguire of Tara acting as guarantor. They pledged to travel together to Mons Aigli (Croagh Patrick) and

---

[113] T. M. Charles-Edwards, *Early Christian Ireland* (Cambridge, 2000), p. 615, 627.

[114] Ludwig Bieler, *The Patrician Texts in the Book of Armagh* (Dublin, 2004), p. 123 ff.

Patrick agreed to pay the price of fifteen men [as he states in his writings] in silver and gold, so that no wicked person should obstruct them, for by necessity they had to arrive at the Wood of Foclut before the end of a year's time, at the second Easter, because of the children crying with a loud voice, whose voices he had heard from their mothers' wombs saying, 'Come Holy Patrick, to save us.'[115]

This is the first clear sign that Tirechán had reworked Patrick's account of the dream and was using this to bolster the claims of the church in Armagh and the *Patricii Paruchia* by locating the Wood of Foclut in his own diocese. When Patrick recalled his dream, he heard "the Voice of the Irish" calling out to him from the Wood of Foclut. There is no mention of them being children, or that they were still in their mothers' wombs.

Tirechán's St Patrick is soon back, across the River Moy in the west of Ireland with the Amolngaids, where he met two maidens and 'he blessed for them a place in the Wood of Foclut'. Tirechán arranged all these journeys to bring St Patrick into Connacht by the 'second Easter'. This suggests some degree of complicity or familiarity with Muirchú, who brings St Patrick to Tara for the 'first' Easter. Connacht may have been claiming the second place of honour, after Armagh, in the *Paruchia Patricii*.

Tirechán was writing towards the end of the seventh century, two hundred years after St Patrick's death. Like Muirchú, his narrative was created with a specific hagiographical agenda in mind which was to safeguard the claims of his own diocese to inheritance rights and support a reform movement for greater Romanisation which was being sponsored at that time by the church in Armagh. Nothing Tirechán said about the Wood of Foclut should be viewed as historically or geographically reliable. To associate the 'sons of Amolngaid' with St Patrick must have served Tirechán's political and ecclesiastical purposes but what he says about St Patrick and the Wood of Foclut is not to be trusted. There are probably snippets of truth tucked away in the crevices and folds of his narrative but the vast majority of what he writes is entirely fabricated. These stories are

---

[115] Tirechán 15. Bieler, *PTBA*, p. 136.

so graphic, they sound authentic and plausible; such was the genius of Irish hagiography in the seventh century.

The influence of these stories on our image and understanding of St Patrick in general and the location of the Wood of Foclut in particular, cannot be underestimated. Tirechán's influence on the development of an ecclesiastical tradition concerning the location of the Wood of Foclut has been enormous.

In *St Fiacc's Hymn*, which is viewed as one of the earliest documents, no specific geographical location is given. The author simply says:

A help to Ireland was Patrick's coming. Afar was heard the cry of the Children of Fochlud's wood.[116]

In notes attached to *Fiacc's Hymn* by the Scholiast, however, which were written much later (at least five hundred years after St Patrick's death) we find a more detailed statement which promulgates the claims made by Bishop Tirechán. These notes show how the Irish church had embraced and been entranced by the Tirechán tradition:

The Wood of Fochlut *[Caill Foclaid]* is the name of the district which is in Tirawley in the north-east of Connacht, and there is a church there to this day.[117]

The Scholiast follows Tirechán's narrative closely, claiming that the Wood of Foclut was in Hy-Amalgaidh (tribal lands associated with the Amolngaids) around Tirawley, near Killala in County Mayo. A similar claim appears in the *Tripartite Life of St Patrick* and many of the other ancient manuscripts that adopted the Tirechán tradition. As we examine these stories more closely, we can see how the ancient writers developed their material, guided not by any information that could be considered historically reliable, but by the imagination and creativity of pure hagiographical genius.

---

[116] Stokes, *Tripartite Life*, p. 407.

[117] Notes on *Fiacc's Hymn* in Stokes, *Tripartite Life*, p. 421.

In the *Lebar Brecc* Homily on St Patrick, for example, the original account given in St Patrick's *Confession* is alluded to but extra descriptive detail is added. The author refers initially to St Patrick's dream, which took place after he had escaped from Ireland and was reunited with his family. The voices now come, not simply from those associated in St Patrick's mind with the Wood of Foclut, but from their mothers' wombs. Foclut is again geographically located in the west of Ireland.

> His (St Patrick's) parents begged him now to stay with them. Never-the-less the angel came to him in his sleep having many letters in Gaelic. And when he was reading them out he heard a great cry from the infants in their mothers' wombs in the region of Connacht. Those children were of *Caille Fochlad* (Wood of Foclut) and this is what they were saying: 'Come, Holy Patrick, to make us whole.'[118]

In notes attached to *St Fiacc's Hymn* by the Scholiast, we can detect a further development of the story, which is now completely embellished by hagiography to support a particular agenda and emerging tradition. The children are given names. Pope Celestine heard the voices too, when he was conferring orders on St Patrick. Patrick heard the voices 'coming from their mothers' wombs and the voices could be heard all over Ireland and as far away as Rome.

> Now when orders were conferred on Patrick (Pope) Celestine heard the voice of the children calling him. These are the children here mentioned, namely Crebiu and Lesru are their names ... And this is what they said out of their mother's womb: 'All the Irish are crying unto thee.' And they are often heard repeating that throughout all Ireland even as far as Rome.[119]

This elevates the children of Foclut to a very high place of esteem and creates a link with the Papacy and the Roman Church. It also serves to confirm an established tradition that the Wood of Foclut

---

[118] Stokes, *Tripartite Life*, p. 421 ff., p.445, n.1.

[119] Stokes, *Tripartite Life,* p. 420 ff.

was in Ireland.

As the story develops further, St Patrick is said to have baptised the children in the Wood of Foclut, at Cell Forcland to the west of the Moy, where their remains can still be found. From a comparison of these stories we can see how Patrick's original account of the dream was used by some of the ancient writers to link St Patrick not only to Rome but also to Germanus of Auxerre.

Patrick is alleged to have told St Germanus about many visions he had about the voices of the children who came from the Wood of Foclut. Germanus instructed St Patrick to go to Pope Celestine so that holy orders could be conferred:

> After Patrick had read the canon with Germanus and the ecclesiastical order, he told Germanus that he had often been invited (to Ireland) in heavenly visions and that he had heard the voice of the children (from the Wood of Foclut).
>
> Germanus said, 'Go to (Pope) Celestine so he may confer orders on you, for he is proper to confer them.' So St Patrick went to him, but he did not give him that honour, for he had previously sent Palladius to Ireland to teach.[120]

None of these extra details can be found in St Patrick's own writings. They are a clear reflection of the Romanising influence.

By the ninth century, the meaning and significance of the original dream had become embellished by ecclesiastical fables and, as a result, the true location of the Wood of Foclut may have been lost to historical memory.

Many of the accounts about this wood found in the later secondary sources are entirely fictional and the only purpose they serve is to support the claims of the church in Armagh and strengthen the Romani movement in the Diocese of Connacht and elsewhere, locating the Wood of Foclut in Ireland and associating St Patrick and his mission more closely with the authority of St Germanus and Rome. The development of these hagiographical accounts can be viewed as part of the 'Romanising' process which

---

[120] Notes on *Fiacc's Hymn* in Stokes, *Tripartite Life*, p. 419.

deeply affected St Patrick's biography, especially towards the end of the seventh century, more than two hundred years after St Patrick's death. This was promoted by the church in Armagh to provide St Patrick in particular, and the Irish church in general, with the credentials necessary to safeguard its image and future. An essential requirement was that St Patrick's mission to Ireland was supported by the Papacy and that St Patrick himself was always in communion with Rome.

This process of later hagiographical development is clear to follow. An original historical reference (as it was given by St Patrick in his *Confession*) is shaped to suit a political and ecclesiastical agenda. This creates false 'information' or 'fake news' which in historical terms is essentially fraudulent.

Muirchú and Tirechán were highly skilled, political and ecclesiastical spin doctors who applied their genius to completely reinvent Patrick's 'biography'.

Tirechán was followed by others, whose religiously creative imagination reshaped St Patrick's original account of his dream. In the hagiographical process the first stage of development takes place when the Wood of Foclut is identified with a specific geographical location: Bishop Tirechán's own diocese in the west of Ireland. In his own writings, St Patrick does not give enough information to identify any one particular location.

In the next stage, the 'Voice of the Irish' that St Patrick heard in his dream calling to him from the Wood of Foclut is said to have been the voice of children who lived beside the wood. Then the voice is said to have come from the children while they were still in their mothers' wombs.

As the hagiographical process develops, the children are given names and then baptised by Patrick, as are their mothers.

Finally, the original account of the dream is woven into an elaborate story of St Patrick's meeting with Germanus of Auxerre and later with Pope Celestine.[121] While he is conferring holy orders on St Patrick, Pope Celestine hears the voices himself. The children of Foclut are now recognised as saints and their voices could be

---

[121] Stokes, *Tripartite Life*, ii, p. 419 See also p. 445.

heard all across Ireland and even as far as Rome. The final 'spin' takes place when all the choirs of heaven join in, to celebrate St Patrick's ordination in Rome and sing the praises of Ireland's apostle.

The mysterious 'Voice of the Irish' which Patrick heard calling to him from the Wood of Foclut in a dream that sounds more like a nightmare, now becomes a fully-fledged church choir. It is the last masterful stroke from the brush of hagiography through which St Patrick's story becomes entirely embellished and Romanised. In these accounts, it is St Peter's successor who sends St Patrick to preach the gospel in Ireland:

> When they were conferring the rank of bishop upon him [Patrick], the three choirs answered, namely, the choir of heaven's household, the choir of the Romans and the choir of the children of the Wood of Foclut. This is what they sang, '*Hibernensis omnes clamant ad puer*' [All the Irish are calling for you]. So Peter's successor sent Patrick to preach to the Gael.[122]

We have included these references about the Wood of Foclut not only because they reveal the growing influence of the *Romani* movement but also because they perpetuated Tirechán's claim that the Wood of Foclut existed in Ireland.

Just as most writers accepted Muirchú's claim that St Patrick came from Britain so there has been widespread acceptance of Tirechán's claim, which locates the Wood of Foclut in the west of Ireland. This now forms part of an established tradition which has never been seriously questioned.[123]

The only reliable historical source for information about the Wood of Foclut is the account given in St Patrick's *Confession* and even this must be viewed with caution, because St Patrick remembered this place in the context of a dream. His description of that wood is part of his memory of that dream, which he had experienced many years before. Some scholars have recognised the

---

[122] Stokes, p. 33.

[123] Patrick MacNeill, 'The Identification of Foclut', *Journal of the Galway Historical Society*, 22 (1947).

historical and geographical difficulties.

The Tirechán tradition, together with the established interpretation given to Patrick's dream, implies that Patrick was held captive in the west of Ireland, where he must have known people who were now calling him to return there.

Tirechán's account, therefore, has implications for the location of St Patrick's place of captivity. Dr Lanigan was one of the first to recognise the difficulty when he suggested that if Patrick was held as a slave in Antrim or Down in the north-east of Ireland as many of the ancient sources suggest, then why would he hear voices coming from a Wood in Connacht, in the far west of Ireland?

From what he says in the *Confession*, St Patrick appears to have been held captive more or less in complete isolation on a remote hillside where he tended animals for his slave master. He does not give the impression that he got to know many other people. In his landmark biography of St Patrick Bury accepted Tirechán's claim, saying the Wood of Foclut must have been in the west of Ireland and that St Patrick (because of what he said when describing his dream) must, therefore, have been held captive in that region. Bury may have misunderstood the meaning and significance of this dream when he wrote, 'It is certain, from his own words, he (St Patrick) served near the Forest of Fochlad.'[124] The following statement shows just how widely the Tirechán tradition has been accepted even by reputable historians:

When the boats of his captors reached their haven, Patrick was led — so we should conclude from his own story — across the island into the kingdom of Connacht, to serve a master in the very furthest parts of the 'ultimate land'. His master dwelled near the Wood of Foclut, 'nigh to the Western Sea' in north-western Connacht, to this day a wild and desolate land, through the forest has long since been cleared away ...

A part of this land belonged to Amolngaid, who afterwards became king of Connacht and it is still called by this name, Tir-awley, 'the land of Amolngaid'. But the Wood of Foclut was probably of larger extent than the district of Tirawley.[125]

---

124 Bury, *The Life of St Patrick*, p. 42.

125 Bury, *The Life of St Patrick*, p. 29.

Bury appears to have swallowed some of the claims of hagiography, hook, line and sinker when he writes, 'the cry that pierced his heart was uttered by the young children of Fochlad' and 'even by children that were still unborn.'[126]

Established traditions concerning St Patrick's origins have had a powerful influence on our understanding of his biography and this has influenced the views of many writers, despite the lack of evidence to support them. Even Todd accepted Tirechán's narrative as trustworthy. Having crossed the River Moy and entered the district of the Amolngaids (*Tír Amalgaidh*) Todd describes how Patrick 'made his way to the Wood of Fochlut, of which he had dreamt many years before, and which had clung ever since to his imagination'.[127]

Hanson suggested that if both Muirchú and Tirechán had not described Patrick's captivity as taking place in County Antrim, rather than Connacht, no one would have questioned Tirechán's claim, which located Foclut in the west of Ireland. Yet still, he says, 'there is no reason to doubt Tirechán's statement that it was in Tirawley, on the borders of Sligo and Mayo.'[128]

Professor T. M. Charles-Edwards of the University of Oxford, who recently helped to republish Bury's *Life of St Patrick*, also affirms the historical integrity of the Tirechán tradition and attempts to solve the dilemma as to where Patrick was held captive by following Bury and locating this in the west of Ireland. Discussing Patrick's escape, he then states that this was not an easy feat, for the district in which he was living as a slave was beside the Wood of Voclut, near Killala in the north of the modern County Mayo, close to the Atlantic coast.[129] Professor Charles-Edwards is one of the leading authorities in Celtic Studies and the history of Ireland in the early medieval period. Tirechán's statements about the location of the Wood of Foclut are accepted to such an extent, however, that he is willing to discard another tradition (which was supported even by Tirechán)

---

[126] Bury, *The Life of St Patrick*, p. 27 ff. See also p. 334 ff.

[127] J. H. Todd, *St Patrick, Apostle of Ireland*, p. 313, n. 4., p.447.

[128] R. P. C. Hanson, *St Patrick His Origins and Career* (Oxford, 1997), p. 91.

[129] T. M. Charles-Edwards, *Early Christian Ireland*, p. 217.

that St Patrick was held in captivity in County Antrim. This gives an indication of the powerful influence of hagiography, leading to potential errors in more scholastic historical analysis.

Once Tirechán's claim about the location of the Wood of Foclut is accepted, then St Patrick's place of captivity is also identified with that region. This traditional view is constructed on what is essentially a risky and misguided form of dream interpretation which a number of high profile scholars have accepted as trustworthy. Tirechán wrote his narrative about two hundred years after St Patrick's death. He claimed that Foclut was in his own diocese in the west of Ireland. Understandably for a bishop of his time, he does not provide reliable evidence to support this.

Medieval hagiographers were not constrained by the same standards which apply to modern historical analysis. The linguistic evidence which has been given in support of the Tirechán tradition is not convincing. In Tirechán's narrative the Wood of Foclut is identified with Fochloth (Fochlad) in Connacht, a place name which is said to have survived in modern Eoghill (Fochoill) near Killala, Tirawley, County Mayo. One or two astute scholars remained sensibly cautious and sceptical about Tirechán's claim. Macneill suggested the existence of such a forest in Connacht was 'a gratuitous assumption'. He recognised that 'Fochlud' was not a clear or easy name to identify because so many different forms of spelling are preserved in the ancient manuscripts and decided it was best simply to call it the Forest of 'U'.[130]

O'Rahilly examined the origins of the name 'Foclud' and thought it came from an archetype, spelled 'Voclitu'. He lists all the various forms in which this name appears in the *Book of Armagh* and other sources. The extent of these variations alone suggests the meaning of the original name was uncertain.

O'Rahilly doubted the connection between the name 'Fochloth' and modern Foghill in Connacht which he suggested could only be due to the 'deceptive resemblance' between these names. Despite these uncertainties, he held firmly to the established tradition. O'Rahilly said the context of St Patrick's dream makes it clear, 'the

---

[130] Eoin MacNeill, 'Silua Focluti', *Proceedings of the Royal Irish Academy, Section C: Archaeology, Celtic Studies, History, Linguistics, Literature*, 36 (1923), p. 249–55.

Wood of Voclut was close to the place of Patrick's captivity, the one place in Ireland that was quite familiar to him after he had spent six years there as a slave'.

He continues, 'There is not the slightest reason to suppose that the Irish tradition was wrong in locating the Wood of "Voclut" near Killala'.[131]

Ludwig Bieler regarded any attempt to locate the Wood of Foclut outside Connacht as 'guesswork' and criticised those who were pushing aside 'traditions of considerable antiquity'.[132] The weight of scholarly opinion has always favoured locating it in Ireland.

Such opinions are based on two equally gratuitous assumptions. The first is that 'Foclut' is the only Irish place name mentioned by St Patrick in his own writings and the second is that Bishop Tírechán was telling the truth and could be trusted when he claimed that it existed within his own diocese. In the context of the local tradition preserved in Brittany, another possibility has to be considered. Perhaps the name 'Foclut' or 'Foclud' was not originally Irish but rather the Irish form of a Brythonic/Celtic name which may have been familiar to St Patrick from his experiences on the continent.

Unlike St Patrick's homeland *in Britanniis* and the family estate at Bannavem Tiburniae, as far as I am aware, at the time of writing, no ancient or modern author has ever suggested that the Wood of Foclut may have existed on the continent, in Brittany.

If 'Foclut' can be identified with the ancient Forest of 'Quokelunde' in Brittany, this would present a radical alternative to challenge our traditional understanding of St Patrick's story.

Before we continue, let's remind ourselves of the claims of a local tradition preserved in Brittany today that describes how St Patrick's family were resident there from the time of the Emperor Magnus Maximus in 383 CE.

These accounts are significant because they provide a historical context for some of the key events that shaped St Patrick's life and destiny.

---

[131] O'Rahilly, *The Two Patricks*, p. 35.

[132] Bieler, 'The Problem of Silva Focluti', p. 352.

Breton historians writing before the nineteenth century claim that Bannavem Tiburniae was located on or close to the present site of Château de Bonaban, now in the village of La Gouesnière -Bonaban. Irish pirates are said to have crept up through a local forest called Quokelunde before they attacked the estate, killed St Patrick's mother and father and dragged Patrick away to be sold into slavery in Ireland. This is the information that was once provided for guests staying at the Château, which is worth reading again:

> The first castle or rather fortress that was built here dates from the Roman period, during the fourth century. At that time, this place was called *Bonavenna* [or *Bonabes*] *de Tiberio*. It belonged to a Scottish prince, Calpurnius [St Patrick's father] who had come here to avoid Saxon forces who were invading Britain. One night, Irish pirates arrived in nearby Cancale. They spread through the Wood of Quokelunde, which stretched under Gouesnière-Bonaban as far as Plerguèr...

> Armed with pikes and axes, they slaughtered the prince and all his family. His property was looted and the castle burned to the ground; only his youngest son, Patrice, survived from this slaughter. He was taken captive to Ireland. There he looked after sheep and learned the language of the country of which he became the oracle and disciple.[133]

This now raises an intriguing question that has never been considered before as an historical possibility. Could the Forest of Quokelunde be the Wood of Foclut, that Patrick remembered in a dream he experienced a few years later, after escaping from Ireland? The geographical details given in this story are significant and worth further consideration. Before such a possibility can be seriously considered, the first task is to establish whether a forest called 'Quokelunde' actually existed in this region at the time of St Patrick.

Considering the uncertainties which exist in records from the fifth century, the Forest of Quokelunde is well documented.[134] It was part

---

[133] Historical information provided for guests at Château de Bonaban, 35350 St Malo, Brittany (2013).

[134] Quinault found many remains of a forest, 'La Forêt de Qokelunde' which after 1734 was called Scissy by L'Abbé Rouault. See L'Abbé Rouault, *Abrégé de l'Histoire des Solitaires de Scissy* (St Malo, 1734).

of a much larger forest called the Forest of Scissy.[135] In the late Roman period, a huge oak forest covered much of Brittany. The forest of Scissy stretched along the coast from the Isle de Chaussey to Mont St Michel. Near the edge of this forest there were seven military roads which consolidated Roman power throughout northern and western Europe.[136] This forest was held sacred by the Druids in the pre-Christian period. In early Christian times it was known 'the Desert of Scissy', because of the large number of hermits who lived there. One French writer described it as a *Thébaid Celtique* or 'Celtic Desert' referring to a place in Upper Egypt where desert monasticism originated in the fourth century.

In his seventeenth-century *Histoire de Bretagne*, M. Deric describes it as the largest forest in Brittany. Part of this vast forest covered the coastal region of north-east Brittany at the time of St Patrick, stretching from Alderney, Chaussey and Les Mintiers, as far as Dol. It surrounded 'Dolomhoir' now Dol-de-Bretagne.[137]

The forests of Brittany have long been associated with folk lore and legend, but they are also remembered as a place of seclusion, religious worship and sanctuary. Valerosi describes it as the 'Forest of a Thousand Oaks'. Many hermits or aspiring monastics are said to have lived in this forest during the late Roman period. The Forest of Quokelunde formed part of this larger, more widely documented Forest of Scissy. [138] A monastery existed at St Pair, called the Monastery of Scissy. This was associated with a holy man called St Senior, identified as a disciple of St Paterne, who is recorded as one of the earliest founders of local Christian monastic settlements.

Breton historians claim that after St Patrick escaped from slavery in Ireland he returned to his homeland in Brittany and that eventually

---

[135] Gilles Manet, *De L'etat Ancien et De L'etat Actuel dans La Baie de Mont Saint Michel* (St Malo, 1829). Manet includes old maps of the Bay area on pp. 146 ff.

[136] John O'Hanlon, *Lives of the Irish Saints* (Dublin, 1875), iii, p. 455, n. 258.

[137] Gilles Deric *Histoire Ecclésiastique de Bretagne*, ii (Paris, 1778). *Histoire de Bretagne*, p. 15–17.

[138] The location of the ancient Forest of Coquelunde is also mentioned in *Memoires des Antiquaries de France* for 1817–1869, vol. 17, p. 383. For other references to Quokelunde see Edouard le Hericher, *Histoire de L'Avranchin*, ii, p. 230. Also: *Les Annales du Mont St Michel*, i (1874), p. 109.

he was ordained as a priest by St Senior, the founding bishop of Dol.[139]

Probus records that Patrick was ordained as a bishop by St Senior. In his *Confession*, Patrick refers to those who had made accusations against him and were seeking to have him removed from the mission in Ireland, as his 'seniors'.

Séigneur is a title traditionally applied to holy men in France, clergy as well as nobles. It is also the word used in French to address Christ as the "Lord".

The earliest reference to the Forest of Quokelunde that we can find (apart from Patrick's Confession) is mentioned by Guillaume de Saint-Pair, a twelfth-century monk at Mont St Michel who wrote *Le Roman du Mont St Michel* around 1160 CE.[140] Here are the verses in Old French, with an English translation kindly provided by David Parris, specialist in Old French at Trinity College, Dublin:

Desouz Averenches vers Bretaigne

Below Avranches towards Brittany

Eirt la forest de Quokelunde,

Was the forest of Quokelunde

Don grant parole eirt par le munde.

Much talked about in the world.

Cen qui or est meir et areine,

Where there is now sea and sand,

En icel tens eirt forest pleine

In that time (it) was all forest

De meinte riche venaison;

---

[139] Joseph de Garaby, 'St Patrick' in *Vies des Bienheureux et des saints de Bretagne* (Saint-Brieuc, 1839). L'Abbé Desroches also records the local significance of 'Saint Senier', the church of 'St Senier' de Beuvron and ancient parish of 'St Senier', which is about two miles from Avranches.

[140] Guillaume de Saint-Pair, *Le Roman du Mont-Saint-Michel* (Caen, 1856).

With much good game;

Mers ore il noet li poisson:

Now fish swim there:

Dunc peust en tres bien aler,

So you can easily travel,

N'I esteust ja crendre meir,

There was no need to fear the sea,

D'Avrenches, dreit a Poulet,

Going straight from Avranche to Poulet,

A la cité de Ridalet.

To the city of Ridalet [Aleth].

En la Forêt aveit un mont

In the forest there was a mount (vv. 49–61)

Guillaume de Saint Pair was describing part of an established medieval pilgrimage route to Mont St Michel. In this poem 'Avrenches' can easily be identified with Avranches, an ancient ecclesiastical centre which is located on the other side of the Bay of Mont St Michel from Dol-de-Bretagne. In the final verse of the passage quoted above (v. 60) the poem mentions the city of Ridalet (*la cité Ridalet*) known also as 'Quidalet', which refers to the city of Aleth (still known as *la cité*) now St Malo, on the opposite side of the bay from Mont St Michel.

Guillaume's poem is recognised as one of three Medieval Latin histories written at Mont St Michel. He was a twelfth-century monk resident in the monastery at Mont St Michel who was familiar with the pilgrimage route and the ancient traditions associated with it. He had local knowledge and came from a place nearby called St. Pair. He describes how the forest was renowned for its venison, and the rivers and sea nearby for the fish.

When David Parris, a specialist in Old French from Trinity College, Dublin kindly sent me a translation of these verses I asked him whether they perhaps contained any *double entendres* or hidden meanings, that perhaps would suggest the influence of romance or

Grail legends. His view was that Guillaume was writing 'pretty straight-down-the-middle Old French' which is a language that is simple in tone. In his opinion, hidden meanings and subtle twists came later with a group called *les grands rhétoriqueurs*.

If this is correct, then he can be trusted in his descriptions of the local landscape and pilgrimage routes that were familiar to him, confirming that an ancient forest called Quokelunde definitely existed in this region, at least in the twelfth century. According to Guillaume de Saint-Pair, the Forest of Quokelunde existed in the Bay area around Mont St Michel, between Aleth and Avranches, well known to pilgrims en route to Mont St Michel. It would be helpful to know whether this knowledge about Quokelunde formed part of an oral tradition preserved at Mont St Michel or if he was drawing on earlier, written records which have been lost or perhaps still preserved elsewhere?

Although disputed by some writers in the past, the existence of this ancient forest is now acknowledged by historians. Archaeologists have found evidence for a cataclysm, which may have taken the form of devastating flood caused by an encroaching of the sea. As a result, the ancient Forests of Quokelunde and Scissy were submerged.[141] This affected the low-lying coastal region between St Malo and Mont St Michel. Breton fishermen, who farm mussels in the shallow waters of the Bay, frequently encounter old tree trunks preserved only a few inches under water in the Bay. Some of these trees have been carbon dated and found to be very ancient (2700–250 BCE). There is disagreement as to when exactly this forest was submerged. M. Manet and René Henry, amongst others, have dated the rise in sea level to 709 CE. This is also said to be the date when St Aubert built a new church on Mont St Michel.

Chateaubriand dated the inundation of the sea during the reign of Childebert (511–558 CE). Archaeological excavations have documented the remains of these ancient forests and the Gallic-Roman roads made of wattle and stone that once passed through them. Remains of other Roman roads can be traced from Dol to St Pair and Corseul (Dinan), and Corseul to Aleth.

---

[141] Desroches, *Histoire du Mont St Michel*. See also Loïc Langouet, 'La Forêt du Scissy et La marée de 709, Légende ou Réalité?' *Dossiers du Centre Régional d'Archéologie d'Alet*, 24 (1996), pp. 49–54.

In a more recent study, French author René Henry has explored the historical and archaeological evidence concerning the Forest of Quokelunde and provided a number of informative maps and illustrations of the local topography, which are fascinating, not least for the study of Patrick.

Archaeologists have identified the ancient course of the River Couesnon, which now flows into the sea at Pontorson, the gateway to Mont St Michel.[142] At the time of St Patrick, it flowed between the Forests of Scissy and Quokelunde. Local historical, geographical and archaeological evidence, therefore, allows for the possibility that Bonaban could be the location of Bannavem Tiburniae, the place from which St Patrick was taken captive, since pirates travelling by ship from Ireland would have had direct access to the site. The short walk from Château de Bonaban to Bois-Renou allows for a clear view of the local landscape and especially the low-lying area of agricultural lands along the coast, called Le Marais. This is where the ancient Forest of Quokelunde once existed. Celtic axes, pottery, coins and other remains from the late Roman period have been discovered here and are now preserved in local archaeological exhibitions. Geological surveys of this region confirm that the ancient site of Bonaban is on a raised granite escarpment, once accessible by sea and a river. These studies document the coastline at the time of St Patrick, before an inundation of the sea which is said to have taken place in 709 CE. Local research has identified a tributary of the River Rance which once flowed from its mouth at Aleth to where Château de Bonaban is now located.

The course of another old river has been detected between Cancale and the present site of Château de Bonaban. This allows for the possibility that if pirates had arrived near Cancale before they attacked the estate where St Patrick's family was resident, they may have been able to reach this site by sailing up this river. These ancient river courses have been affected by recent local land-drainage schemes, but they can be seen clearly on René Henry's original map. Local history and geography are, therefore, consistent with the specific details of the local tradition which describes how St Patrick was taken captive, as pirates landed near Cancale then crept up through the Forest of

---

[142] René Henry, *Au Péril de la Mer* (Paris, 2006).

Quokelunde before they attacked the Calpurnius estate.

The map below is based on the work of M. Manet and René Henry. It is designed to show the region where St Patrick's father owned an estate between Aleth (St Malo) and Mont St Michel. It shows the coastline today and the coastline as it existed at the time of St Patrick, before an inundation of the sea caused the Forests of Quokelunde and Scissy to be submerged. The remains of a Gallo-Roman road that linked Dol to St Pair and Corseul (Dinan) and the site of Château de Bonaban are marked on the map.

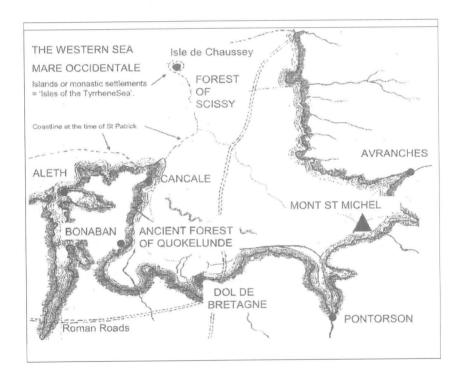

All these local geographical and topographical details are significant in relation to the location of the villa owned by St Patrick's father, because they appear to confirm that key descriptions recorded in the local tradition preserved at Château de Bonaban are plausible and could be true. If this was the location of Bannavem Tiburniae and if St Patrick grew up there, then he would have been very familiar with this forest. Could this forest have been known to St Patrick and recorded in Ireland as the 'Wood of Foclut'?

According to linguistics expert Christine Mohrman, who made a detailed study of St Patrick's Latin, there are definite Gaulish influences in Patrick's writings; influences that in her opinion, could not have come from Scotland, Wales or anywhere else in Britain.[143] This raises the question of Philology which is regarded as one of the most exact and reliable sciences. The names 'Quokelunde' and 'Foclut' show an intriguing similarity but are they linguistically connected to the extent they could refer to the same forest?

When a Brythonic (Breton) name was transcribed into Latin and Old Irish, certain letters would have been changed. Brythonic Celtic (Welsh and Gaulish) has traditionally been classified as a 'P' Celtic language whereas Irish and Scots Gaelic is a 'Q' Celtic language. The difference between them is the treatment of the proto-Celtic 'k' which became 'p' in the P-Celtic languages but 'k' in Irish.[144] For example, in Welsh and Breton the word for head is 'pen' but it appears as 'ceann' in Irish and Scots Gaelic. The name for son is 'mab' (earlier 'map') in Brythonic but 'mac' in Goidelic. More recently, Goidelic and Brythonic have been linked as insular Celtic languages and distinguished from continental Celtic. Old Welsh and Breton spellings reflect the fact that while the sounds of Latin had changed, the spelling of Latin was retained, so that written words often required new pronunciation. A good example would be when a 'c', 'p' and 't' occurring after a vowel was pronounced 'g', 'b', 'd' respectively. This helps to explain the variety of spellings for Foclut which can be found in the ancient manuscripts, sometimes written 'Foclud' or 'Fochlad'.

A Breton word beginning with a 'Q' could be changed to begin with a 'U' or 'V' when written in Latin but appear with an 'F' in Old Irish. The name *Quokelunde* could therefore reflect a Brythonic or continental (Gaulish) tradition. The difference in spelling might be accounted for by the transposition of letters or syllables that occurred when the name spoken by Patrick was recorded in Latin or transferred into Old Irish.

In relation to a connection between the names '*Quokelunde*' and '*Foclut*', the following information was kindly sent to me by David

[143] Christine Mohrmann, *The Latin of St Patrick: Four Lectures* (Dublin, 1961).

[144] [website] Wikipedia: P-Celtic and Q-Celtic languages.

Parris, specialist in Old French at Trinity College, Dublin. Dr Parris advised that Latin did not distinguish between V and U (nor between I and J) and that these two vowels could also, on occasions, be consonants. Eventually, the distinction between the vowels U and I and the consonants V and J was reflected in writing, but we still call a W a "double U" when it is obviously a double V.

He said there was a known difficulty in representing W sounds at the beginning of a word. Thus what we call a "wasp" and the Italians a "vespa", in French is a "guepe" originally pronounced something like "gwesp". Similar correlations are at work as between the English "warder" and French "gardien" which was originally pronounced something like "gwardien".

Dr. Parris recommended that the 'unde' or last part of the name Quokel-unde should be removed and seen as a later, probably Frankish (or Norse) addition, then he suggested that the original name of the forest in Brittany was probably pronounced something like Kwokel to represent an initial W, as in the Latin 'Uoclut', which would have been recorded in Irish as Foclut or Foclud. Dr Parris's knowledge and expertise in this matter was greatly appreciated, not least because it gives support to the case for locating the Wood of Foclut in Brittany and also therefore the integrity of the local tradition about St Patrick which is preserved at Château de Bonaban.[145]

When linguistics expert Christine Mohrman came to Dublin in 1960 to speak about the Latin of St Patrick, she made some very interesting remarks about Patrick's recollection of the Wood of Foclut. She said there was a deeply human element in the way St Patrick described his dream in which some memories associated with this wood were recalled. She suggested that Patrick dreams 'the Irish' call him and that this call is realised and individualised by the voice of a people he had once known, from his youth:

---

[145] L'Abbé Gervais de la Rue, writing in 1834, said that the name Quokelunde includes the common Scandinavian 'lundr' which means 'grove' or forest, attached to an older Celtic name. See Margaret Gelling, *Place-names in the landscape* (London, 1984).

'When he [St Patrick] reads from the letters that the Irish call him, an image of his youth comes back to him and he hears the voices of the people he has known.' [146]

Could the 'image from his youth' that came back to haunt St Patrick in this dream perhaps have been a memory of traumatic events that took place in the forest surrounding his father's estate on the day it was attacked rather than the traditional view that suggests these voices came to him from the place where he was held captive in Ireland?

If so, this would not only support a Gallic theory of origins but also confirm Charles de Gerville's view about the location of Patrick's 'Bannavem Tiburniae' on or close to the present site of Château de Bonaban, which at the time of St Patrick was surrounded by the ancient forest of Quokelunde.

What implications might this have for understanding St Patrick's dream and the meaning of his *Confession*? St Patrick tells us when this dream occurred. He had just returned to his homeland and been reunited with his extended family after many years of separation. Reading his account of the dream, there is immediately a sense that whatever memory Patrick had of the Wood of Foclut it was disturbing and traumatic for him. He tells us that he woke suddenly from the dream, feeling 'heartbroken'.

This was no ordinary dream; judging by St Patrick's description of his feelings when he woke up it sounds more like a nightmare. Despite this trauma, in the midst of this 'night vision', as he describes it, he received what he experienced to be a calling from God to return to Ireland and carry the gospel to those in need who were there. 'Thank God,' St Patrick said, 'after many years their cry was heard by the Lord.'

As with other places mentioned by St Patrick, and despite the claims of Muirchú and Tirechán, the location of the Wood of Foclut is one of the great unsolved mysteries of St Patrick's biography. There is nothing in this dream which should lead us to assume that the Wood of Foclut must have existed in Ireland, and we must also be wary of drawing any historical or geographical conclusions about

---

[146] Christine Mohrman, *The Latin of St Patrick* (Dublin, 1961). *Emphasis ours.

what was remembered in the context of a dream that took place several years before he wrote about it. Having said that, could it be possible that St Patrick was remembering events which had taken place in the woods around his father's estate on the day he was taken captive?

The trauma of being abducted by pirates and dragged from his home and family as a teenager would certainly have created difficult memories and affected him for the rest of his life. St Patrick would never have been able to forget this experience of hearing the shouts and screams of those who cried out in the face of outrageous violence, then being dragged away through the woods by barbarians from a foreign country. In his *Letter to Coroticus*, St Patrick tells us that on the day the raid took place, those who took him captive 'devastated the male and female servants' of his father's house. Those cries alone may have continued to haunt St Patrick even when he was an older man, especially if, as many of the early Breton historians record, he witnessed his own parents being killed during the attack. Patrick's suffering would account for the traumatic nature of his memory and waking up suddenly, feeling 'heartbroken'.

Could the voices that haunted him in this dream have been the cries of those who were taken captive with him, many of whom were still being held captive in Ireland? It had not been too long since Patrick's escape from captivity; perhaps it troubled him in the depths of his own heart and conscience that he was free while they still suffered in captivity. Could the 'Voice of the Irish' have been the voices of those taken captive with him in the turmoil and violence of that fateful day, his own country men and women who were still held captive in Ireland? Is this how God called him, through the pain of a broken heart, to return to the land of his own captivity for the sake of those others who were still in captivity and for the sake of the gospel of Christ? For someone as courageous and faithful as Patrick, that would certainly have been one good reason to go back. Hanson said:

Far be it from any historian to attempt the task of psycho-analysing St Patrick, but it is clear even to the most austere and dispassionate investigator of his writings that in his captivity, at the age of sixteen, Patrick suffered what we now call a severe psychological trauma from which, in a sense, he never recovered ... Even when as an old man he is writing the *Confession*, at least forty and perhaps fifty years after the event, he still cannot stop regarding himself as a helpless adolescent, cruelly torn from home and family ... Hanson continues...

Patrick does not pity himself because as he himself tells us, in his moment of helplessness and extreme need he found a helper and friend in God. He could never forget his terrible experience of being taken captive in his youth, but neither could he forget that through this experience he had met 'the one above all who is powerful, in all and through all, the one who drew him out of the deep mire and set him on top of the hill.[147]

This is one of the most remarkable qualities of St Patrick's personality, revealing his strength and depth of spiritual maturity. However much trauma there had been with all the danger and difficulties he experienced in his life, however much personal grief, loss, suffering and rejection, he never harbours a grudge against those who took him captive, or did him harm. St Patrick even ends his *Letter to Coroticus* offering the olive branch of forgiveness and reconciliation to those who had abused him.

If there is genuine and sincere reparation for wrongdoing, however evil it may have been, the message St Patrick wanted to proclaim is that God always forgives. Hanson said this is the real motive and keynote of St Patrick's *Confession*, not primarily written to hit back at his opponents or justify himself, but to declare gratitude to God.[148]

From the evidence gathered so far, it appears that we may have identified three possible locations from the geographical references mentioned in Patrick's Confession. These include *Britanniis*, *Bannavem Tiburniae* and *The Wood of Foclut* which can all plausibly be identified within a very specific local region, on the north-east coast of Brittany, between Aleth (St Malo) Dol de Bretagne and Mont St Michel. A final clue to support the possibility that all these places existed in the same local area is the meaning of the Latin name '*Mare Occidentale*' or 'Western Sea'. Those who support Tirechán's claim that the Wood of

---

[147] R. P. C. Hanson, *St Patrick His Origins and Career* (Oxford, 1997), p. 208.

[148] Hanson, *St Patrick*, p. 202 ff.

Foclut existed in the west of Ireland have understandably assumed that Patrick's *Mare Occidentale* must be a reference to the Atlantic Ocean off the west coast of Ireland. In Roman geography, the term 'Mare Occidentale' applied to the whole ocean west of the Empire, including that which existed off the west coast of France and Spain.

In his *Confession*, St Patrick describes the Wood of Foclut as being 'close beside the Western Sea'. This is a rare coupling of geographical references. At the time of St Patrick, however, the Forest of Quokelunde was also situated 'close beside the Western Sea' which matches St Patrick's description perfectly. Patrick's *Mare Occidentale* could be a reference to the sea or ocean that existed off the coast of Brittany.

Is it possible that Irish raiders and slave traders could have travelled that far to attack the Calpurnius estate and carry St Patrick back with them to be sold as a slave in Ireland, towards end of the fourth century?

CHAPTER EIGHT

PIRATES OF THE

MARE OCCIDENTALE

When captured by an Irish band
He took their Isle for fatherland
Succat by Christian birth his name
Heir to a father's noble fame[149]

When trying to interpret a dream Jungian analyst Jeremy Taylor warns against the dangers of what he calls 'mistaken literalism'. The advice he gives is that we must be careful not to base any specific geographical or historical claims on whatever a person has described to us in the context of a dream.

Ever since the seventh century, when Bishop Tirechán claimed

---

[149] St Fiacc's Hymn, v 2.

the Wood of Foclut existed in his own diocese in County Mayo, a particular form of dream interpretation has been applied to a passage in St Patrick's *Confession* which quickly became part of an established tradition continued to this day.

This is based on an essentially speculative and misguided form of dream analysis. An initial error of interpretation that assumes the Wood of Foclut must have existed in Ireland because St Patrick describes in his dream how he heard the 'Voice of the Irish' calling to him from that wood, was compounded by further error when it was also assumed that when Patrick said the Wood of Foclut was close beside the Western Sea (Mare Occidentale) he must have been referring to the Atlantic Ocean off the west coast of Ireland.

In the context of his own writings, is it possible Patrick was referring to the ocean off the coast of Brittany? In Roman geography, the 'Mare Occidentale' did not refer exclusively to the Atlantic Ocean off the west coast of Ireland. In Latin, *occident* means west, and *orient* is east. For Roman geographers, who approached the world from a continental perspective, the 'Mare Occidentale' meant, 'the sea of the setting sun'. It applied to the whole ocean west of the Empire, including that which existed off the west coast of France and Spain.[150]

Apart from ancient maps in which the name appears, there are few historical references to the *Mare Occidentale*. Those which do exist, suggest this refers not just to the ocean off the west coast of Europe, but to the seas adjacent to the coasts of France and Spain in particular. The *Mare Occidentale* appears on a Piri Reis map dated to 1513, together with an interesting commentary. Piri Reis was a Turkish captain who later became the Chief Admiral of the Ottoman Navy. Notes in the margin attached to one of his maps include accounts of those who took part in the discovery of places shown on the map.

The following passage is a translation of these notes as they apply to section XXII of the map, which deals specifically with the *Mare Occidentale*:

---

[150] Ludwig Bieler, *Clavis Patricii II: Libri Epistolarum Sancti Patricii Episcopi* (Dublin, 1993), p. 150; also *Irish Historical Studies*, iii (1943), pp. 351–64.

This sea is called Western Sea [Mare Occidentale] but the Frankish sailors call it the *Mare d'Espagne* which means the Sea of Spain. Until now it was known by these names, but Columbus, who opened up this sea and made these islands known and the Portuguese have given it a new name, *Ovo Sano* [*Oceano* – Ocean], round like egg. Before this it was believed this sea did not have aim or limit, except that on the other side was dusk and darkness.[151]

Ireland was at the margins of the known world, beyond which there was only dusk and darkness. The ocean to the west of Ireland was basically an unknown and uncharted territory for classical geographers. It was always stretching the evidence beyond reasonable limits to assume that St Patrick must have been referring to such a remote part of the western ocean, when he described the Wood of Foclut as being 'close beside the Western Sea'. Valorosi described the Mare Occidentale as the ocean which 'bathes all the west of the Empire':

Until now, nobody has pushed beyond the Island of Egamin [Erin/Ireland?] However, there are a series of estuaries for the greater part unexplored that are used as bases for pirates who manage in this way to escape the boat vessels of the imperial military navy.

Ludwig Bieler investigated the origins of the Latin 'Mare Occidentale' as part of his research into problems associated with the traditional location for the Wood of Foclut. He notes that in classical geographical records the word *mare* is often substituted by the word *oceanus*. On various ancient maps the name 'Oceanus Occidentale' appears far more frequently than 'Mare Occidentale' but it still designates the sea which extends westwards from continental Europe, which we now call the Atlantic.

The paucity of references suggests that '*Mare Occidentale*' may have been a more familiar term within local or ethnic rather than classical geography.

---

[151] From notes concerning the *Mare Occidentale*, attached to Piri Reis Map, 1513, Legend xxii. See J. Hapgood, *Maps of the Ancient Sea Kings* (Illinois, 1966), p. 224.

Is there any evidence which might provide clues to help clarify how St Patrick may have understood the meaning of this name? If there is any truth in the geographical descriptions given by Probus in his *Life of St Patrick*, the answer is yes. Probus includes a very significant remark when he describes Bannavem Tiburniae as being 'close beside the Western Sea' in the province of Neustria. He makes no claims regarding the geographical location of the Wood of Foclut but it is significant that Probus uses the same Latin phrase to describe the location of Bannavem Tiburniae that St Patrick used when describing the location of the Wood of Foclut. Both are described as being 'close beside the Western Sea' and the Latin phrase used by Probus – *haut procul a mare occidentali* – is exactly the same phrase as that given by St Patrick in his *Confession*. If what Probus said is true, and if a local tradition recorded by the Breton historians is reliable, that pirates who attacked the Calpurnius estate crept up through a local forest called Quokelunde, which can be identified as the Wood called 'Foclut' in Patrick's *Confession*, then it is undoubtedly also true that when St Patrick tells us that the Wood of Foclut was 'close beside the Western Sea', he must have been referring to the ocean off the north east coast of Brittany. Could Irish pirates have travelled that far?

A number of references can be found which help confirm the existence of piracy on the Mare Occidentale during the time of St Patrick.

Stories recorded in the ancient *Lives of St Patrick*, link an important event in St Patrick's biography to a particular sea, which is called the Iccian Sea or 'Sea of Icht'. The event in question concerns the circumstances in which St Patrick was taken into captivity. The family are said to have crossed the Iccian Sea as part of a journey they made by ship from Strathclyde to Brittany, where St Patrick was taken captive. The *Iccian Sea* was a name given to the stretch of water between southern Ireland, south-west Britain and the northern coast of Brittany. For the Romans, this sea formed part of the Western Sea or 'Mare Occidentale'. Today, the French call it *La Manche*. The location of the Iccian Sea is well documented and can be clearly identified. It was linked to the Roman port of Iccius (Boulogne-Sur-Mer) from which Caesar embarked, during the invasions of the island of Britain in 55 and 54 BCE. It is mentioned in the ancient annals of Ireland where it appears in Old Irish as 'Muir n-Icht', again connected with the Port of Iccius, located in northern Gaul.

The annals record that towards the end of his reign (379–405 CE) one of the most famous of all Irish chieftains Niall of the Nine Hostages was engaged in seafaring expeditions on the Iccian Sea before he was killed during his second or third expedition in Gaul.

The Age of Christ 405: Niall of the Nine Hostages had been twenty-seven years in the sovereignty of Ireland. He was slain at Muir-n-Icht.[152]

In his book, *Oxygia*, Roderick O'Flaherty discusses the reign of Niall and says he was killed by a poisoned arrow when he was fighting on the River Loire. If this is true, it links Niall's excursions even more directly with Brittany.[153]

St Patrick tells us in his *Confession* that he was taken captive at sixteen years of age when pirates attacked his father's estate at Bannavem Tiburniae. If Patrick was born in 385 CE he would have been sixteen years old in 401 CE, which is precisely the period the Irish chieftains were raiding in Brittany.

It is therefore possible that St Patrick was taken captive during one of Niall's raids in Gaul. In his *History of Ireland*, Keating accepted this to be the case and it interesting to note that Keating describes Patrick as a 'noble' youth. Breton sources say St Patrick's family had a royal pedigree and that two of his sisters were founding members of the Breton aristocracy.

He [Niall] sent a fleet to Brittany in France which is called Armorica, for the purpose of plundering that country; they brought 200 noble youths as captives to Ireland with them and it was in this captivity they brought Patrick who was sixteen years old. [154]

---

[152] Donovan, *A4M*, for the year 405 CE. See also O'Hanlon, *Lives of the Irish Saints* (Dublin, 1875), p. 488.

[153] Roderic O'Flaherty, *Oxygia* (Dublin, 1775), pp 393–412.

[154] Geoffrey Keating, *History of Ireland*, ii, in Irish Texts Society, ed. and trans. P. S. Dineen (Dublin, 1908. For a study of St Patrick's royal pedigree see Marcus Losack, *St Patrick and the Bloodline of the Grail: The Untold Story of St Patrick's Royal Family*, (Annamoe, Wicklow, 2012).

The Irish were not the only pirates operating in these waters. Piracy was rampant on the Western Sea or 'Mare Occidentale' during the late Roman period, especially in those final years which preceded the fall of Rome, when there were constant attacks along the north-western coasts of Gaul. Several groups were engaged in piracy and slave trading in the violent, unstable period during the late fourth and early fifth centuries. Slavery was a marked feature of native Irish and Caledonian-Pictish societies, as it was throughout the Roman Empire at the time of St Patrick.

Slave trading provided a lucrative income. With the breakdown of law and order in the Western Empire, the number of young men and women taken captive must have been enormous. In his writings, St Patrick tells us that he was taken captive along with thousands of others. In his *Letter to Coroticus*, he mentions the policy of the Christians in Roman Gaul, which was to pay generous ransoms to the Franks for the release of Christians taken hostage. [155]

This suggests that he was familiar with the situation on the continent.

The busy Roman port at Aleth and its wealthy rural hinterland would have been a prime target for those seeking plunder especially after the legions had been recalled from Gaul around 405 CE.

The soldiers of the Legion Martenensis, who had been stationed at Aleth, were recalled to defend Rome. Attacks were more common as the legions withdrew and lost whatever control they once had in Brittany.

In 407 CE the Vandals, Alans and Suevi and other Barbarian tribes ravaged Gaul and the coastal region was constantly plundered until 417 CE. There were increasing attacks from pirates and Barbarian tribes arriving from the north. These attacks involved British, Irish and Frankish groups.

In the political and military chaos, this region may have been denuded of people and resources. If St Patrick's family home was located near Aleth, at the 'mouth' of the River Rance, then from a historical point of view, Irish pirates could have been responsible for the attack.

---

[155] LC:14

Long before the Roman period there were established trading routes between Ireland and Gaul and archaeological evidence confirms significant exchange between these two regions. With the prevailing westerly winds, the journey from southern Ireland to the coast of Brittany, in reasonable weather, would have taken no more than three days.

Writing in the twelfth century, Gerald of Wales describes Ireland as three days sailing from Spain when he says, 'The farthest island of the west (Ireland) has Spain parallel to it in the south at a distance of three ordinary days sailing.' If Spain could be reached in three days sailing, the same would obviously have applied to Brittany.[156]

After escaping from slavery in Ireland, intending to return to his homeland, St Patrick tells us he sailed for three days and nights before the ship on which he was travelling made land. This indicates that Patrick's homeland was probably on the continent. If his home had been in Scotland or anywhere else in Britain, surely it would have made sense for him to travel there? The journey from Ireland to Wales would have required less than one day's sailing. Boats would have been readily available for such a crossing which is much closer to where he was held captive. It is most likely that Patrick landed somewhere on the continent in Gaul, as Bury suggested.

The place where they landed seemed like a wasteland, almost devoid of people. Patrick and the crew had to walk for several days without food until they reached some kind of human habitation. It is possible the ship sailed to Brittany. If so, Patrick may have been an eye witness to devastations caused by Barbarian invasions of the Gallic peninsular.

Driving along the coast road from Château de Bonaban to St Malo it is possible to enjoy wonderful views of the ocean which stretches out to the west. Could this have been the sea that Patrick described as the Western Sea or 'Mare Occidentale'? If so, the evidence invites us to consider a radical new alternative to our traditional understanding of St Patrick's biography. Four of the key geographical references mentioned in the *Confession* can all plausibly be identified within a specific local coastal region of Brittany between

---

[156] Gerald of Wales, *The History and Topography of Ireland*, trans. John J. O'Meara (London, 1982), p. 33.

the ancient Roman port of Aleth (St Malo) and Mont St Michel. This includes St Patrick's homeland in *Britanniis*, the family estate from which he was taken captive at Bannavem Tiburniae, the Wood of Foclut and the 'Mare Occidentale' or Western Sea. If these identifications are correct, then St Patrick's father and grandfather owned an estate on an elevated site close to the present site of Château de Bonaban, only a few kilometres from the Roman port of Aleth where the Legion of Mars was once stationed.

René Henry's maps identify a large flat area of open ground at Cézembre close to St Malo, which would have been ideal for the Roman military. Soldiers could have pitched tents there during the winter months. Some ancient writers record that St Patrick's 'Bannavem Tiburniae' was identified with such a facility. Remains of Roman and Viking camps have been found on the prairies at Cézembre. Much of the local area, covered by forest at the time of St Patrick, has been cleared for agriculture and new housing and road developments.

A small part of the old Forest of Quokelunde may have survived, however, in the grounds that surround Château de Bonaban.[157] It is possible that some of the oak trees growing on the estate are the descendants of trees which grew there at the time of St Patrick. For those who may wish to visit, these oaks can be viewed as a natural remnant of the forest which once surrounded the Calpurnius estate from where St Patrick was taken captive. Patrick may have played in this forest as a child and through his early teenage years, until that fateful day when he was abducted and sold into slavery in Ireland. Perhaps different memories of this forest, those which haunted St Patrick in his dreams and those which have shaped our understanding of its geographical location, can both now be freed from the shackles of historical uncertainty.

One of the most uncertain periods of St Patrick's biography includes the so-called 'missing years' between the time St Patrick returned to his homeland after escaping from slavery and the moment he set sail to return to Ireland as an apostle. This is the time when St Patrick undertook religious training and spiritual formation. The question as to where St Patrick was trained and which church or

---

[157] See René Henry, *Au Péril de la Mer* (Paris, 2006), p. 43 ff.

religious group supported his mission to Ireland is an essential part of his biography which has always been controversial.

According to these accounts, after Patrick escaped from slavery in Ireland and had returned home to his surviving relatives, he joined the community of St Martin of Tours in the Loire Valley and received his initial religious training there. After leaving this community (perhaps because of dangers surrounding the fall of Rome in 409 CE), Patrick joined a community of 'barefoot hermits' who lived on the *Isles of the Tyrrhene Sea*.

It was here that St Patrick is said to have been ordained by St Senior and commissioned for the mission to Ireland and where he was given the *Baccaill Jesu* or 'Staff of Jesus', as a sign of his authority to preach the gospel as an apostle in Ireland. St Patrick does not mention the *Isles of the Tyrrhene Sea* in his own writings, but these mysterious islands are consistently mentioned in many of the ancient documents related to Patrick. Despite the huge number of books written about St Patrick, their location has never been securely identified. In the next chapter we will explore these references and try to find evidence to show where the *Isles of the Tyrrhene Sea* were located.

Some ancient sources suggest they existed in the Bay of Mont St Michel, off the north-east coast of Brittany, which is very close to the present location of Château de Bonaban. If so, St Patrick may have had a much closer relationship with this local coastal region in Brittany than has so far ever been acknowledged or understood.

LA BAIE DU MONT SAINT-MICHEL AVANT LE RAZ-DE-MARÉE DE MARS 709

CHAPTER NINE

ISLES OF THE TYRRHENE SEA

Truth has its own gravity
And eventually draws people back.[158]

According to some of the ancient *Lives of St Patrick* published by John Colgan, after Patrick had escaped from slavery in Ireland (probably around 405 CE) and as a direct result of a dream in which he heard 'The Voice of the Irish' calling him to return, St Patrick joined the community of St Martin of Tours, located in limestone caves at Marmoutier, on the banks of the River Loire. It was there he began his formal religious training following the early monastic ideals pioneered by St Martin. Martin died in 402 CE (some say 405 CE) so Patrick may not have met St Martin at this time, but the community founded by Martin was vibrant and very well known. Some of the ancient documents record that after leaving St Martin's monastery, Patrick spent several years undertaking spiritual formation and further religious training with a group of 'barefoot hermits' who were

---

[158] Dan Brown, *The Lost Symbol* (New York, 2009), p. 61.

resident in the 'Isles of the Tyrrhene Sea'.

The geographical location of these islands has never been securely identified but they play an important part in several of the ancient accounts given for this period in St Patrick's life. A sense of confusion and contradiction is compounded by the fact that these 'islands' could refer to actual islands, early forms of monastic settlement, or both. The Latin word *insula* applied not only to islands but also to groups of hermits living in remote places such as islands or forests, especially in Gaul.

Modern geography locates the Tyrrhenian Sea in the Mediterranean, in the triangle between Italy, Sicily and Sardinia. Some of the ancient writers appear to have assumed this was its location. Other references exist, however, which provide an alternative theory, that these islands were located in what is now the Bay of Mont St Michel, off the north east coast of Brittany, very close to where Château de Bonaban is located today. If so, this region was not only the place where St Patrick lived and from which he was taken captive, it may have been associated with much of his religious training and spiritual formation.

Like Nemthor and Armoric Letha, the *Tyrrhene Sea* is not mentioned directly by St Patrick in his own writings but several references are preserved in the ancient secondary sources which provide clues to identify its true location. Todd referred to these as "curious fragments of a forgotten geography that lead to the suspicion of their possible authenticity". [159]

These fragments were part of some archaic material that pre-dated Muirchú and Tirechán and the Armagh Movement of the seventh century.

If these 'islands' can be identified, a little more of the truth as to where St Patrick was trained and commissioned for the mission to Ireland can be established. The challenge is to separate the threads of historical possibility from the tangled web of legend, hagiography and tradition.

---

[159] J.H. Todd, *St Patrick, Apostle of Ireland*, p. 310 ff. See especially p. 335.

Muirchú

According to Muirchú, when Patrick was thirty years old he went to Rome to honour the 'the head, certainly of all the churches in the world', in preparation for his mission to Ireland. Pope Celestine held office from 422 to 432 CE. Muirchú describes how St Patrick travelled from Britain to Gaul by ship, journeyed overland through Europe and was about to cross the Alps to go to Rome when he met St Germanus, the bishop of Auxerre. Patrick is said to have spent a long time under the guidance of St Germanus – some said thirty or forty years – learning 'obedience, wisdom and charity'. Then Victor (an angel or spiritual mentor who had appeared to St Patrick in frequent visions) told Patrick that the time had come for him to go to Ireland to preach the gospel.

Muirchú describes how steps were taken to prepare for this journey.

St Germanus arranged for an older man, a priest called Segitus, to travel with St Patrick as a companion because he (Patrick) 'was not yet ordained in the Episcopal grade by the holy lord Germanus'. When news reached St Germanus that Palladius had died, Patrick changed direction and went towards 'a certain wondrous man, the highest bishop, Amathorex by name, dwelling in a neighbouring place' and according to Muirchú it was he, not Germanus, who ordained Patrick a bishop.[160] The ordination as it is described appears to have been characteristic of Celtic customs which required only one bishop to be present. Rome required at least three for episcopal orders to be conferred. The identity of Amathorex is uncertain. He was probably a Gallic bishop. Etymology suggests that he may have been a local king or associated with a royal family, as well as being a bishop. His name is possibly derived from the prefix *Amator* and the suffix *rex*, which means 'chieftain' or 'king'.

The bishop in Auxerre before Germanus was called Amator. He fled Auxerre in 418 CE, after an altercation with St Germanus.

Following his ordination as a priest and bishop by Amathorex, 'according to the order of Melchizedek', Patrick travelled to Ireland to begin his mission.

---

[160] David Howlett, *Muirchú Moccu Mactheni's 'Vita Sancti Patricii'* (Dublin, 2006), pp. 55-58.

In Muirchú's account St Patrick never made it as far as Rome and there is no mention of St Patrick being ordained by Pope Celestine. Muirchú locates all Patrick's ecclesiastical training with Germanus in Auxerre and his ordination by the mysterious Amathorex at an unspecified location on the continent.

St Germanus (380–448 CE) was born from one of the noblest families in Gaul. His grandfather had been Prefect in Gaul. He was educated in the schools of Arles and Lyons then went to Rome to study law. Having developed a successful legal practice in Rome, his professional talents and the reputation of his family brought him in contact with the imperial court. The Emperor sent him back to Gaul, appointing him as one of the six dukes, entrusted with the government of the Gallic provinces with a residence in Auxerre.

Germanus loved hunting and for this reason is said to have incurred the displeasure of St Amator, who was still the bishop in Auxerre at that time. Germanus used to hang the heads of all the animals he killed on a tree that was sacred to local people as a place of worship. Amator challenged him about this behaviour, which led to conflict between them. One day when Germanus was out of town, Amator cut the tree down and burned the trophies. Fearing for his life because Germanus wanted to kill him, Amator fled from Auxerre to Brittany. If Amathorex can be identified with Amator of Auxerre, he could have been the one who ordained Patrick.

Tirechán

In Tirechán's narrative, which is preserved alongside Muirchú's *Life of St Patrick* in the *Book of Armagh*, we find the following account, which includes a tradition not found in Muirchú. Tirechán describes how St Patrick escaped from slavery in Ireland when he was twenty-two years old. After that, he spent the next seven years walking and travelling by water 'through Gaul and all of Italy and in the islands of the Tyrrhenian Sea'. Bishop Ultan had informed Tirechán (his pupil) that St Patrick 'spent thirty years on one of these islands, which is called Aralensis'. Some writers have suggested this name refers to Arles or Lerins, because the Tyrrhene Sea was understood to be part of the Mediterranean. Modern geography locates it in the triangle between Italy, Sicily and Sardinia but as we shall see, this was not always the case.

St Fiacc's Hymn

Fiacc's Hymn is said to be one of the earliest documents after St Patrick's own writings but in this document which was written as a hymn or poem, there is great geographical uncertainty and confusion:

> He went over all Albion (the Alps or Alba?)
>
> Great God it was a marvellous journey
>
> Until he left himself with Germanus in the south;
>
> In the southern part of Letha.
>
> In the Isles of the Tyrrhene Sea he fasted
>
> It was there he pondered
>
> He read the canon with Germanus
>
> That is what books declare. [161]

Fiacc is obviously aware that St Patrick was closely associated with a place called 'Letha'. This is what the old books declared. Fiacc links this place to St Germanus in Auxerre. The problem is that Auxerre is about a hundred and fifty kilometres or ninety-two miles south of Paris in the centre of Gaul and a long way from Letha, which comprised all the territories of the western coastal area of Gaul from the mouth of the Rhine to the River Loire. 'The southern part of Letha' is most likely a reference to Armoric Letha, on the coast of Brittany. According to Fiacc's Hymn, after Patrick had completed his religious formation with St Germanus he then went to the 'isles of the Tyrrhene Sea' where he fasted for an extended time of spiritual reflection.

---

[161] St Fiacc's Hymn, trans. Whitley Stokes, *Tripartite Life*, p. 405.

The Scholiast

When the Scholiast added notes to *St Fiacc's Hymn*, probably in the ninth century, he attempted to correct or clarify the geographical location of these places. This author knew that Germanus was based in central Gaul, but he identifies 'Letha' in the south of Italy. There was obviously great uncertainty about the location of these places and this confusion affected later writers.[162]

Just as the significance and location of 'Armoric Letha' in relation to Patrick appears to have been lost or forgotten, so the precise location of 'the 'isles of the Tyrrhene Sea' in the context of St Patrick's biography, was misunderstood and lost to historical memory in the centuries after St Patrick's death. This was a direct result of mixing up separate traditions relating to Patrick and Palladius.

Patience is required to identify threads of truth and disentangle these from the tangled web of legends and confusion that surround St Patrick but these efforts will be rewarded when we can finally identify the location of the Isles of the Tyrrhene Sea, as these relate to the life of St Patrick.

The Scholiast repeats the claim that Patrick trained with St Germanus, who advised him to go to Rome so that Pope Celestine could confer orders upon him.

The plot suddenly thickens, showing how creative and contrived hagiography can be. According to the Scholiast, St Patrick went to Rome but Pope Celestine refused to ordain him because he had already sent Palladius as a bishop to Ireland.[163] Palladius had been sent to Ireland by Pope Celestine in 431 CE , as 'the first bishop 'to the Irish believing in Christ'.[164]

After being rejected by the Pope, Patrick went to the 'isles of the Tyrrhene Sea'. The account given here is complicated and extremely jumbled but if we follow the various threads of tradition a little further, something closer to the truth slowly begins to emerge. The Scholiast continues:

---

[162] See Notes on *Fiacc's Hymn* in Stokes, *Tripartite Life,* ii, p. 418, 419.

[163] Stokes, *Tripartite Life,* ii, p. 419.

[164] Prosper's Chronicle, Liam de Paor, *St Patrick's World*, p. 72 ff.

So Patrick went to the Islands of the Tyrrhene Sea after Pope Celestine's refusal [to grant him holy orders] and there he found The Staff of Jesus [*Baccail Jesu*] on the island called Alanensis... Mount Arnon.[165]

The *Baccail Jesu* or 'Staff of Jesus' is said to have been a staff given to St Patrick as a symbol of his authority to preach the gospel and be an apostle in Ireland, perhaps akin to a bishop's staff or crosier. According to the Scholiast, after receiving the sacred Staff of Jesus on Mount Arnon in the 'islands of the Tyrrhene Sea', St Patrick went again to St Germanus who sent him back to Pope Celestine but things were different for St Patrick this time.

Celestine had recently learned that Palladius had died suddenly in Britain, so he ordained St Patrick to take his place, an event traditionally dated to 432 CE, the year after Palladius went to Ireland. In this account, Amathorex is conveniently brought to Rome for St Patrick's ordination:

Patrick was ordained in the presence of Celestinus [Pope Celestine] and Theodosius the Younger [Emperor of Rome] king of the World. Amatorex, Bishop of Auxerre was the one that conferred orders upon [Patrick]. Celestine was only alive for a week after he ordained Patrick.[166]

In another account found in the *Lebar Brecc Homily* on St. Patrick, there is no mention of Patrick returning to Rome and meeting again with Pope Celestine. After leaving Auxerre, Patrick 'went upon the Tyrrhene Sea' until he came to an island where he received the sacred Staff of Jesus from two hermits living there. Patrick went to an archbishop living nearby who ordained him bishop. As the story unfolds it gets even more complicated, when angels get involved. After news had reached Rome that Palladius had died (after less than a year in Ireland) the Papal authorities ordered Patrick to go to Ireland. Angels told him to go to Ireland promptly, but St Patrick

---

[165] Stokes, *Tripartite Life,* ii, p. 421.

[166] Stokes, *Tripartite Life*, p. 421,445.

refused to leave, until he had spoken directly with Jesus Christ:

> So the angel brought him to Armoric Letha, to the city named Capua, on Mount Arnon, by the shore of the Tyrrhene Sea and there the Lord spoke to him as he had spoken to Moses on Mt Sinai.[167]

It is the geographical reference in this version of the story that is significant. Here, *Mount Arnon* and the *Tyrrhenian Sea* are both given the same geographical location, which is nowhere near Auxerre, Italy, or the south of France. Mount Arnon and the Tyrrhene Sea are both identified with Armoric Letha. This leaves no doubt that as far as this document is concerned the Tyrrhene Sea was located off the north-east coast of Brittany. Mount Arnon is described as being located '*by the shore of the Tyrrhene Sea*' and if so, this could be a reference to Mont St Michel.

Colgan's Third and Fourth Lives

In the *Third Life* published by Colgan, another version of the story records that after having first been with St Germanus and then spending four years with St Martin's community at Tours, the angel told St Patrick to go to Mount Arnon in Armoric Letha. This mountain is described as 'a big rock in the Tyrrhene Sea' near a city called 'Capua'. The Latin description *ad Montem Arnon in Airmairch Letha super petram Maris Tyrreni* can be rendered into English as 'St Patrick was told to go to Mount Arnon in Armoric Letha; a big rock beside the Tyrrhene Sea'.[168] Once again, the Tyrrhene Sea is clearly identified with the coast of Brittany. The description given in this passage also strongly suggests that Mount Arnon can be identified with Mont St Michel. In the Latin phrase *supra petram Maris Tyrreni*, which describes Mount Arnon, *supra petram* means 'a high or pinnacled rock'. Since this was in Armoric Letha, Mont St Michel matches the description perfectly.

---

[167] The Lebar Brecc Homily on St. Patrick, in Stokes, *Tripartite Life*, ii, p. 447.

[168] See Bieler, *FLL*, p. 222, note c. 25.

The identification of Mount 'Arnon' or 'Hernon' with Mont St Michel appears to be confirmed by another copy of Colgan's *Third Life* which uses a slightly different phrase, *montem Arnon in Armairc Lete super ripam maris Tyrreni*. This translates as 'Mount Arnon in Armoric Letha a large (rock) beside the shore'.[169] The description applies aptly to Mont St Michel, which is very close to the shoreline, as those who have visited can testify.

The *Fourth Life* of St Patrick published by John Colgan also identifies the Tyrrhene Sea with Brittany.[170] Although they appear in the secondary sources and cannot be taken as reliable historical evidence, these references provide some of the missing pieces in a geographical jigsaw puzzle which helps to identify where St Patrick's religious training and ordination took place. We can see that all these missing pieces are fragments of a forgotten geography but they are clearly connected and all point in the direction of Brittany.

As these ancient document continue the story, St Patrick sails through the 'Tyrrhene Sea' where he receives the Staff of Jesus from two hermits living on an island. Patrick speaks to God on a mountain and is told to go to Ireland but first he goes to Rome, where this time he is well received by Pope Celestine, who gives him relics of saints before sending him to Ireland. As with Muirchú's account, nothing is said about St Patrick's ordination in Rome.[171]

Probus

At an earlier stage in our study it was suggested that the true location of St Patrick's homeland was known to Probus, who identified it with a coastal region in north-east Brittany. If this author proved to be

---

[169] *Ad ripam* means 'by the shore (stream or river)'. *Ripa*: river, stream, bank, river. This comes from *arripare*, to 'touch the shore', in the sense of coming ashore after a long voyage. Bieler, *FLL*, p. 132.

[170] In this document, the Tyrrhene Sea is located adjacent to Armorica *terram quae Armorica dicitur iuxta mare Tyrrenum possideret*. 'Vita Quarta', Bieler, *FLL*, p. 51 and Todd, *St Patrick*, p. 323. See note 1.

[171] Bieler, *FLL*, p. 77. See Todd, *St Patrick*, p. 324.

reliable in relation to the location of Bannavem Tiburniae, can he also be trusted as to where St Patrick was trained and ordained?

Probus includes an intriguing account that is very different to those we have encountered so far. He describes how, when Patrick returned to his homeland after escaping from slavery in Ireland, he did not go to Rome or St Germanus in Auxerre as other accounts suggest. Instead, St Patrick went immediately for religious training to the community of St Martin of Tours, based in those famous limestone caves at Marmoutier on the banks of the River Loire.

This is where he spent the next four years. Probus records that St Patrick was trained within St Martin's community and that he was tonsured there. It was here that St Patrick was first ordained in holy orders and learned about doctrine and the lectionary.[172] When St Patrick left the community of St Martin, Probus records that he spent the next eight years on an island with 'the people of God' who are described as a community of 'barefoot hermits'. Then Patrick went to another group of solitaries, living on an adjacent island which is described as being 'between the mountain and the sea'.[173]

According to Probus, after being on this island for several years, Episcopal orders were conferred on St Patrick by a bishop called 'St Senior'.[174] This name strongly suggests a local connection to Brittany. Breton historians record the first bishops established in Brittany during the settlement under Maximus in 383 CE were called 'Senior' or 'Seigneur'. This title is still applied to senior clerics and the nobility in France. In his *Confession*, Patrick refers to the religious leaders who were involved with his ordination as 'seniors'.

---

[172] Probus, *Liber* I: 14; Bieler, *FLL*, p. 195

[173] *Vade ad illos qui sunt in insula inter montes et mare.* Probus, *Liber* I:16, Bieler, FLL, p. 195. A similar description in the *Tripartite Life* is more geographically specific and locates this place in the Tyrrhene Sea. *Quodam tempore dum esset S Patricius in Mari Tyrrheno venit ad locum, in quo errant tres alij Patricii. Erant enim hi in quodam solitario specu inter montem et mare.* Stokes, *Trip. Life*, i, p. 26 ff.

[174] Lanigan notes (from Martiniere) that hermits were resident on Mont St Michel and surrounding islands, long before a church dedicated to St Michael was built by St Aubert of Avranches in 705 CE. See Lanigan, *Ecclesiastical History of Ireland*, 4 vols (Dublin, 1822; 2nd edn, Dublin, 1829), p. 166 ff.

Probus provides geographical clues to identify where St Patrick was ordained as a bishop. St Senior was based on 'Mount Hermon', a mountain 'on the right side of the ocean' known as 'the city with seven walls'.[175] He describes how St Patrick had to climb steeply up this mountain so that he could speak with God. The geographical descriptions given are significant, especially the use of the Latin word *ascende*, which means to ascend, or climb up steeply.[176] This could be another reference to Mont St Michel. It also matches the description Nennius gives for Mons Jovis, one of the landmarks that designated the boundaries of Armoric Letha in which this mountain is described as *super verticem* or 'rising almost vertically'.

Mont St Michel is a precipitous, pyramid-shaped rock which ascends very dramatically, almost 'vertically' from the sea. It was once an island, close to the shoreline but is now joined to the mainland by a causeway. Mont St Michel was probably one of the most famous of the 'islands in the Tyrrhene Sea'. It remains a major landmark in the local topography today, as those who have visited can testify. Probus records that St Patrick was ordained as a bishop there. But there is no mention of this in the official guide book.

The reference to 'seven walls' is significant. Those who have visited Mont St Michel, which is now a world heritage site, will be familiar with the steep climb to the church on the summit. Several walls have been built over the centuries, primarily as retaining walls for buildings and paths, also for safe access, helping to separate the religious or monastic areas above from the more secular activities taking place below. Models on display today for visitors to the abbey, attempt to show the development of structures on this rocky island over the centuries. This confirms the existence of several ancient walls.

At Mont St Michel, the retaining walls are intersected by a path which directs pilgrims towards the summit, known as the Merveille. It is possible that there were seven walls on Mont St Michel at some stage, if not at the time of St Patrick then perhaps by the time Probus was writing in the ninth century.

---

[175] Probus, *Liber* I, pp. 17–25. Colgan, *Trias Thaumaturga*, ed. De Burca, pp. 48–9; Stokes, *Tripartite Life*, i, p. cxxxvii ff. See Bieler, *FLL*, p. 196.

[176] Probus 18:15, Bieler, *FLL*, p. 196. 33. See Dr Lanigan, *Ecclesiastical History of Ireland*, p. 109, n. 129.

In a detailed study of the history of Mont St Michel, French author Louis Blondel records that a College of Druidesses, in the Gallo-Roman period, was established on the rock now called Mont St Michel. It was a sanctuary to the Celtic God of fire and the Sun Belenos. After the Romans occupied Gaul, it became a sanctuary for the Roman god Jupiter.

The holy mountain then became known as Mont Jou or Mont Jovis, which appears to have been the name familiar to Nennius. After the fall of the Roman Empire, the mount became known locally as 'Mont Tumba'. Blondel describes an early Christian religious community on Mont St Michel or 'Mount Tumba', founded by St Paterne and St Pair, the first apostles of Neustria, in the fifth century. This pre-dates the first church said to have been founded on Mont St Michel by St Aubert in the early eighth century. [177]

St Paterne and St Pair established a monastery called *The Monastery of the Two Tombs*. The identity of the person or persons buried there is uncertain. The island adjacent to Mont St Michel is called Tombelaine (Tomb-Elaine) or Helen's Tomb. This could have referred to Helena, the Mother of Constantine the Great, or perhaps to Ellen or Helen, the widow of Magnus Maximus.

In 705 CE St Aubert, the Bishop of Avranches, built a new church on the rock dedicated to the Archangel Michael. Custody fell to the expanding monastic order of the Benedictines and since that time, this sacred mount has been known as Mont St Michel. If 'Mount Hermon', as mentioned by Probus, can be identified with Mont St Michel, we may be coming very close to knowing where St Patrick received spiritual training and was ordained as a bishop for Ireland. St Patrick appears to have belonged to a spiritual community of 'barefoot hermits' who practised asceticism on certain islands off the coast of Brittany in the vicinity of Mont St Michel and Dol. These islands and early 'monastic' communities were known to ancient writers as the 'isles of the Tyrrhene Sea'.

From a historical point of view, can we be confident that we have identified the location of the Tyrrhene Sea correctly?

---

[177] Louis Blondel, *Notice Historique du Mont-St-Michel, Tombelaine et d'Avrenches* (1823), p.7.

In the '*Cosmographia*' of Julius Honorius, the 'Mare Tyrrhenum' is part of the 'Oceanis Occidentalis', the Western Sea, which associates it with the coast of Brittany. In an anonymous *Life of St Patrick* published in Paris in 1870, it is stated that 'The Western Ocean (Mare Occidentale) is in another part called the Tyrrenian Sea or *Turonian Sea* located at the mouth of the Loire opposite the country inhabited by the Turones also called the people of *Turaine*, whose capital, Tours, was a great city even in the time of the Romans'. [178] This concurs with Murphy's *Life of St Patrick* published in 1853.

One reference in an ancient Irish source identifies the Tyrrhene Sea closely with the Iccian Sea, which we know refers to the stretch of water between Ireland, south-west Britain and Brittany.

In this passage, the reference to the Archangel Michael suggests a possible link with Mont St Michel. It confirms that some of the early Irish writers understood the Tyrrhene Sea to be located off the coast of Brittany.[179]

Scholars have wrestled with these enigmatic and elusive geographical descriptions concerning St Patrick and some accepted the identification with Mont St Michel. In an *Ecclesiastical History of Ireland*, published in 1823, John Lanigan suggested that the geographical descriptions mentioned above refer to Mont St Michel.[180] When J. H. Todd published a controversial but magnificent study of Patrick in 1864, he recognised the significance of these geographical descriptions and he accepted that they applied very aptly to Mont St Michel.[181]

In fact, Todd's scholarly eye had penetrated deeply into all these

---

[178] *Life of St Patrick*, (Paris, 1870), Anon., p. 13.

[179] 'The sons of Muirchú of Connaught made this hymn to [the archangel] Michael to save themselves from a tempest on the Iccian Sea or to save themselves from famine on 'the island of the Tyrrhene Sea' *(tempestate Mare Icht no ara soerad de fame in insola Maris Tyrreni).* Stokes, *Tripartite Life*, i, p. cvi; Louis Blondel, *Notice Historique du Mont-St-Michel, de Tombelaine et d'Avrenches* (Avrenches, 1823).

[180] See Lanigan, *Ecclesiastical History of Ireland*, p. 165 ff.

[181] See Todd, *St. Patrick, Apostle of Ireland*, p 323 ff., p. 338, n. 1. Todd was concerned that he could find no record of this place ever being called 'Mount Hermon', 'Arnon' or 'Morion' and so identified the Tyrrhene Sea with the Mediterranean. He placed a question mark over this, accepting the uncertainty.

confused and contradictory accounts about the location of St Patrick's religious and spiritual training, far enough for him to suggest that confusion had arisen because two different stories had been woven together, one relating to the ordination of Palladius and the other, to Patrick. Todd had therefore anticipated O'Rahilly's theory of the Two Patricks. The fusion or confusion between separate traditions associated with Patrick and Palladius greatly affected the church's understanding of Patrick's biography.

People and places integral to the life of Palladius (St Germanus, Pope Celestine, the church of Auxerre, Arles, Lerins, Capua, Italy and Rome) appear to have been transferred to St Patrick by many of the ancient writers.

If we remove these from the list of other people and places associated with St Patrick, we are left with St Martin of Tours, the Isles of the Tyrrhene Sea, a community of 'barefoot hermits', Armoric Letha, Mount 'Hermon' or 'Arnon' (Mont St Michel), the city of seven walls, Amathorex and St Senior. Since there is no historical record of Palladius being associated with any of these places, it would seem reasonable to suggest these references belong to material that applies to St Patrick. They help to identify the places where St Patrick received his religious training and was commissioned for the mission to Ireland.

We can only be grateful to the ancient writers and scribes who faithfully compiled or copied the ancient manuscripts down through the centuries. These documents preserved certain names, geographical descriptions and traditions without which the truth about St Patrick's place of origins and where he was ordained and received religious formation, might never have been identified.

If the ancient manuscripts collected and published by John Colgan and his colleagues at Louvain had not survived, it would not have been possible to compare them and thereby glimpse patterns, which can help to separate history from hagiography and put some of the more difficult pieces of the puzzle together. Scribes intervened and made changes but they retained old names and traditions that have been passed down faithfully to us through many centuries. Without them, the truth about Patrick may have been lost forever.

The Staff of Jesus

Some of the ancient legends attached to St Patrick are intriguing and very mysterious. The following account describes a remarkable experience Patrick is said to have had during his time in the Isles of the Tyrrhene Sea when he met a holy couple who were living together on one of the islands. They gave St Patrick a sacred staff, which they had been keeping for some time. This staff was known in Ireland as the Baccail Isu or Staff of Jesus.

'When Patrick went to sea nine was his number. And it is then that he came to the island and he saw the new house and the young married couple inside. In front of the house he saw a decrepit old woman on her hands. 'What is wrong with this old woman?' Patrick asked. 'Great is her feebleness,' the young man replied, 'She is my grand-daughter but if you could see her mother, she is even more feeble.' 'How did that come to pass?' said Patrick. 'Not hard to answer' said the young man.

'We have been here since the time of Christ, who came here and dwelled amongst us. We made a feast for him. He blessed our house and us but that blessing did not come upon our children. Because of his blessing, we shall abide here without aging or decay until the Day of Judgement'. The young man said to Patrick 'Your coming to us has been foretold for a long time. God left us with knowledge and understanding that you would be the one to come and that you would preach to the Gaels [Irish]. He left this token with us that is His staff, and said it was to be given to you.' 'I will not take it', said Patrick, 'unless Christ himself gives me his staff.'

St Patrick stayed three days and three nights with them and then went to Mount Hermon in the neighbourhood of the island. And there the Lord appeared to him and told him to go and preach to the Gael and gave him the Staff of Jesus. He said that it would be a helper to him in every danger and in every unequal conflict in which he should be …

St Patrick asked that three promises should be given to him if he went to preach the gospel in Ireland. Firstly, that he [Patrick] would be at Christ's right hand in the kingdom of heaven, secondly that Patrick alone would be judge of the Irish at the End of Days and thirdly, that he should be given as much gold and silver as nine companions could carry to support and further St Patrick's mission in Ireland'.[182]

The drama of this event and conversation is embellished by myth and great storytelling, but it is certainly possible that when Patrick came to Ireland as an apostle, he carried a staff as a sign of the authority given to him to preach the gospel in Ireland. The existence of such a staff has been recorded in Ireland from an early date. It is one of three famous relics associated with St Patrick, together with St Patrick's Bell which is preserved in the National Museum of Ireland in Kildare Street, Dublin and a sacred book, thought to be the *Book of Armagh*, preserved at Trinity College, Dublin. This staff was said to have been reserved for St Patrick because he was designated to be the 'Last of the Apostles' through whom the Lord's commandment would be fulfilled, that the Gospel should be preached 'to the ends of the Earth' – at that time a reference to Ireland. The 'Baccail Isu' was treasured by the Irish Church until it was lost (possibly destroyed) in Dublin at the time of the Reformation.

St Bernard of Clairvaux, writing in the twelfth century, refers to St Patrick's Staff as conferring more power than the highest canonical sanction. He describes it as being overlaid with gold, adorned with the most precious jewels. If there is any truth in the legend that surrounds it, the Staff of Jesus was not just carried by Patrick as a sign of his authority as an apostle in Ireland; it was the staff that had once been carried in the hands of Jesus Christ himself.

The Missing Years

There is so much about St Patrick that we do not know. One of the most uncertain periods of St Patrick's biography includes the so-called 'missing years' between the time St Patrick returned to his homeland after escaping from slavery and the moment he set sail to return to Ireland as an apostle. This is the time when St Patrick undertook religious training and spiritual formation. The ancient *Lives*

---

[182] See Stokes, *Tripartite Life*, ii, p. 445 ff.

of St Patrick published by Colgan preserve several confused and contradictory accounts which mention different people in various contexts and a number of different geographical locations.

Many of these record that St Patrick's spiritual formation was associated with and guided by senior figures within the church of Rome, including St Germanus and Pope Celestine. These particular strands of tradition say Patrick was trained for many years under Germanus in Auxerre, that he may have spent time at the Monastery of Lerins or Arles, that he visited Rome on more than one occasion and was ordained by Pope Celestine before he went to Ireland as an apostle. This is not based on any reliable historical evidence, but appears to form part of the 'Legend' of St Patrick.

Some ancient sources contradict these traditions and present an alternative version of events. According to these accounts, after Patrick escaped from Ireland he joined the community of St Martin, where he was tonsured and received his initial religious training. After four years there, Patrick joined a community of 'barefoot hermits' who lived on the 'isles of the Tyrrhene Sea'.

A *Life of St Martin of Tours* written by Sulpitius Severus was published in 405 CE. A copy of this book was included in the *Book of Armagh* together with other material directly related to St Patrick. The Irish Church was aware of a close connection between St Martin and St Patrick and Severus was greatly respected as a writer by St Augustine and St Jerome who were his contemporaries. This author is very important for our study because he was writing towards the end of the fourth century and was an eye witness to events that took place during the rebellion of Magnus Maximus in 383 CE.

Severus was a close friend and devoted disciple of St Martin and had visited the community at Marmoutier on several occasions. He tells us that many young nobles were attracted to St Martin's monastery. St Patrick may have been one of them. It's time to find out what was happening in those famous limestone caves on the banks of the River Loire and see if there is any evidence to support the possibility that St Patrick may have been there.

CHAPTER TEN

MARTIN OF TOURS

Jesus did not predict that he would come clothed in purple with a glittering crown on his head. I will not believe Christ has appeared unless he comes in the form in which he suffered, naked and stripped of this world's glory, its power and possessions.[183]

Several of the ancient sources claim that St Patrick was trained and tonsured in the community of St Martin of Tours. The credibility of this connection is strengthened by the claim that Patrick's mother, Conchessa, was 'of the Franks' and that she was St Martin's niece. If this is true, Martin and Patrick were closely related. [184] The primary source for information about St Martin is Sulpitius Severus (363–420 CE). His writings are a contemporary witness for the crucial period from 385–400 CE when both the Emperor Maximus and St Martin

---

[183] Sulpitius Severus, *Life of St Martin,* in *The Nicene and Post Nicene Fathers*, xi, eds Philip Schaff and Henry Wace (New York, 1894), ch. xxiv.

[184] Deric records that Patrick's mother, Conchessa, was Martin's niece. Martin's sister, her mother, was born in Pannonia. In Gaul she married Ochimus, Conchessa's father. See Gilles Deric, *Histoire Ecclésiastique de Bretagne*, ii (Paris, 1778), p. 148.

were still alive. This was the time of Patrick's birth, childhood and teenage years. Severus was a disciple and close friend, familiar with Martin's approach to Christianity and how the teachings of the gospel were being practised in St Martin's community. If St Patrick received initial ecclesiastical training and spiritual formation at Tours, this is where we may be able to find more clues as to St Patrick's real identity.

The accounts given by Severus of the situation relating to church and state during this period reveal there were diverse groups within the church and conflicts which had a direct impact on St Martin and perhaps, therefore, also on St Patrick. Severus provides insight into these disputes and conflicting approaches to the requirements of Christianity and the teachings of Jesus, which may help explain why St Patrick was perhaps rejected by the church and excluded from historical records for two hundred years after his death.

The key to the truth about St Patrick's biography is the link with St Martin. Severus calls St Martin 'a truly blessed, holy person, in whom there was no badness, judging no one, condemning no one, returning evil for evil to no one'. He says, 'Never was there a feeling in his heart except for piety, peace and tender mercy.' Martin was a very spiritual person, who understood Christianity to be essentially an ascetic religion.

Christian discipleship required the renunciation of personal wealth and a willingness to follow the essential teaching of Jesus, to avoid temptations associated with material grandeur. St Martin understood the command of Jesus to 'sell everything you have, give to the poor and come follow me' as an essential foundation for discipleship.

To become a Christian, seek spiritual perfection and try to be worthy of eternal life, this command had to be put into practice. Martin embraced the teachings of (Coptic) Egyptian Desert Spirituality, following the example of St Antony, to the extent that all members of his community wore simple garments made from camel hair which had been imported directly from Egypt. Severus shows us how important the Egyptian Desert Tradition was for them when he said, 'As long as I live and retain my senses, I will always celebrate the monks of Egypt.' [185] Severus tells us that Martin continued to dress in

---

[185] Severus, *Life of St Martin*, ch. x, p. 9. See 'Dialogues' in *The Nicene and Post Nicene Fathers*, xi, eds Philip Schaff and Henry Wace (New York, 1894), i, ch. xxvi, p. 36.

the Egyptian way even after he became a bishop, which infuriated some clergy who thought ecclesiastical leaders should retain a sense of status which belonged to a more 'dignified' classical lifestyle.

He describes how Martin's approach to Christianity was influenced by Paulinus of Nola, who parted with his material possessions (which were substantial) and 'following Christ, showed himself the only one in these times to have fully obeyed the precepts of the gospel'. A favourite disciple of St Martin's, called St Victor, was sent by Martin to visit St Paulinus of Nola; Martin and Victor together persuaded Paulinus to withdraw from the world. Could this be the person called 'Victor' who helped St Patrick escape from slavery in Ireland and then appeared again to St Patrick in his dreams? [186]

Severus also describes Martin's hermitage, two miles outside the city of Tours. This spot was so secret and retired that he enjoyed the chance for solitude, in the midst of other responsibilities. On one side it was surrounded by a precipitous rock; the River Loire had shut in the rest of the plain by a bay extending back for a little distance and the place could be approached only by one person at a time through a very narrow passage.

Martin built a cell constructed of wood. The other monks also built cells, although most were dug out of the rock in the overhanging mountain, which they hollowed out into caves. [187] Similar limestone caves occupied by monks at the time of St Martin can be seen near the village of Candes Martin, where St Martin died. His death is portrayed on a beautiful stained glass window in a chapel dedicated to him in the local parish church.

At these early monastic settlements, no one had anything called his own; all things were possessed in common. It was forbidden to buy or sell anything, which Severus claims was the custom among most monks. No art was practised except by the scribes. Rarely did anyone go beyond the cell, except when they assembled at the place designated for prayer. They ate food together, after the hour of fasting was past. No one drank wine, except when illness compelled them. Severus says there were about eighty monks in Martin's

---

[186] Severus, *Life of St Martin*, ch. xxvi, p. 16. See O'Hanlon, *Lives of the Irish Saints* (Dublin, 1875), p. 502.

[187] Severus, *Life of St Martin*, ch. x, p. 8 ff.

community, many from noble families. If St Patrick went there, we can imagine that he would not have felt out of place.

Severus also provides a reliable contemporary witness to the conflicts and difficulties which existed between St Martin and other church leaders. He tells us that some of the diocesan clergy despised Martin's appearance and his Christian way of life, as a result of which there was controversy over Martin's election as Bishop of Tours. Some bishops accused Martin of being unworthy of the episcopate on the basis that his appearance was despicable, saying that his clothes were poor and shabby, that he was 'a contemptible person' and 'his hair was disgusting'. We can only try to imagine what was so despicable to them about St Martin's hair. For some reason it was offensive to other clergy and bishops. Perhaps it was long, following the orthodox tradition, which required a monk never to cut his hair or shave the face again after monastic vows were taken. Martin's hair was obviously not compatible with what was expected or accepted by other clergy. This sheds some light on the kind of tonsure that was distinctive in his community. If Patrick was trained in St Martin's community and tonsured there, as some of the ancient records claim, then Patrick would probably have worn his hair in the same style as St Martin.

If so, this would have been equally offensive to those church leaders. Tonsure was to become one of the key issues of conflict between the Irish tradition and the Roman Church together with the calculations of a cycle related to the appropriate time for the celebration of Easter.[188]

Severus tells us that some of the bishops attacked St Martin and 'sought to slander him'. Someone called The Avenger opposed Martin's election as bishop of Tours. The appointment was ratified by popular demand, in controversial circumstances. This did not go down well in some quarters.

There was serious conflict within the church of Gaul at this time. Severus reveals something of the danger when he states openly that those who hated St Martin included many bishops, although he did not want to name names, saying, 'a good many of these people are

---

[188] Severus, *Life of St Martin,* ch. ix, p. 8.

still venting their spleen against myself'.[189] Severus was treading on a dangerous political and ecclesiastical tight rope. Whatever these conflicts and differences were they had created a dangerous situation for Martin and those associated with him.

Severus was a well-known writer, respected by the highest authorities in the church at the end of the fourth century but when approaching this subject he was clearly concerned to watch his words carefully. He tells us that he had originally intended to keep his record of St Martin private 'confined within the walls of my own house' but he thought it was disgraceful that the excellence of so great a man (St Martin) should remain concealed.[190]

His *Life of Martin* was written when St Martin was still alive but Severus may have sensed danger and delayed publishing it until after his death.

This shows how complex and potentially sinister the situation was.

What was so dangerous about things happening in the church?

We don't have to read too far between the lines to find out what was going on and who Severus was talking about. Severus describes an emerging conflict between those who supported a simple form of monasticism of the kind sponsored by St Martin and those clergy, who were linked more closely to a politically influential diocesan hierarchy.

Monastic groups advocated the practice of asceticism and poverty, characteristic of Egyptian Desert Spirituality. Others, including some very wealthy and powerful bishops, were more attached to classical Roman social and economic values. This conflict appears to have been a very serious issue for senior members of the church. Ambrose of Milan refused to visit Gaul because of the conflict there between monks and diocesan clergy but this conflict was not restricted to Gaul. It was characteristic of those areas where an expanding authority of the Roman hierarchy was interfacing with monastic expressions of Christianity in the 'Celtic' heartlands of Britain, Ireland and Gallic parts of Spain. St Patrick's life cannot be understood in isolation from these issues which were affecting the whole western church at this time.

---

[189] Severus, *Life of St Martin,* ch. xxvii, p. 17.

[190] Severus, *Life of St Martin*, p. 3.

Some of those associated with Martin were accused of being Pelagian. This included Severus himself. St Martin may have died before Pelagius visited St Augustine in North Africa, but views expressed by Pelagius were characteristic of the monastic movement at this time. Those who sympathised with him would soon be targeted by Pope Celestine, St Germanus, and Palladius, amongst others who strongly supported the teachings of St Augustine.

In relation to our study of St Patrick it is interesting to note that Severus is also said to have incurred charges of heresy because he embraced Pelagian opinions. Severus lets us know very clearly where he stood in relation to these disputes. As far as he was concerned, in their behaviour some bishops and a powerful clergy group within the church were betraying the essential teachings of the gospel and the original teachings of Jesus. He says, 'in Martin alone Apostolic authority continued to exert itself'. [191]

This is a remarkable statement, which shows his profound respect for Martin's way of being Christian. Severus describes St Martin as a truly blessed and holy man 'in whom there was no falsehood – no lies or deception – judging no one – condemning no one – returning evil to no one'. He writes, 'never was there a feeling in his heart except piety, peace and tender mercy'. But there were those who 'as he led his retired and tranquil life, slandered him with poisoned tongue and viper's mouth.' [192]

In one of his books, Severus records a dialogue between himself and a 'man of Gaul'. He invites this person to speak the Celtic language or 'Gaulish'.

This was Brythonic Celtic, now preserved in Welsh and the Breton language. Severus was from Aquitania but this monk was a Celt from Gaul who was a disciple of St Martin and a member of Martin's community. We know this because he speaks about fishing on the River Loire and catching a huge pike when he was responsible for finding food for the other monks who lived in the monastery. [193] The monk from Gaul speaks about the serious conflict taking place

---

[191] Severus, *Life of St Martin*, ch. xx, p. 13.

[192] Severus, *Life of St Martin*, ch. xxvii, p. 17.

[193] Severus, *Dialogues*, iii, ch. x, p. 50.

in the western church at this time. St Martin's community had come under serious attack from Jerome, in a dispute related to issues of authority that manifested themselves shortly afterwards in the Pelagian controversy. When speaking about St Jerome the monk from Gaul says:

> He [Jerome] is in truth but too well known to us, for some five years ago I read a certain book of his in which the whole tribe of our monks is vehemently assaulted and reviled by him.[194]

Jerome and Augustine were powerful and very influential figures in the church at this time. Anyone on the receiving end of Jerome's caustic criticisms would be vulnerable to condemnation and ridicule. Severus describes a church Council at which three hundred and fifty bishops were present and Jerome was in very high standing. At this council, heresies were condemned. Severus adds an intriguing comment that 'Jerome is said to stand in high favour with certain people who I am unwilling to name'. If this is a reference to St Augustine, which is possible, this reveals how precarious the situation was for St Martin's community and any other forms of 'Celtic' monasticism.

To have Jerome attacking you in his racist, vitriolic diatribes was one thing, but to have Augustine and Jerome teamed up against you, as Pelagius did, was sufficient to guarantee a theological death sentence, if not worse.

Telling of his conversion in 383 CE, St Augustine recalls a conversation in Milan with an imperial officer called Potitanus. This man told how, when he was stationed at Trier he and some companions walked together in the park outside the city walls. He entered one of the monastic huts, where he picked up a copy of the *Life of St Antony*, written by St Athanasius. When Augustine read this book it changed his life and led him and his wife to embrace celibacy. It brought about St Augustine's conversion to Christianity.

It is interesting to note that Potitanus was associated with members of the greatly feared Imperial Secret Police – known as *Agentes in Rebus*. Augustine was the first to develop a theological

---

[194] Severus, *Dialogues*, i, ch. viii, p. 27 ff.

justification for the use of the secular powers and military agencies of the state to increase the church's influence and authority, including its ability to combat those deemed to be heretical.[195]

In relation to how these disputes were affecting monks in Gaul, the 'man from Gaul' is afraid to name names or speak in greater detail, noting somewhat despondently, 'Submission procures friends while truth gives rise to hatred.'[196]

Severus knew that by writing too openly about these matters he would be walking 'barefoot' into a political minefield, but he shows great courage by entering that field far enough for us to catch glimpses of how the western church was developing.

Severus was an accomplished writer, well respected by established authorities. Jerome called him 'our friend Severus'[197] and St Augustine referred to him as 'a man excelling in learning and wisdom'.[198]

Severus was also a disciple of St Martin and visited the monastery at Marmoutier on many occasions, so his writings are a priceless historical record of events taking place around him. The following passage describes the kind of approach to Christianity and spiritual formation that must have been typical of St Martin's community. It appears in a letter that may have formed part of extensive correspondence between Severus and St Paulinus of Nola.

This letter provides an excellent summary of the essential teachings of St Martin and early Gallic monasticism, the kind of environment in which St Patrick probably received spiritual formation and training. If he was trained in St Martin's community, this is how St Patrick would have been taught to believe and practice the Christian faith:

If you wish to be with Christ, you must live according to the example of Christ, who was so far removed from all evil and wickedness, that he did not render a recompense, even to his enemies, but rather even prayed

---

[195] Gerald Bonner, *St Augustine of Hippo: Life and Controversies* (2002), p. 89.

[196] Severus, *Dialogues*, ch. ix, p. 28.

[197] Jerome*, Comm.* 36th ch. Ezekiel.

[198] St Augustine, *Letters*, 205.

for them ...

For I do not wish you to reckon those souls Christian, who [I do not say] hate either their brothers or sisters but who do not, before God as a witness, love their neighbours with their whole heart and conscience, since it is a bounden duty for Christians, after the example of Christ himself, even to love their enemies.

If you desire to possess fellowship with the saints, cleanse your heart from the thought of malice and sin. Let no one circumvent you – let no one delude you by beguiling speech. The court of heaven will admit none except the holy, the righteous and simple, the innocent and pure.

Evil has no place in the presence of God. It is necessary that those who desire to reign with Christ should be free from all wickedness, hypocrisy and deceit. Nothing is so offensive and nothing so detestable to God, as to hate anyone. While nothing is so acceptable to him as to love everyone.

The prophet knowing this bears witness when he teaches, 'Ye who love the Lord, hate only evil.' [199]

Everything is unrighteous which goes against the gospel of Christ and that is the case if you will quietly permit anything to be done to another which you would feel painful if done by anyone to yourself ...

Let grace grow in you with years. Let righteousness increase with age and let your faith appear the more perfect the older you become. [200]

There are shades of St Patrick and St Francis and Pope Francis here. In Patrick's writings, we find a strong emphasis on simplicity and purity of heart. [201]

Another intriguing similarity between the letters of Patrick and the teaching of St Martin concerns the relationship between good and evil. Severus tells us an important aspect of St Martin's preaching and teaching concerned the possibility of repentance and salvation, even for the Devil. In a saying with Pelagian overtones, St Martin told Severus a religious parable, centred on a dialogue between Martin and

---

[199] Severus, *Letter 2*, ch. xv, in Schaff and Wace, p. 65.

[200] Severus, *Letter 2*, ch. xvii. See also ch. xix in Schaff and Wace, p.66ff.

[201] 'Written on your hearts.' C:11; 'turn sincerely with all your heart.' C:19, 'troubled in heart.' C:23; 'sincerity of heart.' C:48; 'the unseen honour which is believed in with the heart.' C:54; 'exultation of heart.' C:60.

the Devil. Martin told the Devil, 'Past sins could be cleansed by the leading of a better life.' The Devil replied, 'No mercy was shown by the Lord to those who had fallen away.' Martin said to the Devil, 'If you, O wretched being, would repent of your deeds with a true confidence, the Lord would promise you the mercy of Christ.' [202]

This is essentially the same kind of teaching we find in Pelagius and the Egyptian Desert Tradition, that good or evil comes through thoughts expressed in actions but through the agency of free will as human beings we have the opportunity to choose one path over another. We can be guided by the heart to act and think in a certain way or to refrain. According to this philosophy, even the Devil can be saved and redeemed through love, repentance (recompense made for evil actions) and forgiveness.

St Patrick takes a similar approach in his *Letter to Coroticus*. Even though the soldiers of Coroticus had attacked and killed some of Patrick's newly baptised converts, stolen goods and taken others as slaves to be sold into prostitution, the gospel standard of forgiveness for those who repent and make genuine redress for wrongdoing, is never lowered. St Patrick 'excommunicates' Coroticus for his evil actions while offering forgiveness and reconciliation if appropriate action was taken to restore what was stolen and redress the imbalance of the evil or wrongdoing committed.

This is what makes St Patrick's understanding of Christianity so profound. It is very similar to the teaching of St Martin.

Severus includes another intriguing statement which might help shed light on St Patrick's decision to 'give up his nobility' for the sake of the gospel. He claims he got this saying from the lips of St Martin himself, and that it was not fabricated:

The Lord Jesus did not predict that he would come, clothed in purple with a glittering crown on his head. I will not believe that Christ has come unless he appears in the form in which he suffered – naked and stripped of this world's glory, power and possessions.[203]

---

[202] Severus, *Life of St Martin*, ch. xxii, p. 14.

[203] Severus, *Life of St Martin*, ch. xxiv, p. 16.

If this saying is a reflection of Martin's approach to Christian teaching, it may hold clues to the origins of early Irish monasticism. It reveals real differences between traditional Roman customs and values (purple as a sign of imperial power and ecclesiastical authority) and early forms of Christian monasticism such as that practised by St Martin, in which a different kind of nobility was expected – the nobility of a truly loving and compassionate heart, wearing only simple clothes, without the trappings of imperial power and wealth.

In relation to the origins of Irish monasticism, it is significant that the same story and very similar teachings appear in documents of the Céile Dé, an eighth-century monastic reform movement in Ireland. The following story appears in the Legend of St Moling from the *Book of Leinster*:

> On one occasion as he [St Moling] was praying in his church, he saw the youth coming towards him into the house. A purple garment was about him and he had a distinguished countenance. 'That is good, O Cleric,' the youth said. 'Amen,' said Moling. 'Why do you not salute me?' said the youth. 'Who are you?' said Moling. 'I,' said he, 'I am Christ, the Son of God.' 'That is not possible,' said Moling. 'When Christ approaches to converse with the Céile Dé, he never comes in purple, but in the form of the lowly, the sick and the poor.[204]

The same legend is recorded in the *Book of Lismore*, an Irish manuscript dated to the fifteenth century which contains material from a much earlier period.[205]

---

[204] William Reeves, *The Culdees of the British Islands* (Dublin, 1864; fasc. edn, Llanerch, 1994), p. 74 ff.

[205] *Lives of Saints from the Book of Lismore*, trans. Stokes, (Clarendon 1890) facs. Ed., (Llanerch, 1995).

Martin and Maximus

St Martin was Bishop of Tours at the very time Magnus Maximus was being dressed in purple and hoisted onto the shoulders of the Legions in Britain, before making his bid for imperial power. Breton historians record that St Patrick's family came to Brittany at this time – around 385 CE. Maximus led a rebellion from Britain against the incumbent Emperors, Valentinian and Gratian. Gratian was killed by soldiers loyal to Maximus, who became Emperor of the West, establishing his residence at the royal palace in Trier. Gratian's brother, Valentinian, fled for his life but eventually returned with the support of Theodosius, Emperor in the East. Maximus was executed in 388 CE, beheaded at the third milestone from Aquilaea.

Breton historians record that during his short reign as Emperor, Maximus established a British colony in Brittany and that one of his relatives, Conan, was crowned as the first king of Brittany and Duke of the Armorican Tract. Conan is said to have been related to Maximus through the latter's marriage to Ellen or Helen, daughter of a high king in Britain, who was called Eudes or Eudav Hen. Several Breton historians who were writing before the end of the nineteenth-century claim that St Patrick's father, Calpurnius, was a cousin of Conan and that Conan married St Patrick's sister, Darerca.

If there is any truth in these claims, then St Patrick and Conan were brothers-in-law and both Calpurnius and St Patrick were also not far removed as blood relatives of the Emperor himself.

Sulpitius Severus does not mention St Patrick in his writings, but anything Severus tells us about St Martin, the Emperor Magnus Maximus and what was going on at this time in the church in Gaul, is relevant to the study of Patrick.

Severus records in great detail the close relationship that St Martin had, first with the Emperor Valentinian and then with his successor, Magnus Maximus. This is a priceless record of events which took place at the Palace in Trier from 380–395 CE. In his role as bishop, St Martin met on several occasions with both Emperors. Severus describes them both as kings, which suggests that he recognised the sovereign or royal lineage of the Emperor, Magnus Maximus. Severus tells us that Martin had warned Maximus that Valentinian was plotting to kill him. He pleaded with the new Emperor to show compassion towards two supporters of the former Emperor, Gratian.

This was the time when Patrick was still a young infant.

Severus published his book in 405 CE, which is around the time Patrick escaped from slavery in Ireland. The following information helps to shed light on events and relationships which may have had a significant impact on St Patrick's life and destiny.

When Martin became a bishop, his new responsibilities brought him into contact with the Emperor Valentinian on the eve of the British rebellion, which took place in 383 CE. Martin had to visit the imperial court. Severus tells us that Valentinian was initially unhappy when he realised Martin was asking for things which he did not incline to grant, so 'he ordered him to be kept from entering the doors of the royal palace'. St Martin fasted for seven days then represented himself and managed to gain entry. The King did not rise to greet him but they were soon reconciled. Severus writes:

> Afterwards the King [Valentinian] often invited the Holy Man to the conferences and entertainments. The King offered him many presents which Martin totally refused, maintaining his poverty, as he did on all occasions.[206]

In 383 CE, after his brother Gratian had been killed by soldiers loyal to Maximus, Valentinian had to flee from the Palace at Trier, where Maximus now established his imperial headquarters. Martin's relationship with the new Emperor would be even more significant than it was with his predecessor. Severus had to be especially careful about what he wrote at this point. The rebellion of Maximus was viewed by the imperial families ruling on the continent not simply as 'usurpation' but a gross act of treason. As he begins this part of his narrative, Severus chooses his words very carefully to avoid causing offence and to minimise the damage and dangers to himself and others that publication would have caused. He gently invites us through what he writes, to approach this controversial subject and enter the political and ecclesiastical minefield with him by saying:

---

[206] Severus, *Dialogues*, ii, ch. v, Schaff and Wace, p. 40 ff.

And here to insert some smaller matters among things so great … such is the nature of our times when all things have fallen into decay and corruption is almost a pre-eminent virtue. Often invited [to the Palace at Trier] Martin kept away from the King's entertainments saying he could not take a place at the same table of someone who out of two Emperors had deprived one of his kingdom and the other his life.[207]

Trying to explain and justify the recent rebellion, the new King (Maximus) told St Martin that he 'had not of his own accord assumed the sovereignty', but was encouraged by his supporters in Britain. He simply 'defended by arms the sovereign requirements of the Empire' and a decision to bid for imperial power had been imposed on him by his soldiers 'according to the divine appointment'.

The Latin phrase *regni necessitatem* meaning 'a sovereign requirement', 'sovereign necessities' or 'requirements of the kingship' probably refers to the Imperial responsibilities associated with 'divinely appointed' kingship.[208] Severus may be revealing his sympathy towards this rebellion when he says, 'it was as if he had the favour of God'. He then presents us with an intriguing record of meetings which took place between St Martin and the new Emperor. A number of bishops from various parts had assembled at the request of Maximus who was 'a man of fierce character' and who was elated at that time in the victory he had won in the civil wars. Severus describes the rebellion as 'illegal' but he places it in the context of a civil war. Severus says:

Maximus ruled the state — a man worthy of being extolled in his whole life, if only he had been permitted to reject a crown thrust upon him during an illegal rebellion by the soldiers, or had been able to keep out of the civil war. The fact is a great Empire cannot be refused without danger or preserved without war. And as we have, once for all, entered the Palace, I shall string together events that took place there, although they happened at different times. It does not seem right not to mention the Queen's admiration for Martin.[209]

---

[207] Severus, '*Life of St Martin*', ch. xx, Schaff and Wace, p. 13 ff.
[208] See Schaff and Wace, p. 13, n. 1.
[209] Severus, *Dialogues,* ii, ch. vi, p. 43.

Martin agreed to come to a royal banquet held at the palace in Trier and what follows is probably as close as we can get to an eyewitness account of what happened. At the banquet, Martin's 'presbyter', a respected elder in the church, sat between Maximus's brother and uncle. St Martin sat near to the King. Maximus ordered the goblet to be given to Martin 'accepting and hoping that he should receive the cup from his right hand'. Martin gave it to his presbyter instead. This caused a great stir and news about the incident spread like wildfire. Severus describes this incident in greater detail:

> Martin was given a seat close to the King. About the middle of the banquet according to custom one of the servants presented a goblet to the King, who ordered it to be given to Martin, expecting he should receive the cup back from Martin's right hand.

> When Martin had drunk from the goblet, however, he gave it to his own presbyter, because he said there was no one worthier to drink next to him, saying it would not be right for him to prefer either the King himself or those who were next to the King, before the presbyter.

> The Emperor, as well as those who were present, admired this conduct so much, this very thing, by which they had been undervalued, gave them pleasure. A report then ran through the whole Palace what Martin had done at the King's dinner which no bishop would have dared do even at the banquet of the lower judges.[210]

This story is reminiscent of Saint Aidan's conduct in Northumbria with King Oswald, at the royal palace in Bamburgh and shows the close connection between St Martin and the development of early Irish monasticism.

Severus also us tells about the close relationship which developed between Martin and the Emperor's wife, who now became Queen. Unfortunately, he does not name her but in Welsh tradition she is called Ellen or Helen:

---

[210] Severus, Life of St Martin, ch. xx, p. 13.

The new emperor frequently sent for Martin, received him into the palace and treated him with honour. His whole speech with him was concerning things present, things to come – the glory of the faithful and the immortality of the saints. In the meantime, the Queen hung upon the lips of Martin and no less than the woman mentioned in the gospel she washed the feet of the holy man with her tears and wiped them with her hair. She did not think of the wealth of the kingdom, the dignity of the Empire, the crown, or the purple. She could not be torn away from the feet of Martin.

At last she begged of her husband that all the other attendants should be removed from the holy man and that she alone should wait upon him at meals. Martin could not refuse. His modest entertainment was arranged for him by the Queen.

She arranged his seat for him, set his table, gave him water to wash his hands, and served the food which she herself had cooked. While he ate, she fixed her eyes on the ground, stood quietly at a distance, like a servant, mixed his drink and gave it to him.

When the meal was over she collected leftovers and crumbs of bread which became her banquet. A Blessed woman worthy by this display of piety to be compared to she who came from the ends of the earth to learn from Solomon.[211]

After this, the sequence of events recorded by Severus becomes more sinister, violent and dangerous, almost leading to Martin's execution. If St Patrick was a family relation to Martin and a member of his monastic community, the following account may provide clues not only to the kind of Christianity St Patrick may have been trained to observe but also the complex political and ecclesiastical factors which may have impacted on his life.

St Martin's life was threatened because of his support for the Priscillians, a group that was strong in Spain and the first to be denounced by leaders in the western church as heretics. The Priscillians were an ascetic sect, named after the leader, Priscillian, who was the Bishop of Avila. A synod held at Bordeaux in 384 CE

---

[211] Severus, *Dialogues*, ii, ch. vi, p. 43. Welsh tradition holds that after the death of Maximus, Helen returned to Wales where she was an influential figure in the development of Welsh monasticism.

had condemned his doctrines, but he had appealed to the new Emperor. The Bishop of Ossanova, Ithacius, had attacked Priscillian and urged Maximus to put him to death. This dispute caused great conflict within the church. Neither Ambrose of Milan, nor Martin of Tours would hold communion with Ithacius or his supporters, because they had appealed to the Emperor in a dispute over doctrine and were now trying to punish a heretic with death. Martin wrote a strongly-worded letter to reprove Ithacius for appealing to the state authorities in a matter that concerned the church.

St Martin said it would be sufficient punishment if Priscillian was branded a heretic and excommunicated by the bishops, without punishing him with death. Maximus yielded at first to Martin's lobbying on behalf of Priscillian by ordering the trial to be deferred and even promised there should be no bloodshed, but afterwards he was persuaded to turn the case over to his prefect Evodius. Priscillian and some others were found guilty on several charges and were beheaded in 385 CE. This was the first judicial death sentence for heresy and had the effect of spreading Priscillianism in Spain.

At this news, Martin went to Trier to plead for the lives of the Spanish Priscillianists who were threatened with a bloody persecution, and also for two men under suspicion as adherents of the late Emperor Gratian. As a condition, before granting this request, Maximus stipulated that St Martin should resume communion with Ithacius and his friends.

Since they were not excommunicated, the Emperor said this was no violation of any canon and Martin accordingly promised the Emperor he would do so, provided Maximus would pardon the two who were supporters of Gratian and recall the military tribunes he had sent to Spain. The next day Martin received communion with the Ithacians, an action which he thought was needed to save many people from death. Martin explained to Severus how deeply troubled he was by these events because he felt he had compromised too much and not followed his own conscience to stay away.

Priscillian was the leader of a controversial Christian group thought to be heretical by certain authorities within the church and it is intriguing to learn that St Martin was prepared to go to such great lengths to support them. Severus tells us that the leader of this sect had been condemned to death along with two others 'who, when they were clerics, had recently adopted the cause of Priscillian and revolted from the Catholics'. Some were beheaded; others were transported to the Island of Sylina, 'beyond the Britains', a reference to the Scilly Isles. The Latin phrase used by Severus *ultra Britannias*, 'beyond the Britains', could also be a reference to Brittany as well as Britain.

From a strictly geographical point of view, living in Aquitania, it would be strange for Severus to describe the Scilly Isles as being 'beyond' Britain.[212]

For their part in the affair both the Emperor and Ithacius were censured by Pope Siricius. This passage is extremely significant; and the words of Severus speak for themselves:

> I will now come to an event which he always concealed, owing to the character of the times but which he could not conceal from us. The Emperor Maximus, while in other respects doubtless a good man, was led astray by the advice of some priests after Priscillian had been put to death. By his royal power he protected Ithacius, a bishop, who had been Priscillian's accuser, together with other friends and confederates of his who it is not necessary to name.
>
> The Emperor prevented anyone from bringing it as a charge against Ithacius that by his actions a man had been condemned to death. Martin, who was constrained to go to the court wishing to act as an advocate for many situations which had caused serious suffering, incurred the whole force of the storm which was raging.
>
> The bishops retained in Trier were talking every day with Ithacius and had made a common cause with him. And it so happened that under their influence the Emperor had already resolved to send tribunes armed with absolute power into the 'two Spains' to search out heretics and deprive them of their life or goods.[213]

Some of the bishops were aware that such proceedings would not please St Martin. They were concerned that Martin would not commune with them and influence others to take the same approach. These clergy, who clearly represent the great power and influence of

---

[212] Severus, *Sacred History*, Book II, ch. li, Schaff and Wace, p. 121 ff.

[213] Severus, *Dialogues*, ch. xi, p. 50 ff.

the Catholic Church and diocesan hierarchy at this time, tried to persuade the Emperor not to let Martin into the city, unless he would declare first that he would make peace with the bishops who were living there.

He frustrated their plans by saying that he would come with the peace of Christ. St Martin met the Emperor (Maximus) and asked him first to act on behalf of some of Gratian's former colleagues, before making a further request that Roman tribunes with the power of life and death should not be sent to Spain. Martin not only wanted to safeguard from danger all the Christians in these regions who were to be persecuted in connection with that expedition, Severus tells us he was also concerned to 'protect the heretics themselves'.

The Emperor delayed seeing Martin. Some said he did not want to offend the other bishops. Rumours suggested the Emperor wanted properties belonging to the Priscillians. He needed resources as the Treasury was empty and civil wars were about to rage. Bishops in Trier who supported Ithacius then tried to have Martin killed. The Emperor was angry and 'not far from being compelled to assign to Martin the same fate of the heretics'. When this became known to St Martin he rushed to the palace, although it was night. He pledged to the King that he would agree to communicate (with the bishops) if the tribunes who had already been sent to Spain for the destruction of churches were recalled. Maximus granted his requests.

There was an ordination the next day of Felix as a bishop. Martin took part and received communion, judging it better to yield for the moment rather than disregard the safety of those over whose heads a sword was hanging.

The bishops tried to get St Martin to put in writing that he had shared communion with them, but Martin refused. The next day Martin left the palace as soon as he could, filled with sorrow and feeling greatly disturbed that he had allowed himself to have been mixed up with such an 'evil' communion. He felt that his own salvation was in danger and was very troubled. St Martin guarded himself against having any further communion with Ithacius or his supporters, believing it had caused the loss of his own power to heal and cure.

Martin confessed in tears to Severus and his friends, saying that he felt a diminution of his power on account of the evil of that communion in which he had taken part through necessity, going against the instincts of his own heart and conscience. Martin lived for sixteen more years after this incident but he avoided diocesan bishops for the rest of his life and refused to attend another church synod. Severus says, 'Never again did he attend a synod and he kept carefully aloof from all assemblies of bishops'. For a monk to do this was not unusual, but for a bishop to do this was a sign of real conflict between early forms of monasticism and the emerging hierarchy of the diocesan church.

Severus met Martin on several occasions and describes how St Martin washed his feet and spoke great wisdom. He held deep respect for Martin as a person and the genuine holiness that permeated St Martin's approach to Christianity and the spiritual life. Severus tells us that he saw in Martin the model of religious life which revealed a profound and genuinely Christ-like spirituality. His language reflects the educated, formal rhetorical style of his day, so unlike the Latin of St Patrick, but what Severus records about St Martin and the brief five-year period when Maximus was Emperor from 383–388 CE is very significant.

Severus tells us that the way Martin was treated by the bishops also affected him, because of his close association with Martin. This is why he had to make arrangements for a delay in publishing his *Life of St Martin* until after Martin's death. The price of truth and controversial publicity in the church at that time was simply too great. Death was now a real possibility for those accused of heresy, including any supporters. Severus viewed this development as a form of wickedness within the church. Severus uses very strong language to describe these bishops when he speaks of the 'evil communion' of Ithacius.

In a response similar to Patrick's approach to those 'seniors' in the church with whom he was in conflict, Severus chose not to name names. He provides insights into events taking place in the late fourth and early fifth centuries which involved people with whom St Patrick and his family may have been associated and events with which they were familiar. If St Martin died in 405 CE and Patrick was a member of his community from 407 to 411 CE, then Patrick would not have met Martin personally but he may have joined the monastery shortly after Martin's death. Ecclesiastical conflict and division were becoming increasingly significant within the Church at this time.

If Patrick spent four years with St Martin or joined the community shortly after Martin's death, what Severus records about Martin's understanding and practise of Christianity would be very similar to the approach and values St Patrick would have known and practised during his mission in Ireland.

From the way Martin's approach to Christianity is described, we can detect many similarities with the writings of St Patrick. This includes the practice of asceticism through spiritual exercises and fasting leading to self-induced dreams and visions.[214] At the heart of St Martin's approach to the Christian life, as with Patrick, we find the voluntary renunciation of personal property and material wealth. In his own writings, Patrick is very anxious to defend himself against any accusations of simony. He refused material gifts or payments that were offered to him personally, although financial resources were used to foster good relations with the Irish chieftains, since this would guarantee him safe passage when he needed to make a journey in the course of his ministry in Ireland. Sincerity of faith and 'purity of heart' is the essential component of St Patrick's approach to the gospel and how Christian discipleship could be practised. It seems clear that Patrick had significant resources to help him during his ministry in Ireland. He tells us that he paid the local judges 'the price of fifteen slaves' which must have been a considerable sum.[215]

In his writings, he tells us that he spent a lot and wanted to spend more, even to death. It would be interesting to know the source of these mission resources. Did he receive support from benefactors or was Patrick able to draw on his own financial resources? We shall explore this is the next chapter, when we explore the possibility that he belonged to a significant royal family.

If St Patrick was born in 384 or 385 CE, taken captive in 400 CE and escaped from Ireland in 407 CE, his religious training could have taken place from 407–427 CE. If so, there is a possibility that he may have returned to Ireland as an Apostle before the traditional date, which is given as 432 CE.

---

[214] Nora Chadwick, *Age of the Saints in the Celtic Church* (Durham, 1960; facs., Llanerch, 2006), p. 27.

[215] C:53

A pioneering mission by an early 'monastic' community linked to St Martin but based in Brittany could have taken place before 431 CE when Palladius was sent as a bishop 'to the Irish believing in Christ' as part of the first official Roman mission. If such a mission had been sent to Ireland from monastic groups linked to St Martin of Tours' foundations in Brittany, let's say in the 420s, then this may have been the cause, at least in part, of initiatives taken by Rome when Germanus was sent to Britain in 428 CE and Palladius was sent to Ireland in 431 CE, to combat Pelagianism and monks who had 'wandered'.

The approach to Christian discipleship taken by St Martin and St Patrick is very different to the lifestyle adopted by other clergy in the church who preferred to embrace the comforts of an overt material lifestyle which accompanied their privileged social status.

The stark contrast between alternative lifestyles can be clearly seen by comparing St Patrick's writings or the way Severus describes St Martin, with the Letters of Sidonius Apollinaris, c.450 CE who gives a graphic description of an opulent lifestyle as Bishop of Clermont, treasuring classical social values.[216]

Sidonius was a close friend and associate of St Germanus so we can imagine they shared a similar lifestyle. Politics and issues of church and state must also have played a huge part in the development of the church at this time. Severus tells us that in Rome and Gaul there were 'powerful bishops' strongly supportive of the deposed Emperor, Valentinian. If St Patrick and his family were close relations to St Martin, Conan and Maximus then we have grounds to suspect that Patrick's life and mission may also have been embroiled in these events and conflicts which surrounded these controversial figures.

In a detailed study of St Martin, Mary Caroline Watt suggests that St Martin was almost condemned to death as a Priscillianist and that he died a schismatic. She says Martin's 'repugnance and dislike for honours paid to the hierarchy of the church' led him to spend the last years of his life apart from the emerging diocesan structures.[217] Christopher Donaldson writes about the powerful, formative influence of Celtic monks on early English Christianity, acknowledging that

---

[216] O. M. Dalton, trans., *Sidonius Apollinaris, Letters* (London, 1915).

[217] Mary Caroline Watt, St Martin of Tours (London, 1928).

historians are only just beginning to understand that 'the key to it all is undoubtedly St Martin'.[218]

It would be many years before some of the ideals of early Gallic, Irish and Egyptian desert spirituality and monasticism would find more fertile soil and independence within the Benedictine Movement and the Rule of St. Benedict (480-547 CE).

Everything Severus says about Martin's approach to Christian spirituality, early Gallic monasticism and how to practise the demands of the faith is seamlessly compatible with the ethos and values which give such character to St Patrick's own writings. It is, therefore, reasonable for us to suggest that it is far more likely that St Patrick was associated with an early monastic form of Christian community linked to St Martin of Tours rather than any formal training under St Germanus or the bishops and teachers at Auxerre or Lerins.

---

[218] Christopher Donaldson, *Martin of Tours: The Shaping of Celtic Spirituality* (Norwich, 1997), p. xi.

CHAPTER ELEVEN

BRITAIN OR BRITTANY?

The 'problem' of St Patrick can still be seen
To bar the very portals of early Irish history.[219]

Following Muirchú's 'Life of St Patrick' and Tírechán's narrative in the *Book of Armagh,* the manuscripts collected and published by Fr John Colgan in 1647 preserved stories and traditions about St Patrick which had been passed on faithfully for many generations. Some of these were concerned with St Patrick's religious training and spiritual formation, and others related to Patrick's nationality, his place of birth and the family estate from which he was taken captive. Hagiographers were determined from an early date to link St Patrick's spiritual formation to St Germanus in Auxerre and his ordination and commission to be an apostle in Ireland, to Pope Celestine and Rome.

This was part of the Romanising process. There was clearly a strong desire and need to honour the diocesan hierarchy and the

---

[219] Dáibhí Ó Cróinín, ed., *A New History of Ireland* (Oxford, 2005), ch. 4.

175

Papacy, in accounts which appear to sit somewhat uncomfortably beside other records in which there is no reference to Rome. St Patrick and his mission to Ireland had to be seen to be sponsored by the Papal authorities if he was going to be regarded as an apostle with legitimate religious authority, an important issue at the time these later documents were compiled. In his own writings, St Patrick does not tell us the name of the person or persons who commissioned him for the ministry in Ireland or which church or religious group supported his mission.

Patrick does mention that he longed to visit his family *in Britanniis* and then proceed further into the Gauls (*Galliis*) to see 'the faces of the saints of my Lord' – a description of religious colleagues that he loved dearly. Having considered the evidence that is available, we have taken the view that St Patrick's homeland 'in Britanniis' is a reference to Brittany and that his religious colleagues were based at St Martin's monastery near Tours.

In relation to where St Patrick had come from, when Colgan examined the documents in 1647 he knew there were conflicting accounts about Patrick's origins. Two different places had been mentioned. Colgan said they were 'far removed' from each other. There was disagreement and confusion about the location of Bannavem Tiburniae which some said was in Britain and others in Brittany.[220] This created a problem which had to be accounted for.

St Patrick's birthplace was too important to be left unresolved but there appears to have been a reluctance to distinguish between where St Patrick was born and where he was taken captive. Colgan said the associations with Brittany were false and the Strathclyde tradition was more reliable.

Having read, studied and compared all the ancient documents, he was aware that some writers had identified Brittany as the place where St Patrick was taken captive but he said they were mistaken. He decided that Patrick must have been taken captive from Strathclyde in northern Britain and that Nemthor, the alleged place of St Patrick's birth, was also located there.

---

[220] Appendix V, 'On the Homeland and Family of St Patrick', in John Colgan, *Trias Thau.*, p. 220 ff.

Colgan discredited Probus, saying this author was 'not sufficiently skilled in Patrician matters and the location of places'.[221]

An aversion to Probus was shared by the Bollandists who refused to publish his manuscript at first, claiming it was full of lies. There is no rational explanation as to why Probus was singled out for censorship. Political and/or ecclesiastical factors may have intruded into the publication process.

In a recent study of the Irish annals, Bernadette Cunningham concluded that the Louvain manuscripts (which had been edited by Colgan and others) show clear signs of 'something more than a manuscript being tidied up for publication'. Cunningham provides evidence that shows how this affected material directly related to St Patrick and she makes a remarkable statement concerning this material when she says:

> The more extensive revision of Patrician material [in the annals] is not typical of the manuscripts [AFM] as a whole and must be regarded as exceptional. Its importance is that the attempt to alter the traditional chronology to accord with that contained in the printed ecclesiastical annals of Baronius [published in 12 vols between 1588 and 1607] provides evidence of changing attitudes to historical evidence'.

Cunningham suggests that,

> It marks a point where the native Irish historical record was modified in the light of the international standards dictated by Counter-Reformation historiography.[222]

If material relating to chronology was affected in this way, could material relating to geography and social or ecclesiastical background have also been affected? Colgan's views may have been influenced by his loyalty to the Church. He ended his commentary by referring to

---

[221] John Colgan, *Trias Thau.*, p. 220 ff. Translated by John Luce.

[222] Bernadette Cunningham, *Annals of the Four Masters*, Four Courts Press (Dublin, 2010).

official Church teaching as the ultimate authority but even this statement from the Lateran Council is unclear and open to interpretation. Does it mean that Patrick was born in Britain or that he was born to parents who were in Britain or who had come from Britain?

> Truer, however, and received is the opinion of our native and foreign writers *that St Patrick was born in Great Britain.* Thus [it is written] in the official records of the Lateran Canons, printed at Montes in Hanover in the year 1635, Reading 4, of the Office of St Patrick: Patrick, the apostle of the Irish, was born of Christian and Catholic parents from the island of Great Britain.[223]

If St Patrick had come to Ireland from Brittany and not Britain, it is perhaps ironic that John Colgan and his colleagues may have been misled. Having opened St Antony's College as a resource to challenge an established Scots-British interpretation of Irish history, which was offensive to the scholars at Louvain, the decision to reject the claims of France and locate St Patrick's place of origins exclusively in Britain served to sustain rather than reverse the historical momentum of that tradition. In relation to the quest for the truth about St Patrick, conspiracy theorists cannot afford to be denominational.

A belief that St Patrick came from Britain was endorsed by many others including the influential Protestant antiquarian and Archbishop of Armagh, James Ussher and the British theory was subsequently to be accepted by many influential scholars in Britain and on the continent even to the present day.

Despite the sterling efforts by so many writers in Patrician studies over the last two hundred years, the consensus of academic opinion still clings firmly to the established tradition that St Patrick came from Britain and that he was born and taken captive from there. A Gallic theory of origins continues to be discounted by the vast majority of writers. Before we can progress towards any possible conclusion we must consider their position and examine the strength of the evidence on which the theory of Britain is based.

---

[223] John Colgan, *Trias Thau.*, p. 220 ff. Translation by John Luce.

One single Latin word actually holds the key to identify the location of Patrick's homeland and the place where he was taken captive by Irish pirates before he was sold as a slave in Ireland. In the earliest surviving copy of St Patrick's *Confession* in the *Book of Armagh*, Patrick uses 'Britanniis' three times and in two of these references it is given as the name for his homeland. What did this name mean for Patrick? Did it apply to Britain or Brittany or perhaps to both? This is a controversial subject which has never been resolved. Despite uncertainties, 'Britanniis' is still rendered as 'Britain' in the most respected and accredited translations of St Patrick's writings.[224]

The notion that Patrick came from the island of Britain began with Muirchú in the *Book of Armagh* and was supported by those ancient *Lives of St Patrick* that copied Muirchú. When John Colgan published these documents in 1647, he strongly advocates for the British theory and dismisses other claims that Patrick was born on the continent.[225] In the seventeenth century, the highly influential and respected Archbishop of Armagh, James Ussher, strongly supported the theory of Britain and stubbornly resisted any attempts to question it.[226] Camden, one of the most respected Scottish historians of his time, also claimed that St Patrick came from Britain and that he was born in Scotland on the banks of the River Clyde.[227] The ancient claims of Brittany were silenced for a time. Minds became closed to the possibility of any alternative to Britain. The documents suggesting that St Patrick was taken captive from Brittany were rejected. A conservative approach dominated the study of St Patrick for the next two hundred years.

---

[224] For an edition that includes Brittany as the preferred translation, see John Luce and Marcus Losack, *The Letters of St Patrick* (Wicklow, 2013).

[225] John Colgan, *Trias Thaumaturga*, ed. Eamonn De Burca (Dublin,1977), ch.2, p. 221

[226] See Ussher, *Britannicarum Ecclesiarum Antiquitates*, CAP XV11, pp. 426,427.

[227] Camden, *Britannica* (Abridged, London, 1701), p.43.

A Survey of Scholars

In the nineteenth century, the established view was challenged for the first time since Probus by several writers including Irish scholar Dr John Lanigan in 1822, the Irish-American author John Murphy from Baltimore, in 1853, and M. Charles de Gerville from Brittany in 1844, amongst others. De Gerville described the traditional British theory of origins a 'gross historical error'.[228] Lanigan insisted that most of ancient writers had misunderstood the meaning of the name *Britanniis* when they assumed that St Patrick had come from the island of Britain, exclusively. He claimed identified *Bannavem Tiburniae* with 'Bononia Tarvannae' or 'Tarabannae', now Boulogne-Sur-Mer, in France.[229] This stretched etymological evidence beyond acceptable limits and Lanigan failed to provide conclusive historical and local geographical evidence to convince sceptics. But his theory attracted some very interesting converts.

Thomas Moore (1779–1852) a well-known Irish entertainer, poet and singer-songwriter, best known for his lyrics of 'The Minstrel Boy' and 'The Last Rose of Summer', became one of his first disciples. Moore was a man of many talents. Extensive literary achievements included *The History of Ireland*. Moore's comments are worth recalling. Having given the claims of Scotland thoughtful consideration, he strongly disputed them.

Respecting [St Patrick's] birthplace, there has been much difference of opinion – the prevailing notion being that he was born in Al Cluit, now Dumbarton, in North Britain. It is only, however, by a very forced and false construction of some of the evidence on the subject that any part of Great Britain can be assigned as the birthplace of St Patrick. His [St Patrick's] own *Confession* proves him to be a native of old Gallican, or rather Armoric Britain. The country anciently known by this name comprised the whole of the northwest coasts of Gaul.[230]

---

[228] Charles de Gerville, *Lettres sur la communication entre les Deux Bretagnes* (Valognes, 1844).

[229] John Lanigan, *Ecclesiastical History of Ireland*, 4 vols (Dublin, 1822; 2nd edn, Dublin 1829)

[230] Thomas Moore, *History of Ireland*, I, p.203 ff.

Another writer at this time examined the earliest sources and was convinced that St Patrick was resident with his family and then taken captive from Brittany and that he was also born there. John Murphy published his *Life of Saint Patrick, Apostle of Ireland* in 1853 a few years before the Famine in Ireland of 1845.[231] He was convinced that Patrick was taken captive from Brittany although he did not try to identify the exact location or village. Some other writers took this view. Dom Philip O'Sullivan Beare also identified Brittany as Patrick's place of origins.[232] But the majority of scholars were reluctant to support this position and held fast to the theory of Britain.

In 1864, less than twenty years after the greatest sufferings of the Famine, J. H. Todd published a major study of St Patrick. This quickly turned into a catalyst for controversy which exploded into accusations of heresy and sectarianism with verbal attacks that became public and personal. Todd (1805–1869) was a member of faculty at Trinity College, Dublin and President of the Royal Irish Academy. His book *St Patrick, Apostle of Ireland* is credited with being one of the first real biographies of St Patrick. Todd became a lightning rod for controversy when he claimed there was no historical evidence to support the traditional view that St Patrick was sent to Ireland by the Pope as part of any official mission of the Catholic Church.[233] This view aroused anger and resentment in many quarters. Binchy reflects the atmosphere of the times when he said:

> There is a nationalism in religious matters which can be as strong an emotional force as political nationalism and which reacts just as vehemently against any attempt by historians to query its foundations.[234]

Todd was a very disciplined, structural thinker and a scholar of the highest calibre. In relation to uncertainties surrounding Patrick's

---

[231] John Murphy, *The Life of Saint Patrick, Apostle of Ireland*, Baltimore, 1853.

[232] Philip O'Sullivan Beare, *Patriciana Decas* (Madrid, 1629).

[233] J. H. Todd, *St. Patrick, Apostle of Ireland*, (Dublin, 1864).

[234] D. A. Binchy, 'Patrick and His Biographers', *Studia Hibernica*, 2 (1962), p.17.

place of origins he was aware of conflicting claims in the earliest sources and refused to commit to any particular theory. As a historian, he tried to remain faithful to the maxim that all we can know for certain about St Patrick is the information given in Patrick's own writings and he acknowledged the difficulties which exist because of those writings. Most scholars accepted Muirchú's account that St Patrick came from Britain but Todd had studied the manuscripts thoroughly enough to know that some of the ancient authors recorded that St Patrick had been taken captive from Brittany. He allowed for this possibility when he said, 'If this story be true, "*Bonavem Taburniae*" where St. Patrick was taken captive, must have been in Armoric Britain'.[235]

This was a sensitive and controversial subject in the nineteenth century with competing claims and serious political, religious, social and economic rivalries especially between Ireland and Britain and between Britain and France.

It was only a matter of time before Scottish historians would decide enough was enough and seek to defend the historical integrity of the established tradition. In 1872, when J. H. Tukner began a presentation to the Royal Society of Scottish Antiquaries in Edinburgh the case for Britain was so firmly established he exclaimed with great confidence: 'The unanimous tradition of Christendom represents the apostle of Ireland [Patrick] as having been born amongst the Britons of Strathclyde or Clydesdale, south-west Scotland'.[236]

Tukner began his presentation to the Royal Society of Scottish Antiquarians by saying, 'the question of St Patrick's origins should only be approached with the calm and unbiased temper appropriate to the investigation of scientific problems'. The presentation went from bad to worse from an ecumenical and objective perspective. Tukner said Dr Lanigan had attempted 'to deprive north Britain of the glorious St Patrick, of whose apostolic labours and the success which crowned them she has long been proud'. Then he drove his warhorse deeper into the mire when he accused Dr Lanigan of 'hagiocleptsy' (saint stealing) and said Lanigan's theory was an

---

[235] Todd, *St Patrick, Apostle of Ireland*, p.356.

[236] J. H. Tukner, An Inquiry as to the Birthplace of St Patrick, *Archaeologica Scottica*, (1890), pp. 261-84.

attempt to 'undermine the true position of north Britain and Scotland in the history of the Christian Church'.

Switching to more conciliatory remarks, Tukner identified two key issues which had to be resolved if the continental hypothesis could be taken seriously.

Firstly, he said it had to be shown that Bonavem or Bannavem Tiburniae could be identified at a specific location on the continent with evidence that could not be applied equally to Strathclyde or Wales or any other place in Britain. Secondly, he suggested that more evidence was required before it could be accepted that 'Britanniis' or 'Britannia' applied to a region in Gaul at the time of St Patrick, with sufficient historical evidence to support the view that Patrick may have been referring to a place on the continent when he used this name in his writings. Tukner's sharp mind had cut through to the heart of the Patrician problem. These two issues still form the essential historical criteria by which any theory concerning St Patrick's place of origins will be judged. In Tukner's view, Dr Lanigan had failed on both accounts.

After presenting what he considered to be enough evidence to confirm St Patrick's birth in Scotland, Tukner loosened his grip on Lanigan's throat and admitted, 'That St Patrick's family was connected with Armorica, that it may even have been Armorican in its origin, is not impossible.' Tukner was satisfied with his own defence of Strathclyde as the place where St Patrick was born but he expressed grave doubts about the geographical location of Bannavem Tiburniae. He was not the first and would not be the last to admit feelings of frustration and despondency regarding efforts to identify this place. Having summoned the courage to accept this, he speaks as a true Scotsman in claiming that wherever it was it must have been somewhere in Scotland! And he concluded his 'Inquiry into the Birthplace of St Patrick' by agreeing with Dr Wylie and others whose view now forms part of the Scottish historical record.[237]

As we entered the twentieth century and the so-called 'era of modern scholarship', a lingering hope remained that experts would apply their wisdom and academic expertise to this complex subject and resolve some of the uncertainties. Ireland deserved to know the

---

[237] See J. A. Wylie, *History of the Scottish Nation* (London 1887), ii, p. 108 ff.

truth about St Patrick and why the origins of Irish Christianity have been shrouded in so much controversy. Any such hopes would quickly be dashed. Despite a huge renaissance in Patrician literature, the claims of Brittany would continue to be discounted by the vast majority of scholars.

When J. B. Bury's *Life of St Patrick and His Place in History* was published in 1905, it was also acclaimed as a genuine biography of St Patrick, reflecting the more stringent discipline of historical inquiry. Bury's expertise was the late Roman period and although he accepted that Patrick landed in Gaul when he escaped from slavery in Ireland Bury was convinced that St Patrick had come from Britain. He claimed that passages from the *Confession* 'prove that St Patrick regarded Britain as his native land and that his family lived there continuously from the time of his captivity till his old age'.[238]

Bury placed far too much trust in Muirchú's authority when he said, 'His biographer in the seventh century writes unhesitatingly that he was of the British nation or native of Britain and born in Britain.'

We hear strong echoes from Muirchú when Bury exclaims, 'That Patrick's family were British provincials and lived in Britain there can be no question.' He discounted the evidence for Strathclyde on the basis that it was very unlikely the Romans had settlements that far north at the time of St Patrick. Instead, he suggested that Bannavem Tiburniae was in south-west Britain, in the region of the lower Severn.[239]

Bury was not alone in helping the theory of Britain to become more firmly established in the first decades of the twentieth century. Heinrich Zimmer published a controversial study of St Patrick in 1902 which held fast to this view, making a statement that simply cannot be justified by any evidence not least a reference to St Patrick's writings:

> According to his [Patrick's] own statement he was born in the British borough of Bannaventa, which must have been somewhere near the modern town of Daventry.[240]

---

[238] J. B. Bury, *The Life of St Patrick, His Place in History* (London, 1905), p. 290.

[239] Bury, *Life of St Patrick*, p. 16 ff.

[240] Heinrich Zimmer, *The Celtic Church in Britain and Ireland* (London, 1902), p. 43

Bury's reputation as a historian had encouraged others to accept it as 'fact' that Patrick came from Britain, when the conflicting evidence in the earliest sources should never have allowed scholars to make such categorical statements about Patrick's place of origins.

In 1905, when N. J. White produced the first critical edition of St Patrick's *Confession*, the established tradition became enshrined in a respected academic translation. White remained faithful to the plural form 'Britanniis' as it appears in the *Book of Armagh*, translating this as 'in the Britains', but for him it referred exclusively to the island of Britain.[241]

Then an academic bombshell dropped through the roof of Trinity College, Dublin. In March 1942, Thomas O'Rahilly presented a study of St Patrick which shook conservatives and liberals alike. O'Rahilly was convinced that our traditional understanding of Patrick's biography had been created by the fusion or perhaps confusion between the records of two or three different saints, all called Patrick. He suggested that details from the life of Palladius (who had been sent to Ireland by Pope Celestine as part of an official Roman mission in 431 CE) and Patrick (author of the *Confession* and *Letter to Coroticus*) had been woven together to make a composite figure, our traditional St Patrick. Conflicting references in the Irish annals mention several figures called Patrick whose records or legends may have become confused.[242]

According to O'Rahilly, the Patrick we know from Muirchú and the *Book of Armagh* is a contrived figure who exists only in the ecclesiastical 'cyberspace' of seventh-century Irish hagiography. This composite figure is a 'virtual' St Patrick, without historical foundation.

In relation to St Patrick's origins (the Patrick who wrote the *Confession*, that is) O'Rahilly favoured Britain but like Bury he rejected the evidence for Strathclyde. Instead, he came up with yet another suggestion and conjectured that Bannavem Tiburniae was in south-west England. In so doing, it is ironic that O'Rahilly himself may

---

[241] See C:23, C:32, C:43 in N. J. White, *Translation of the Latin Writings of St Patrick* (London, 1918).

[242] Thomas O'Rahilly, *The Two Patricks* (Dublin, 1942; rept. 1981).

have confused the real St Patrick with a later namesake, who is closely associated with Glastonbury.[243]

Once the claims of Strathclyde had been rejected, the uncertainties which surround Patrick's biography became more complex. If Scotland had to be discounted, which part of Britain did St Patrick come from? How would scholars react to this latest challenge to the established tradition?

R. P. C. Hanson (1916–1988) was Professor of Historical and Contemporary Theology at the University of Manchester, regarded as one of the foremost authorities on St Patrick. He began by warning us that from a historian's perspective there are few things we can know about St Patrick. Hanson then insists that the one thing we can know for certain is that Patrick was born in Britain.[244] He suggests Patrick was probably taken captive somewhere along the west or south-west coast of Britain, from a place accessible to Irish pirates but despaired the precise location could ever be discovered:

> The fact is that we do not know where Bannavem Tiburniae was [located] and short of an archaeological miracle, we probably never shall. But the probability is strongly in favour of locating it in the Lowland Zone of Roman Britain and in the south western part of that zone, in Somerset, or Dorset or Devon.[245]

Hanson's contribution to the study of Patrick was immense. In his final chapter, he provides a moving tribute to St Patrick. In relation to Patrick's origins, however, following Bury, he may have relied too much on Muirchú. Hanson rejected the possibility that St Patrick's family came from Strathclyde, claiming there was no significant Roman presence north of Hadrian's Wall during St Patrick's lifetime. The strength of the established tradition shaped the opinions of many writers.

---

[243] For Patrick's alleged connections with Glastonbury, see William of Malmesbury, *The Antiquities of Glastonbury*, trans. Frank Lomax, (Llanerch, 1992).

[244] R. P. C. Hanson, *St Patrick His Origins and Career*, (Oxford, 1997) p. 1.

[245] Hanson, *St Patrick His Origins and Career*, p. 116.

When D. A. Binchy joined the fray in 1962 he began his study by saying the quest for reliable historical information about St Patrick was 'like an effort to solve a jigsaw puzzle from which most of the important pieces are missing'.[246] It was the perfect analogy but Binchy appears to have resigned himself to failure even before he began when he decided that 'most of the essential pieces of the Patrick puzzle have been lost and are unlikely to be recovered'.

Binchy was not the first and would not be the last to quit the table in dismay. He thought the ancient *Lives of St Patrick* were completely untrustworthy and regarded them as worthless for authentic historical information. Historical caution was then thrown to the wind when he exclaimed, 'St Patrick must have been born in Britain'.[247] According to Binchy, Patrick's birth, family, homeland, ecclesiastical training and spiritual formation were all located in Britain. He claimed that the ancient traditions which linked him to France were all spurious: 'So much is certain [Patrick] was consecrated bishop in Britain. His mission was financed by members of the British hierarchy'.[248]

Binchy believed that when St Patrick escaped from Ireland he travelled back to Britain and was supported in his mission to Ireland by the British Church. He says, 'Patrick may never have been in Gaul ... he was consecrated bishop in Britain and his mission to the Irish was organised and financed by certain members of the British hierarchy.' Unfortunately, like so many others who have wrestled with this subject, Binchy does not provide any evidence to support these claims aside from his own opinions. Nevertheless, this view is now reflected in some of the most respected and authoritative, current academic writings.

T. M. Charles-Edwards, Professor of Celtic at the University of Oxford, who recently published a major study of Early Christian Ireland, also states emphatically that St Patrick's family came from Britain. He says St Patrick belonged to the local nobility of a Romano-British *civitas* and that when Patrick escaped from Ireland he returned to Britain and was trained within the British Church, like his

---

[246] Binchy, 'Patrick and His Biographers', *Studia Hibernica* No. 2, 1962.

[247] Binchy, p. 164.

[248] Binchy, pp. 27, 167.

grandfather.[249] Professor Charles Thomas from the University of Exeter says: 'The Apostle of Ireland was himself one hundred per cent Briton, all the indications being that his homeland was beyond Carlisle'... 'From the Britains (de Britanis) geographical plural, in the fourth-fifth century, suggesting the four (or five) Provinciae (provinces) of Britannia (singular)'.

Thomas continues, 'His (Patrick's) return to the Ireland of his youthful captivity can only have been instigated or permitted by a synod of the British Church (conceivably held at York) and his consecration by existing British bishops'. [250] In the same way, Nora Chadwick, Liam de Paor and Máire de Paor excelled in their studies of St Patrick but like so many others they were convinced that Patrick came from Britain.

Chadwick was more sympathetic towards the traditional theory and took the view that Patrick's home at Bannavem Tiburniae was probably Strathclyde or the Solway Firth area.[251] Liam de Paor suggested Birdoswald, which is a short distance west of Carlisle, close to the northern frontier of Roman Britain.[252] Máire de Paor claims, 'We can be sure of only one thing – Patrick was a native of Britain'.[253] Continued uncertainty about the location of Bannavem Tiburniae was reflected in the diverse opinions of scholars, while the notion that St Patrick came from Britain was still taken for granted almost unanimously.

The claim that St Patrick's origins can be associated exclusively with the island of Britain became so firmly established during the twentieth century it is not unreasonable to say that it is now taken as a historical 'fact', even though no conclusive evidence has ever been provided to finally determine this matter.

---

[249] T. M. Charles-Edwards, *Early Christian Ireland* (Cambridge, 2000) p. 217.

[250] Charles Thomas, 'Palladius and Patrick' in *The Island of Saint Patrick*, Ailbhe MacShamhrain (ed.) Four Courts Press (Dublin, 2003), pp 20, 33, 15.

[251] Nora Chadwick, *Age of the Saints in the Celtic Church* (Durham, 1960; facs. Llanerch, 2006) p. 18.

[252] Liam de Paor, *St Patrick's World*, p. 88.

[253] Máire de Paor, *Patrick, The Pilgrim Apostle of Ireland* (Dublin 1988), p. 22 ff.

Thomas O'Loughlin helped pioneer an innovative graduate programme in Celtic Studies for the University of Wales in Lampeter. He is widely respected as a contemporary authority on Patrick, having published his own detailed and in many ways excellent study. After giving the statutory warning that we must be extremely wary of claims made in the secondary sources, O'Loughlin says this view can be taken too far and that we must not dismiss the uniqueness of these documents, to assess their true value. At last we have found a modern writer who is willing to keep the door open and admit the ancient *Lives of St Patrick* might contain some information of value.[254]

O'Loughlin is aware of the difficulties which surround St Patrick's biography but he does not try to examine the evidence for Brittany. When dealing with the geographical place names in St Patrick's *Confession* he warns us to be very sceptical of claims made by Muirchú in the *Book of Armagh*. Muirchú no longer knew where these places were and engaged in 'guesswork'.[255] He repeats the mantra expected from all Patrician scholars, 'The only reliable historical information about St Patrick is that which is contained in St Patrick's own writings', and he allows for the fact that St Patrick's family home at Bannavem Tiburniae has never been positively identified.

Unfortunately, he then makes certain statements which cannot be justified from the evidence of St Patrick's *Confession*: 'Patrick tells us that he was born in Britain.' 'Patrick tells us that his parents' home was in Britain'.[256] These statements are further compounded by somewhat hasty and unjustified conclusions when the author states categorically that 'all we can say with certainty is that Bannavem Tiburniae was in Britain and that the Wood of Foclut was located in Ireland'. St Patrick said no such thing!

The extent to which scholars support the established tradition and made categorical statements about Patrick's British origins as if this overcomes or short-circuits uncertainties in both the primary and secondary sources is very surprising. Most twentieth century writers have taken this position. This is not criticism of their otherwise outstanding scholarship, which greatly enhances our understanding of

---

[254] Thomas O'Loughlin, *Discovering St Patrick* (London, 2005).

[255] Thomas O'Loughlin, *St Patrick: The Man and His Works* (London, 1999), p. 20.

[256] O'Loughlin, *Discovering St Patrick*, p. 47, n. 12. See also p.78.

St Patrick and the origins of the early Irish Church. It is simply to make the point that it is not appropriate for academic theologians and historians to claim on the one hand that the only reliable information we have concerning St Patrick is contained in his own writings (where most of the key geographical references have not been identified and are still uncertain) and then on the other to make categorical statements insisting that the one thing we can know for certain is that St Patrick came from Britain. This is how so many reputable scholars repeat the traditional view, without providing a shred of reliable historical or geographical evidence to support this view.

Throughout the twentieth and now as we enter the twenty-first century, such strong academic opinions have shaped the image of St Patrick that is found today in popular writings, religious publications, heritage magazines, educational resources provided for schools and colleges, and even guidebooks and tourist information services. [257] This raises the possibility that we have all been misled and our understanding of Patrick may have been shaped by what the Breton antiquarian Charles de Gerville called a 'gross historical error'.

The Evidence for Britain

As J. H. Tukner said in 1872, if there is any truth in the claim that Patrick came from Brittany, it has to be shown that the name 'Britanniis' or 'Britannia' applied to the region we now call Brittany at the time St Patrick was born. Before presenting further evidence which supports the case for Brittany and challenges the academic consensus, it is important to investigate the historical foundations on which the traditional theory of Britain is based.

The evidence put forward in support of the established view can be summarised as follows. Firstly, it is argued that the name given for St Patrick's homeland is the name for Roman Britain. The ancient name for Britain was 'Alba' or 'Albion' but after the invasion by Julius Caesar in 67 BCE, the Romans called it 'Britannia'. Those who are convinced that St Patrick came from Britain, claim that when he

---

[257] See *A Course in Irish History*, ed. T. W. Moody and F. X. Martin (Dublin, 1994).

used the phrase *in Britanniis* or *in Britannias*, he must have been referring to Britain. At first sight, this seems very reasonable. The island of Britain was called 'Britannia' by the Romans.

There is a complication, however, that has to be accounted for. The Latin name given in the *Book of Armagh* appears as 'Britanniis', which is a plural form. Those who hold to the traditional view say there is a simple explanation for this. Britain was divided into several provinces by the Romans, hence St Patrick was describing his homeland as being within these provincial regions. It is true that Britain was subdivided by the Romans, a process which took place over a considerable period of time.

It was divided at first by Caracalla in 212–296 CE into two regions, called Britannia Superior (in the south) and Britannia Inferior (in the north). In 296 CE during the reforms of Diocletian, these two provinces were restructured and each was again divided in two. Britannia Superior became Britannia Prima, governed in the west from Cirencester, and Maxima Caesariensis, governed in the east from London. Britannia Inferior became Britannia Secunda governed from York and Flavia Caesariensis governed from Lincoln.

Another Province called Valencia in the far north beyond Hadrian's Wall was added in 369 CE by the Emperor Valentinian, probably including Dumfries, Galloway and the Scottish borders. The boundaries of Valencia are difficult to determine. Security deteriorated rapidly, almost as soon as this region was established. There may have been a brief period of stability when Maximus led a successful campaign against the Picts and Scotti (Irish) in the years before his rebellion in 383 CE but the existence of a well-established Roman settlement that far north at the time of St Patrick is unlikely.[258]

Secondly, those who support the view that Patrick came from Britain claim that no alternative meaning or translation is possible because the region we now call Brittany in France was not known by the name 'Britanniis' in the late fourth century, at the time of St Patrick's birth and teenage years.

In other words, if St Patrick used this word for his homeland, he could only have been referring to the island of Britain and not to any

---

[258] Charles Thomas, *Christianity in Roman Britain to AD 500* (Berkeley and Los Angeles, 1981), p.197.

region on the continent. These are the two essential pillars of evidence on which the theory of Britain is based and with which it continues to be justified.

They provide support for the established view, which is taken by scholars who accept these arguments as trustworthy. This 'evidence' forms the basis for the most accepted English translations of St Patrick's writings. On closer examination, both pillars of evidence appear to rest on very insecure and uncertain foundations. Let's consider first the Roman name for Britain.

It cannot be doubted that the Romans applied the name 'Britannia' (in a singular form) to the island of Britain but there is less evidence to show that the various regions or subdivisions were commonly referred to using a plural form. Only two of the five regions incorporated the name 'Britannia' (Britannia Prima and Britannia Secunda). If St Patrick was born in Strathclyde, this was located in Valencia. Roman Britain was part of a very large island. It seems strange that St Patrick would describe his homeland using such a broad and uncertain geographical reference. If St Patrick came from a specific region within Britain and wanted us to know its location, why did he not simply give us the name for that region in which his family lived?

St Patrick wrote his *Confession* in Ireland at a time when the Irish were familiar with British geography, especially Wales and the north-west.

To regard St Patrick's use of 'Britanniis' as a reference to the island of Britain exclusively would only be appropriate if it can be shown with absolute certainty that no other meaning could possibly be given to this name. The existence of historical uncertainties, especially with regard to the plural form, raises serious and legitimate questions. Those who adhere to the established view claim there is sufficient evidence to show that the name 'Britanniis', was applied to Britain in several classical sources. In response to a controversy about St Patrick's origins which erupted in the Letters columns of the Irish Times, shortly after this book was first published, Dr Terry O'Hagan made a serious attempt to document these sources, to vindicate the established theory.

In a lengthy and controversial article called 'Less DA Binchy Code Please... St Patrick's Origins in his own words', published on the

Irish blog site Vox Hiberionacum [259] he cites a number of classical authors who use Britanniis as a term for Britain. Examples given include Claudian, a Roman poet from Alexandria (370-410 CE), the Roman historian Ammianus (320-370 CE), Orosius (375-418 CE) and Sidonius Apollinaris, a bishop and nobleman who was familiar with Brittany (470-480 CE). All these Roman historians are cited as proof of the "fact" that the Latin name Britanniis was frequently and specifically used to describe the provinces of Roman Britain at the time of St Patrick. Whilst we can agree with O'Hagan's statement that these sources do refer to Britain using the plural form, in my view they do not undermine the case for Brittany and cannot be used to discount the case for Brittany, for the following reasons.

Claudian was contemporary with St Patrick but cannot be regarded as an authoritative historical witness. He was writing as a poet not a historian and his work has been criticised for being distorted by conventions and panegyrics. Claudian lived in Alexandria and Rome and was far removed from events taking place locally in Brittany and Britain at the close of the fourth century. The fact that he does not mention the rebellion of Maximus in 385 CE (which was viewed as a gross act of treason by the Imperial authorities ruling on the continent) suggests he may have been too busy trying to please his imperial benefactors rather than being engaged in a serious effort to establish what on earth was going on in the farthest corners of the western Empire at that time.

Ammianus chronicled the history of Rome from 96-378 CE, although only the period from 353-378 CE survives. His last work was completed in 391 CE but ends with the death of Valens in 378 CE. This is five or six years before Magnus Maximus launched his rebellion from Britain. Ammianus cannot therefore be used to support the case against Brittany, which is based on a hypothesis that the name 'Britanniis' was formally introduced to the region we now call Brittany, at the time of the rebellion of Magnus Maximus in 385 CE.

O'Hagan also relies on statements from Orosius (385-418 CE) who was born at the same time as St Patrick (c. 385 CE) and was

---

[259] *Less DA Binchy Code Please… St Patrick's Origins in his own words.* Blogsite Vox Hiberionacum, posted Nov. 29, 2013. Parts 1, 2.
https://voxhiberionacum.wordpress.com/2013/11/29/patrick-origins1/

therefore just coming out of his mother's womb when the rebellion of Maximus was being launched.

He left Spain to go to Jerusalem and the information we have about him is uncertain because of the great turmoil, with social and military unrest on a massive scale before and immediately following the Barbarian invasions, from which he was anxious to escape. As a result, he cannot be regarded as a reliable witness to what was taking place at a local level in Britain and Brittany.

Orosius collaborated with St Augustine in writing *The City of God* and acted as a go-between, carrying letters from Augustine to Jerome in Bethlehem and also replies from Jerome which Orosius carried back to Augustine in North Africa. Orosius informed St Augustine of a meeting he had with Pelagius when he was in Jerusalem. In fact, the decision to write his most famous work '*Historiae Adversus Paganos*' (A History Against the Pagans) was born from ideas discussed during his meetings with Augustine. He was therefore in close contact with those who had a heavy axe to grind against early Gallic (Celtic) monasticism such as that being practiced by St Martin of Tours.

We must remain cautious about his motives when dealing with controversies that were raging within the church in Britain and Gaul and question his objectivity and appreciation for the dramatic events taking place in Britain and Brittany at that time. The British Rebellion in 383-389 CE was viewed as a usurpation and gross act of treason by Imperial families ruling on the continent and Maximus together with his British and Gallic supporters were historically vilified and discounted; a vilification and discounting that has continued to the present day. The authors cited by O'Hagan are neither contemporary with St Patrick nor trustworthy enough to be viewed as reliable historical sources in the context of this dispute. We can and must give credit to Dr O'Hagan for having the courage to examine the available sources even though we disagree with him about the historical weight that can be given to those sources he relies on.

As I mentioned to him when I replied to his article on his blog site, in my view he is probably the first academic in the last one hundred years to try and document the evidence that is available in support of the British theory.

One of the difficulties that must be resolved in solving what has been called "the problem" of St Patrick is the fact that there was so much turmoil and dramatic change in the Western Empire in general and Britain and Brittany in particular, after the Barbarian invasions of 405 CE and the fall of Rome in 409 CE. This turmoil was followed by the total collapse of the western Empire so that we have insufficient documentation or written records from this period and those which did survive are not sufficiently precise.

Rufus Sextus (also known as Festus) was a classical author who wrote about the provinces existing in the Roman Empire during the period when Valens was Emperor (328-378 CE). His work, *The Breviarium,* covers the entire history of the Roman state from the foundation of the City until 364 CE. He notes that there were eighteen provinces in the western Empire and lists four of these as within Britain (Britannia). He also uses the plural form Britanniis to describe these four provinces. Here we appear to have another classical source who confirms that Britanniis could be and was used to denote the provinces within the island of Britain.[260] Rufus Sextus, however, as with the other classical authors cited above, cannot be used to support the theory of Britain and dismiss the case for Brittany, for the following reasons.

Sextus completed his work in 370 CE which is thirteen years before Magnus Maximus launched his rebellion from Britain. Sextus therefore does not include any reference to that rebellion or the divisions that were taking place in the western Empire as result of civil wars and rebellions.

Sextus had a reputation for being a ruthless secretary and devoted supporter of the ruling Imperial families. This included Valens and his later namesake Valentinian who was deposed by Maximus from the Imperial Palace at Trier before he managed to return with support from the Emperor Theodosius in the East and defeat the British forces at Aquileia where Maximus was captured and beheaded in 389 CE.

Having carefully considered the classical sources excavated by Dr O'Hagan, we have come to the conclusion that the references presented to support the traditional British theory of origins, are not sufficient to change our view that St Patrick's homeland was in Brittany and that it was from there he was taken captive when his

---

[260] J. W. Eadie, *The Brevarium of Festus* (Athlone, 1967).

father's house was attacked by Irish Pirates probably in the year 400 CE. We hold to the view that Patrick's use of the Latin name *Britanniis* is a reference to Brittany rather than the provinces of Roman Britain, as a result of a strategic settlement of the ancient Britons in Armorica at the time of the rebellion of Maximus in 383 CE, when the name *Britanniis* was forcefully established on the continent by Maximus as part of his imperial strategy and hence became more deeply enshrined in local ethnic geography.

This was the main reason that this region became known as "Little Britain" or Britannia Minor, now Bretagne in French, distinguished from Greater Britain (Britannia Major) now Grande Bretagne in French.

If we take into account the civil wars and rebellions that were taking place towards the end of the fourth century and also the collapse of Rome and ensuing chaos that followed in the western Empire following the Barbarian invasions from 405 CE, then we should not be surprised by the fact that St Patrick's *Britanniis* may have meant one thing to him and his family who had moved from Strathclyde to settle in Brittany at the time of the rebellion of Maximus, as so many of the early Breton historians and others record, whilst it meant something completely different to classical Roman authors such as Rufus Sextus who were part of the old regime and greatly detached from events taking place in Britain and Gaul at the close of the fourth century.

Having looked at the evidence which has been given to support the established view, we must now consider other sources which provide evidence to suggest that the name Britanniis was applied to Armorica at the time of St Patrick.

The Evidence for Brittany

One of the earliest and most reliable accounts which refers to a region called 'Britain' on the continent can be found in the writings of Sulpitius Severus (363-425 CE). Severus was a native of Aquitania and is best known for his *Chronicle of Sacred History* (published in 403 CE) and a biography of St Martin of Tours, a copy of which is preserved in the *Book of Armagh*. He was more familiar with events taking place in Brittany than any of the authors cited by O'Hagan and especially the rebellion of Maximus, which he writes about in great detail. The descriptions he gives relating to local, ethnic geography must be taken seriously because he is a reliable historical witness, a writer who was known to Augustine and Jerome and well respected by them.

Severus was a close friend and disciple of Martin of Tours and St Martin provided him with detailed information about matters affecting church and state in the closing decades of the fourth century. He was also contemporary with St Patrick, one of the few sources we have from someone in his prime as a writer and historian when Maximus launched his rebellion from Britain and became Emperor of the West from 383-389 CE. Severus describes a church synod at Ariminum which took place in Italy in 359 CE, shortly before the time of Patrick. He provides some fascinating information about local 'ethnic' geography in the following passage, in which the Latin names given for the 'Britons' and/or 'Britain' are open to interpretation:

> More than four hundred western bishops were summoned. For all of these the Emperor had ordered provisions and lodgings to be provided. But that appeared unseemly to the men of our part of the world that is, to the Aquitanians, the Gauls and Britons [*Britanniis*] so that refusing the public supplies they preferred to live at their own expense.
>
> Three only of those from Britain [Britannia] through want of means of their own, made use of the public bounty, after having refused contributions offered by the rest for they thought it more dutiful to burden the public treasury than individuals.[261]

Severus was a very articulate and careful author who pays close attention to detail. In his record of events taking place at the synod, he appears to refer to two different places both of which were called 'Britain' or associated with the Britons. In the first part of the passage he tells us that men from 'his own part of the world' – namely

---

[261] Severus, 'Sacred History', in *The Nicene and Post Nicene Fathers* (New York, 1894), p. 116, xli.

Aquitanians, Gauls and Britons (*Britanniis*) – refused financial support because they preferred to live at their own expense.

On the other hand, three delegates representing the Church in Britain (Britannia) having no means of their own, made use of the public funds they had been offered. Severus appears to be describing two different regions by his use of the names 'Britanniis' and 'Britannia'. The 'Britons' that Severus identified as being from 'his own part of the world', probably came from a region on the continent most likely to have been Armorica. The three who accepted financial support were from the island of Britain.

Severus refers to the Armorican Britons in Latin as 'Britanniis'. This is precisely the same name which is used to describe St Patrick's homeland in the earliest surviving copy of St Patrick's *Confession*, preserved in the *Book of Armagh*. Did this name refer to a place, a people or to both? For Severus the name 'Britanniis' reflects a cultural as well as a geographical identity. Just as the Aquitanians are from Aquitania, the Galls are from Gallis so he says the Britons from his part of the world (which is on the continent) are from Britanniis. He uses different words to make this clarification.

Severus distinguished these Armorican Britons from the Aquitanians and Gauls and also from those Britons from the island of Britain who availed of the public purse. The geographical distinctions recorded by this author who was writing at the end of the fourth century are very significant as this is the time when St Patrick was born. Severus gives reliable testimony that in his part of the world various ethnic groups existed in three separate regions. Severus was from Aquitania. The person with whom he converses in his *Dialogues* is a Gaul. It is significant that he does not refer to the coastal peninsular as Armorica, suggesting that this region had been renamed or was known as 'Britanniis' at the time he was writing. If this is correct, then our understanding of local ethnic geography on the continent at the time of St Patrick, in relation to regional divisions of Gaul, will need to be revised.

Severus includes another significant reference to Britain, in relation to the rebellion of Maximus in 385 CE. He speaks as a contemporary witness to these events when he says:

A faint rumour had spread that Maximus had assumed imperial power in the Britains [*intra Britannias*] and he would in a short time make an incursion into Gaul.[262]

The Latin name given (Britannias) is again in a plural form which leaves open a possibility that it could be a reference to Brittany as well as Britain.

This would be the case, for example, if Severus was saying the usurpation of Maximus began and was centred in or launched not only from Britain but also from within Brittany. In other words, Maximus had assumed imperial power in or 'within the Britains' (*intra Britannias*). If so, this allows for the possibility that a coastal region in Armorica was known as *Britannia* at the time of St Patrick. Several Breton historians, writing between the seventeenth and nineteenth centuries, record that Maximus landed considerable forces at the mouth of the River Rance at the port of Aleth and subdued Gaul and Spain from Brittany whilst his other forces landed near the Rhine before going north to take over the imperial palace at Trier. They are convinced that the name 'Brittany' or 'Bretagne' was introduced at this time.

Gregory of Tours (539-594 CE)

However, we may interpret the references given by Severus, what is not disputed by anyone is that by the time of Gregory of Tours, writing in 575 CE, a coastal region of Armorica was called 'Britain' and probably had been for a considerable period of time. Gregory frequently and consistently refers to Brittany using both Latin names 'Brittaniis' and 'Britannia'. As far as Gregory is concerned, these names are synonymous and it is important to note that they are both applied exclusively to Brittany, not to the island of Britain.[263]

Those who specialise in local ethnic geography estimate that it takes between one hundred and one hundred and fifty years at least

---

[262] Severus, 'Sacred History', xlix.

[263] See Gregory of Tours, *History of the Franks*, trans. Lewis Thorpe (London, 1974).

for new geographical names to become more widely known and established in historical records. The names familiar to Gregory must have been established for some considerable time to be recognised by his readers.

When Gregory writes about Brittany he uses the two names given for St Patrick's homeland, which can be found in all surviving copies of St Patrick's *Confession*. He includes specific local geographical references that clearly identify 'Britanniis' or 'Britannia' as a local region on the north-east coast of Brittany, close to Aleth, Dol and Mont St Michel.

From the description he gives, this 'Britain' existed as an independent region with its own Breton culture and some unusual religious and political customs.

Gregory describes the great slaughter which took place at this time among the Bretons and Saxons. The troops marched out of Brittany (*exercitu a Brittaniis*). The stronger men crossed the River Villaine but those less strong and the camp followers beside them were not able to wade through. They had to stay on the far side of this river.

Gregory applies the name 'Brittaniis' in this case to a very specific local area in the vicinity of the River Villaine, which is close to the region where Château de Bonaban is located today. The local French municipality is still called Isles et Villaine.[264] He also distinguishes Brittany (which he refers to as 'Brittaniis' and 'Britannia') from the Gauls (*Galliis*). Gregory was based in Tours which for him is clearly part of Gaul but for him, 'Britanniis' is a separate, independent region near the coast around St Malo and Dol de Bretagne.

The same local geographical distinction is present in the *Life of St Maclovius* or St Malo, an early Irish or Welsh saint who travelled to Brittany and placed himself under a hermit named Aaron, who had established the first monastery on the island adjacent to Aleth where the old walled city of St Malo is now located. A disorder on the island had compelled Malo to leave. After being driven away from his monastery, he is said to have cursed Brittany or the Bretons (Britanniis) and travelled into the Gauls.

This suggests that 'Britanniis' and the Gauls – 'Gallias' – were

---

[264] Gregory of Tours, *History of the Franks*, p.287, p. 556, p. 558. See also v.16.

considered as separate but adjacent regions within the area we have traditionally thought of in more general terms, simply as Gaul. These passages help to shed light on a geographical description given by St Patrick, when he also distinguishes Brittany (Britanniis) from Gaul. In his *Confession*, Patrick describes how he would love to have the opportunity to make a journey from Ireland to 'Britanniis' to visit his homeland and family, and then to proceed further into 'the Gauls' (*Gallias*) and see his religious friends. He says:

> As a result, even if I would wish to leave them and make a journey *in Britanniis* and I would most dearly love to make that journey so as to see my homeland and family – not only that but also to proceed into the Gauls [*in Gallias*] to visit the brethren and see the face of the saints of my Lord.[265]

The journey Patrick imagined would make perfect geographical sense if his homeland had been in Brittany and his extended family were resident in Brittany, but the religious friends or 'saints' he longed to see again were based at Tours, which was in Gaul.

Considering the chaos that existed within the western Empire at this time, it is surprising that so many writers have discounted the possibility that Patrick may have been referring to Brittany rather than Britain when he used the Latin name 'Britanniis'. Part of the reason for this is a strong disagreement among scholars as to when the name 'Brittany' or 'Bretagne' was first applied. A real weakness in the position taken by Dr O'Hagan and others who hold fast to the traditional theory of Britain is that they do not give sufficient consideration to the impact of the rebellion of Maximus and events that took place on either side of it, as a possible historical context for St Patrick.

Gildas (516-570 CE) and Nennius (630-688 CE) are two the earliest sources we have for the history of Britain during this period. They both say that a British colony was established in a coastal region of Brittany at the time of Maximus. Gildas identified the first settlement of Britons in Armorica with Maximus and says this region

---

[265] C:43.

began to be called Britannia at this time. Gildas claims that when Maximus entered Gaul with the British legions, launching a bid for imperial power in 383 CE, he broke his vows to the Emperor and discarded Roman laws, 'whilst keeping the Roman name for Britain'.[266]

Nennius wrote his *History of the Britons* in the seventh century; he records that when Maximus launched his rebellion in 383 CE, a large number of British troops were settled in Armorica. He refers to these colonists as 'Armoric Britons' and the region in which Magnus settled his troops is identified as 'Armoric Letha'.[267] These accounts strengthen the case for Brittany.

In 1777, M. Deric published a magnificent *Ecclesiastical History of Brittany*. This includes more detailed, local information about this region, especially valuable for our study because it comes from a Breton perspective. He says,

> The lands that Maximus gave to these foreigners were said to be uncultivated. These migrants were called 'Létes or 'contes'– 'laiti' in Latin [from lætus], which described their status and condition [as serfs or half-free colonists] and which was given to "those Barbarians who were in the service of the [Roman] Empire and who had been granted special military benefits (or favors)". They were required to cultivate their new lands, called 'Létiques', and to provide a certain number of army recruits for the Romans. During this period Armorica was also called 'Letavi' or 'regio læta - land of the Contens' as well as 'Ledaw' or 'Leidaw'.[268]

M. Daru also writes in detail about the army of Britons in Armorica at the time of Maximus. He claims that it changed the whole existence of this region, which he calls *La Bretagne continentale* – a Britain on the continent – and says the name 'Little Britain (*La Petite Bretagne*) was applied to this region at this time, to distinguish it from

---

[266] 'The Works of Gildas' in *Six Old English Chronicles,* ed. J. A. Giles (London, 1868), p. 307.

[267] Nennius, History of the Britons (AD 286-422), in *Six Old English Chronicles,* p. 394.

[268] Deric, *Histoire Ecclésiastique de Bretagne*, p. 136 ff.

the island of Britain, which is still called *Grande Bretagne*, in French.[269] Daru quotes various sources to support this and also documents more ancient texts which support the view that Brittany was called 'Britanniis' at the time of Maximus.[270]

Another early Breton historian, M. Deric, provides what he considers to be etymological and local geographical evidence to support this view that a settlement in Brittany under Maximus was based in the coastal region between St Malo, Dol and Mont St Michel, linked to the names of certain local villages, which still exist today. On the outskirts of Dol-de-Bretagne, we find the local parishes of Baguer Pican, Baguer Morvan and Miniac-Morvan.

According to M. Deric, 'Bagner' is a Celtic word which refers to 'a troop' of soldiers, 'Morvan' comes from the Celtic word for great or large (mor in Gaelic) or sea (mer in French) and 'wan' or 'gan' which derives from a Celtic word for birth. He suggests that the names of these villages refer to 'a large troop of soldiers born from (or close to) the sea'.[271]

Deric is convinced that these names are unequivocal signs of the existence of the British colony established by Maximus and that the centre of administration was at Dol. He quotes the fifth century Prefect of Gaul, Sidonius Apollinaris, when he suggests that the territory covered by the British settlement in Armorica under Maximus was even larger, stretching from the north-east and west coasts of Brittany to the Loire Valley.[272]

The transition from the name 'Armorica' to 'Brittany' is an historically controversial subject riddled with uncertainty, linked to a serious political controversy that relates to the turbulent relationship and historical rivalry between Britain and France.

Dr Christopher Snyder, Head of the Department of History and Politics at Marymount University, says the Breton succession crisis became a permanent part of the continuing struggle between these two great powers and the transition from 'Armorica' to 'Brittany',

---

269 Daru, *Histoire de Bretagne*, i, p. 18.
270 Laccary, *De Colonis in Gallias ab Exterior Ductis*, ch. 24, for 382 CE; (ii) Matthew of Westminister (entry for the years 390-392); (iii) Sigebert's Chronicle, for the year 385. Daru, *Histoire,* p. 54.
271 Deric, *Histoire Ecclésiastique de Bretagne*, p. 133, 147.
272 Deric, *Histoire Ecclésiastique de Bretagne*, p. 135 n, (a).

that is the establishment of the Britons in this region, is a little understood process.[273]

The political, military and cultural hot potato is whether the British occupied this region in the fifth and sixth centuries as refugees or in 383 CE as conquerors, with an independent monarchy that pre-dated the earliest French kings. This was and still is a very sensitive and controversial subject that has affected relations between Britain and France.

Another significant factor is the disdain shown towards the rebellion of Maximus by classical historians. Gibbon was prepared to accept that a settlement of the ancient Britons took place in Gaul under Maximus, saying, 'The youth of the island (of Britain) crowded to (Maximus's) standard; he invaded Gaul with a fleet and an army, long afterwards remembered as the emigration of a considerable part of the British nation'. [274]

Gibbon was aware that many of the early Breton historians understood the government of Armorica was established as a monarchy by Maximus before declaring its independence from the Roman Empire in 409 CE. He examined the evidence given by various French historians concerning an earlier foundation for this 'Britain' and said they were wrong. Gibbon refused to accept that any significant migration and settlement of Britons took place in Brittany before the middle of the fifth century, saying 'beyond that era the Britons of Armorica can be found only in romance'. Gibbon held strongly to this view, following the well-known French historian, Lobineau, who claimed 'Brittany' or 'Bretagne' was not introduced until about 458 CE. Gibbon was even more cautious, insisting this name was not established until after the arrival of Britons who fled to the continent, following defeat by the Anglo-Saxons in 550 CE. [275]

Sharon Turner takes a similar position, claiming that the coastal region of Armorica was not called Britain or 'Brittany' until 513 CE. At

---

[273] Dr C. Snyder, 'The Medieval Celtic Fringe', *The ORB: Online Encyclopedia Book for Medieval Studies* [website] pubd online 2 June 2003.

[274] Gibbon, *Decline and Fall of the Roman Empire*, 8 vols (London, 1862, iii, p. 360).

[275] Gibbon, *DFRE*, iv, p. 130 ff. See G. A. Lobineau, *Histoire de Bretagne*, 2 vols (Paris, 1707), i.

the same time, she admits that 'the first British colonists of Armorica have been excluded from European history, and wherever they did appear, their history has been wrapped in legend and fable'.[276]

Gibbon's authority and reputation as historian of the Roman Empire was strong enough to shape prevailing opinion. Naturally, his views are accepted as trustworthy by those who hold that St Patrick came from Britain.

Unfortunately, Gibbon had no real interest in St Patrick. He mentions Patrick and Ireland only briefly in dismissive, racist remarks, when he says, 'The meanest subjects of the Roman Empire assumed the illustrious name of Patricius, which by the conversion of Ireland has been communicated to a whole nation.' [277] Gibbon also had a very negative attitude towards the ancient *Lives of St Patrick* and although he must have been familiar with their writings, his stance towards most of the early Breton historians is equally dismissive. Dean Milner is one of few authors to mention alternative accounts recorded by Breton historians, that the monarchy and name change came into effect at the time of the usurpation of Maximus.[278]

Thankfully, Gibbon's attitude towards events taking place in Britain and Brittany in the fourth and fifth centuries did not go unchallenged. Others took a different view, providing alternative historical evidence to support their claims. Dr Lappenberg (1759-1819) placed the first British settlement in Armorica much earlier, during the rebellion of Maximus in 383 CE. He describes this as a *milites laeti* consisting of British warriors in Armorica, which gave the region a distinct character and new name, Bretagne.[279] Scholars on both sides of the Channel and in Ireland also take the view that Brittany became independent during the settlement of Maximus and was called 'Britanniis' or 'Britannia' at that time. In Ireland, John O'Hanlon recognised the significance of the settlement under Maximus when he said:

[276] Sharon Turner, *The History of the Anglo-Saxons* (London, 1852), p.179.

[277] Gibbon, *DFRE*, iv, p. 300, n. 26.

[278] See Gibbon, *DFRE*, iv, p. 131, n. (a) added by Milner.

[279] Johann Martin Lappenberg, *A History of England under the Anglo-Saxon Kings,* i, trans. Benjamin Thorpe (London, 1865), p. 59 ff. See editorial notes by W. Smith in Gibbon, *DFRE*, iv, p. 391–2.

Several ancient and modern writers have derived the Armoric Britons from the followers of Maximus, who appear to have spread along and ravaged the northern coasts of France, to their remote extremity of Brittany. The Bretons of this province, however, have an obscure history; *but after the time of Maximus, the westernmost corner of Gaul began to be styled Britannia.*[280]

Detailed consideration has now been given to the controversial historical question as to whether the Latin names 'Britanniis' or 'Britannias' could refer to Britain or Brittany in the context of St Patrick's writings. Although to some extent uncertain because of the lack of historical records, the evidence that is available to us suggests that either or both of these names could have applied to a region on the continent in the closing decades of the fourth century.

The origins of Brittany or 'proto-Bretagne' are still cloaked in historical uncertainty and political controversy, but from the variety of sources considered above, it seems irrefutable that the name 'Britanniis' or 'Britannia' was applied to Brittany at the time of the rebellion of Maximus in 385 CE.

The establishment of a colony in Brittany may have been one of the most significant events in European history at the time of St Patrick, shortly before the fall of the Rome. This is most likely to have been Patrick's homeland and the place from which he was taken captive.

We consider the writings of Severus, Gregory of Tours, Nennius and Gildas to be primary historical evidence to support the Brittany theory, together with all the circumstantial evidence from the secondary sources that has been documented during the course of this enquiry.

The map below has therefore been designed to show the regional divisions of Britain and the location of this settlement on the continent.

---

[280] O'Hanlon, *Lives of the Irish Saints* (Dublin, 1875), ii, p. 447. See notes 164–8.
*Emphasis added.

Caledonia

Strathclyde

Valencia

Hadrian's Wall

Hibernia

IRELAND

Maxima
Cæsarensis

Flavia
Cæsarensis

Britannia
Secunda

Londinium

ROMAN BRITAIN
Showing the Rebellion
of Magnus Maximus
383 - 388 CE

Britannia Prima

Iccian Sea

British forces land at the
Roman port of Aleth at
the mouth of the River
Rance, establishing
a settlement in Brittany
known to ancient Irish
writers as Armoric Letha

Aleth

BRITTANY
(Britanniis)

Tours

Gaul

If a strategic settlement of the ancient Britons in Brittany took place under Maximus, when he took control of the western Empire from 383-389 CE, this would support the case that a name change occurred and was introduced more forcefully at this time, at which point a coastal region in Armorica would have been known as 'Britanniis' or 'Britannia'.

This provides an historical context for St Patrick's life and legacy and a deeper understanding of his biography. If St Patrick was born around 385 CE, as Bury suggested, this is precisely when the settlement in Brittany was established by Maximus. If Patrick's family moved to Brittany from northern Britain at this time, as the majority of Breton historians claim, then Patrick would have grown up knowing 'Britanniis' as the name for his homeland. This would be the case if he was born in Brittany or moved there when he was a very young infant.

CHAPTER TWELVE

SAINT PATRICK'S FAMILY

Was it without God or according to the flesh that I came to Ireland? Who compelled me? I was bound by the spirit not to see any of my family. Can it be held against me that I have deep spiritual compassion for those who once took me captive and devastated the male and female servants of my father's house? I was born free according to the flesh, my father was a Decurion. I sold my nobility for the sake of others and I have no regrets and am not ashamed of this.[281]

During the course of this enquiry, a determined effort has been made to explore the uncertainties that surround Patrick from a balanced historical perspective. Much of what has been written about Patrick takes the form of legend and stories passed on through the centuries in 'secondary sources' that cannot be viewed as reliable historical information. At the same time, these sources have preserved treasures of truth, tucked inside the tangled web of confusion and tradition, including fragments of a forgotten geography that may have helped to solve part of the puzzle of St Patrick. If the established tradition has been in error with regard to the location of Patrick's

---

[281] LC:10

homeland and other places mentioned in his *Confession* and if we have been 'misled' as to where St Patrick received his religious training and the real identity of those who sponsored the mission to Ireland, could it also be possible that we have not fully understood the whole truth about other aspects of St Patrick's life and real identity?

Breton historians record intriguing and detailed information about St Patrick's family, which links him even more directly to Brittany. They claim that St Patrick's father, Calpurnius, was a 'Scottish' prince from Strathclyde in northern Britain but that two of Patrick's sisters were founding members of an independent monarchy in Brittany that was established at the time of the settlement that took place during the rebellion of Magnus Maximus in 385 CE.

Apart from accounts given by early Breton historians, genealogical tables are the only resource we have to pursue these matters further. These are well attested from around the ninth century but uncertain before that, so they cannot be taken as reliable historical evidence but like the ancient *Lives of St Patrick* they may have preserved some of the missing pieces in the puzzle.

In their account of the settlement under Maximus, Breton authors include information about St Patrick's family that appears to have been neglected or excluded for some reason by those Patrician scholars whose writings are more familiar to us in English. This begins with Calpurnius and Conan, an elusive historical figure who can perhaps be identified with the Welsh 'Cynan', the son (or nephew) of Eudes (Eudav Hen), a leading member of the nobility in Britain at the close of the fourth century.[282]

Welsh tradition holds that Conan or Cynan (Meriadog) led a large army of Britons over to Gaul. This is recorded in the Welsh Triads as one of the *tair cyuordwy* or three emigrations that left Britain and never returned.[283] Welsh tradition also preserves the 'legend' that Magnus Maximus married Helen or Ellen, the daughter of Eudes who was Conan's father (or uncle).

This was understood to have been an arranged marriage, by which

---

[282] Gilles Deric, *Histoire Ecclésiastique de Bretagne*, ii (Paris, 1778), p. 138.

[283] Robert Williams, *Enwogion Cymru: A Biographical Dictionary of Eminent Welshmen*, p. 216.

Maximus was invited to become part of the royal family in Britain because of their imperial ambitions.[284] After Maximus launched the rebellion and entered Gaul with the legions under his command, Conan is said to have been appointed Duke of the Armorican Tract and appointed as the first 'king' of Brittany as part of a new monarchy. Breton historians record the close family ties that are said to have existed between Conan and St Patrick's father, Calpurnius. Both came from noble families in Albany (Scotland) and were related as cousins. If there is any truth in this claim, then St Patrick's family were closely related to the Emperor, Magnus Maximus.

Such a possibility might explain why St Patrick went "missing" from historical and ecclesiastical records for more than two hundred years after his death. The rebellion by Maximus was viewed as a gross act of treason by Imperial families ruling on the continent and as we have seen, these families held great power and influence over developments that were taking place in the Church. It is not unreasonable to suggest that certain details concerning St Patrick and his family may have been lost or suppressed during such a period of political conflict and controversy. This is what makes the following information recorded by several early Breton historians, so interesting.

In a section of his *Histoire de Bretagne* entitled 'Calpurnius goes to Armorica' Dom Morice records the following story:

Calpurnius, the father of St Patrick, was a powerful lord in Albania (Scotland). In Gaul he had married one of St. Martin's nieces, named Conchèse. He was also the cousin of Conis or Conan, to whom Maximus had given part of Armorica [Brittany]. Since Conan was a widower he remarried with Darerca, Calpurnius's daughter, who was St Patrick's sister. Through this marriage Calpurnius inherited land in the territory of the Diablintes close to the sea but he barely had time to enjoy this as he was murdered in 388 by pirates from Hibernia [Ireland].[285]

---

[284] For Helen and Maximus and the events in Brittany, see Matthew Hall, *Lives of the Queens of England Before the Norman Conquest*, (Blanchard and Lea, 1859), ch. 8, 'Helena'.

[285] P. H. Morice, *Histoire de Bretagne*, (Paris, 1744), translated by Francine Bernier, i, p. 8.

M. Deric also records that Conan married Darerca and that Calpurnius had inherited an estate 'close to the sea' in the territory of the Diablintes near Aleth, on the ancient site where Château de Bonaban is now located.[286]

The Diablintes was a Celtic or Gallo-Roman tribe that inhabited a coastal region between St Malo and Mont St Michel.

In a detailed historical study of the Château and nearby village of La Gouesnière, Joseph Viel records the opinion of various authors that the settlement at Bonaban dates back to the late Roman period. He includes the following statement about the migration of Patrick's family from Scotland to Bonaban in 385 CE which suggests that Calpurnius came to Brittany with an established noble pedigree and some impressive resources:

> Calpurnius, a little prince of Scotland and cousin of Conan [Meriadec] was one of these exiles. He had a large family, slaves, a whole nation [or following]. Conan received him magnificently [in Brittany], married his daughter, the beautiful Darerca and gave him a large and fertile territory, located near the sea, in the country of the Diablintes or Aleth that a few authors, including M. de Gerville, believe to be Bonaban.[287]

Breton historians record that Calpurnius and Conan were cousins and that both were members of an ancient Scots-British royal family. Similar claims are recorded in Britain. The *Legend of John of Tinmouth* describes Calpurnius as one of the chief Lords of Scotland as does as the *Aberdeen Breviary*. This suggests that St Patrick's father may have had a royal pedigree.[288]

An established tradition has always linked Patrick's family to Strathclyde. This still forms part of the Scottish historical record and

---

[286] Deric, *Histoire Ecclesiastique de Bretagne*, p. 193 (see n. 3).

[287] Joseph Viel, *La Gouesnière et Bonaban* (Dinan, 1912), pp. 114–119, trans. Francine Bernier.

[288] *Patricius Hiberensium apostolos expatre Calphurnio de Scottorum nobili familia ortus*: Macnab, Duncan, *Archaeological Dissertation on the Birthplace of St Patrick* (Dublin, 1865).

has to be accounted for. Could St Patrick's father, Calpurnius, have been a 'Scottish' prince?

The country we now call Scotland was not known by that name at the time of St Patrick. 'Scotti' was a name originally applied by the Romans to the Irish, including those who had settled in northern Britain. 'Alba' was an ancient name for Scotland. At the time of St Patrick, Strathclyde can best be described as a kingdom occupied by various tribes of the ancient Britons who were Welsh. It was located close to the northern boundary of Roman influence between Valencia and the Pictish kingdoms of Caledonia. This was Dalriada, an ancient kingdom of the Scots and Irish. It included lands on both sides of the Irish Sea. Dalriada existed in the north-east of Ireland around Antrim and in the Highlands and Islands in Western Scotland (Argyll).

The capital of the kingdom of Strathclyde was the heavily fortified Rock of Dumbarton (Dun Briton, the fort of the Britons). It separated the Britons to the south from the Scots-Irish of Dalriada, in the north.

According to the ancient *Lives of St Patrick*, Calpurnius also had family ties in Gaul. Irish and Breton sources record that St Patrick's mother, Conchessa, was 'of the Franks'. They claim she was also a close relative of St Martin of Tours:

> Now Patrick's kin were of the Britons of Dumbarton. Calpurn was his father's name, an arch presbyter was he. Otid was the name of his grandfather ... Conchessa was his mother's name. She was the daughter of Ochbas, of France was her kin ... she was a sister of St Martin.[289]

This suggests that Patrick's family were Britons from Strathclyde on his father's side and Franks from Gaul through Conchessa. If Calpurnius was from Strathclyde, then most likely he would have been related to some branch of the early kings of Wales or Scotland, perhaps even those who had intermarried with the Irish who settled from an early date on the north bank of the Clyde, near Dumbarton. The most significant royal families in this region are the early kings of

---

[289] 'Lebar Brecc Homily' in Whitley Stokes, *Tripartite Life of St Patrick* (London, 1887), ii, p. 433.

Strathclyde and Scots Dalriada.[290]

There is no direct reference to Calpurnius in any of the genealogical charts currently available but some records are worth exploring further, because they suggest a possible connection to a particular Scottish lineage.

The first clue is the name itself. Calpurnius is a Latin name, well known in the late Roman period. St Patrick's father may have belonged to that group of the ancient Britons who had been Romanised. This does not discount the possibility that his name had Gaelic origins. This would be the case, for example, if 'Calpurnius' was a Latinised version of 'Calpurn' or 'Calpin', as recorded in many of the ancient documents related to St Patrick.

In the Highlands and Islands of Scotland, St Patrick was remembered as Patrick McAlpin.[291] In Gaelic, Patrick's name appears as Padraig M'Alpin (pronunciation: Pawrig). 'Mac', or the abbreviated 'Mc', means 'son of' and, therefore, he was remembered as Patrick 'Mac Calpurn' (son of Calpurn), which became Patrick McAlpin when anglicised. Patrick is frequently called Patrick McAlpin in the ancient poems of Ireland.[292]

This suggests that his father may have been associated with the McAlpins in the minds of local people. The Alpins or McAlpins represent one of the most important royal families in Scotland. Most of the kings of Scotland down to the twelfth century came from the McAlpin dynasty.

This includes: Alpin (736–740 CE); Alpin, King of Scots (839–841 CE); Kenneth I (844–859 CE); Donald I (859–863 CE); Constantine I (863–877 CE); Constantine II (900–942 CE); Constantine III (995–997 CE); Duncan I (1034–1040 CE); Macbeth (1040–1057 CE).

---

[290] For information on the kingdom of Strathclyde, see Skene, *Celtic Scotland* (Edinburgh, 1886), p. 237.

[291] 'Patrick M'Alpain as he was designated by the Highlanders.' Dugald Mitchell, *History of the Highlands and Gaelic Scotland* (Paisley, 1900), p. 36. 'Patrick son of Alpurn' (Mac Alpurn), Stokes, *TL*, p. 561.

[292] See *Transactions of the Royal Irish Academy*, Dublin 1787, p. 80 (n. c) and p. 104. Also, 'Patrick, son of Alpurn' (Old Irish, *Patraic maicc Alpuirn* in the Lebear Brecc, Stokes, *Tripartite Life*, p. 552; 'Patrick, son of Calpurn' (*mac Calpuirn*), Stokes, *Tripartite Life*, p. 427.

Malcolm III (1058–1093) was the last representative of the royal line of McAlpins.

The origins of this clan go back to Aedhan mac Ghabran who was anointed as King of Scots Dalriada by St Columba of Iona in 574 CE. This is the first record we have in Western Europe of the anointing of a king by a Christian cleric.

If Calpurnius was a 'Scottish' prince as Breton historians claim and his family was based in Strathclyde, this is the lineage he is most likely to have been related to. Another clue which suggests that Calpurnius may have been related to progenitors of the McAlpins is the name of Patrick's sister, Darerca. Dar-erca is a Gaelic name carrying a particular meaning that suggests a possible royal pedigree. The prefix *Dar* means 'oak' in Irish and Scots Gaelic. The suffix *Erca* suggests a link to Erc, the high king of Ireland from whom the kings of Scots Dalriada and the McAlpins are descended.

Darerca is a Scottish name of feminine gender that means 'daughter of Erc' or 'daughter from the oak of Erc'. Names always carried special significance for indigenous people including the Celts, as they still do.

King Erc or 'Eirca' was the royal progenitor of the McAlpins. Such genealogical connections cannot be verified historically owing to the lack of reliable records but names are usually chosen for a purpose, especially in royal families. If St Patrick's father, Calpurnius, was linked to the ancient Irish dynasty associated with King Erc of Dalriada, then genealogical records for the kings of Scots Dalriada may provide further clues to shed light on uncertainties that surround his family origins.

The table given below is a simplified version of an original chart compiled by Laurence Gardner, who was Presidential Attaché to the European Council of Princes and Jacobi Historiographer Royale. It shows only key figures in the main line of descent, as this appears relevant to the origins of St Patrick.[293]

---

[293] For the original charts see Laurence Gardner, *Bloodline of the Holy Grail* (New York, 2006), pp. 342 ff.

THE KINGS OF SCOTS DAL RIADA
ERC of Dal n'Araide
(Dal Riata) Ireland

I	I	I
Fergus Mor	Loarn	Aengus
d. 501 CE	Kingdom of N.	Kingdom of Islay
Kingdom of Alba	Argyll	

I
Domangart
(501–608 CE)

I
Gabran
(537–559 CE)

I
Aedhan mac Gabran
(574–608 CE)
Progenitor of the
McAlpins.
Anointed by St Columba
of Iona on the 'Stone of
Destiny' in 574 CE

Erc was king of Irish Dál Riata until 474 CE. He was the father of Fergus Mór, one of two sons including Loann Macc Ercc or Macc Ercae.

The surname Macc Ercae may have come from the maternal side, as there is mention of a legendary mother called Erca. In Irish mythology Eochaid is named as 'son of Erc', son of Rinnal, of the Fir Bolg.

St Patrick's sister was born several generations before Erc became the high king of Ireland around 480 CE, but her name allows for the possibility that she was 'from the lineage of Erc'. This ancient royal family is symbolised by the oak tree. If Darerca's name was chosen to honour her father's relatives or ancestors, the lineage of 'Erc' was important to him.

She may have been given this name by her parents to acknowledge the ancient ancestors of Calpurnius who may have been Irish and the significance of her own place in this pedigree.

At this point, the genealogical tables reveal some interesting surprises in relation to St Patrick's experience in Ireland and his writings. The kings of Scots Dalriada trace their lineage directly from King Coroticus of Strathclyde. Coroticus was a British king or 'warlord' who was in conflict with St Patrick. In his *Letter to Coroticus*, St Patrick chastised this king for acts of violence which had been perpetrated against some of Patrick's recent converts. St Patrick threatened to excommunicate him if he did not make redress and return those who had been taken captive. The identity of Coroticus (450–470 CE) is no longer disputed.[294]

His lineage is confirmed by established genealogical records including those compiled by the Directory of Royal Genealogical Data at the University of Hull and the Magoo Centre.[295]

Coroticus (Welsh: *Ceredig* or *Ceretic*) was the ruler of Strathclyde from about 450–470 CE. St Patrick was an older man when he wrote his letter to Coroticus so the date of this king's rule can help to shed light on when Patrick may have died, suggesting the traditional date of 461 CE may be correct.

In a genealogy attached to Nennius's *Historia Brittonum* in the Harleian MS, he is called 'Gwledig' (Guletic) which means 'a ruler' in Welsh. This was a title not simply related to Roman military rank but also a royal pedigree. Magnus Maximus (recorded in Welsh traditions as Maxim Gwledig) is probably the best known holder of this title. Coroticus was the founder of a famous dynasty that ruled Strathclyde

---

[294] See T. M. Charles-Edwards, *Early Christian Ireland* (Cambridge, 2000), p. 227 ff.

[295] Brian Tompsett, University of Hull: *Directory of Royal Genealogical Data*; see also:

[website] http://www.magoo.com/hugh/scotskings.html

down to the eighth century.[296] Coroticus may have held the title 'Dux Britanniarum'.

This was a noble title given to British kings when the island was under Roman occupation. It continued in use for a time after the legions left Britain in 406 CE, when certain British warlords came to prominence as local leaders. Coroticus was one of these. Even though he was King of Strathclyde as we have already noted, it would be wrong to think of him as 'Scottish' since at that time this applied to the Irish (the original 'Scotti'). As far as we know, the country we now call Scotland was not officially known by that name before the tenth century. Coroticus probably belonged to a tribe of the ancient Britons who were Welsh or Cornish although it is also possible that he may have been related to the Irish who had settled around Strathclyde.

At the time of St Patrick, the kingdom of Strathclyde extended from the River Derwent in Cumberland in the South, to the Firth of Clyde in the North. The River Clyde separated the Britons to the South from the Scots (Irish) of Dalriada in the North. Its population came from two British peoples (as opposed to Anglo-Saxons, Picts or Scots/Irish). These were the Cymric or Welsh to the south while the northern part of the kingdom was occupied by the Damnonii who belonged to the Cornish. The capital of this kingdom was the heavily fortified rock on the Clyde, called by the Britons 'Alcluid' and known as Dumbarton (Dun Briton) the 'Fort of the Britons'.

When Britain was administered by the Romans, Hadrian's Wall provided the most stable line of defence against the marauding Picts and Scots (Irish). Built at the time of Hadrian in 120 CE, this wall extended between the Solway Firth (Carlisle) and Tynemouth (Newcastle). In c. 380 CE Maximus led a successful military campaign against the Picts, before he left for Gaul. During that campaign, the Romans may have been able to protect an area further to the north possibly as far as the Antonine Wall, which extended between the Firth of Forth and the Clyde estuary (Strathclyde). This was an earthen rampart built in 138 CE when Antonius succeeded Hadrian. Security disintegrated rapidly and Britain lost all her defensive capability following the rebellion of Maximus when the

---

[296] Skene, *Celtic Scotland*, p. 184.

legions under his command crossed to Gaul.[297]

This was a period of social disorder and lawlessness especially in northern Britain. Strathclyde was beyond Hadrian's Wall and vulnerable to attack. Breton historians record that St Patrick's family moved from there to Brittany at this time. In light of the deteriorating security situation, this would have been a sensible decision, especially for a young family.

As a Decurion, a position that held significant military responsibilities, Calpurnius would have been well informed about the broader political situation and if he had close family relationships with Conan and Maximus, as the early Breton historians claim, then he may even have been privy to plans for Maximus to become Emperor and the new settlement in Brittany that would take place as a consequence of this development.

The Kings of Strathclyde

In genealogical tables for the Kings of Strathclyde, Coroticus holds a prominent position. He was a direct descendant of Confer of Strathclyde. The McAlpins trace their lineage back to Aedhan mac Gabhran (574–608 CE). Aedhan was a descendant of Coroticus. If Calpurnius belonged to the noble lineage of King Erc of Dalriada from whom the McAlpins trace their origins, this suggests that St Patrick and King Coroticus of Strathclyde were related. They appear to have belonged to rival or 'dislocated' branches of the same noble lineage. This introduces the possibility that there may have been underlying reasons for the conflict between them, the precise details or extent of which have not been recorded. This cannot be verified historically, but even the possibility that it could be true would have significant implications for St Patrick's biography. It is one of the reasons why these genealogical tables are so intriguing and potentially significant for the study of St Patrick.

We know that Coroticus was sufficiently aware of Patrick's location in the north of Ireland, to launch an attack on the

---

[297] Skene, *Celtic Scotland*, p. 59 ff., p. 97.

congregation which was probably based in Patrick's Church at Saul, near Downpatrick.

We also know that Patrick was familiar with King Coroticus's location at the palace in Strathclyde, enough to send emissaries to him with a letter. These facts are evident from Patrick's Letter. In his *Letter to Coroticus* St Patrick more or less told King Coroticus that he would be excommunicated and damned forever if he did not seek forgiveness from God and make redress for his evil actions. We can only imagine how this letter was received.

A British king and his soldiers and supporters would react strongly to being challenged so publicly in this way, especially from a self-proclaimed bishop in Ireland. This letter probably placed St Patrick's life in even greater danger.

The following is another abbreviated version of Gardner's original chart. Only key figures in the main line of descent have been included here, as these relate to the study of St Patrick.[298]

Gardner had no specific interest in St Patrick when compiling these charts. He was dealing with the claims of the Jacobites and the lineages of certain European royal families that traced their ancestry back to the House of Constantine and the family of Jesus. That is what makes these charts so interesting in relation to our study of St Patrick.

Readers should be warned that these charts are controversial and would not be accepted or appreciated by some historians because the subject Laurence Gardner is dealing with is controversial. Genealogical tables can be unreliable and are usually controversial. They were and still are prone to manipulation, to enhance the claims of certain royal families and even to support a particular political, ecclesiastical or military agenda. At the same time, the lives of many of the historical figures who appear in these charts have already been well documented. The significance of the charts is that they include various figures directly or indirectly associated with St Patrick in a variety of sources, which is surprising and perhaps more than coincidental.

---

[298] For the original charts see Laurence Gardner, *Bloodline of the Holy Grail* (New York, 2006).

SCOTS IMPERIAL DESCENT
Lleiffer Mawr (King Lucius) – *Gladys* c.180 CE

I	I	I
Caradawc (Caratacus)	St Helena (Elaine) Married Constantius I	Cunedd
I	I	I
Eudes (Eudaf)	Constantine I (The Great) 312–337 CE	Confer of Strathclyde
I	I	
Elen (Orienne) Married to Magnus Maximus Emperor of the West (383–388 CE)	*Helen of Hosts*	
	I	
	Cinhil, etc.	
	I	
	Gratiana Married Tudwell of Galloway	

I	I	I
Severa Vortigern 418–464 CE	Descent to Aedhan mac Gabhran, 574 CE and the Kings of Scots Dalriada	Coroticus of Strathclyde (Ceretic Guletic) 420–450 CE

The chart above claims to be a record of 'Scots Imperial Descent'. It reveals possible links between several important figures who have appeared in our study so far, including the ancient kings of Strathclyde and Scots Dalriada, Eudes, Maximus and the Imperial House of Constantine.

THE HOUSE OF WALES AND BRITTANY
St Helena — Constantine Chlorus

I	I
Caradawc	Constantine (The Great)

I	I
Eudes (Eudaf)	Magnus Maximus
I	Married *Ellen*, daughter of Eudes.
Cardawc	

I
Conan
Conan Meriadec (Cynan)
Duke of the Armorican Frontiers
First king of the Bretons, d. 421 CE
Married St Darerca, grand-niece of
St Martin of Tours*

I		I
Istrafael		Urbien
I	I	I
Cunedda	Gwawl (Grallon)	Solomon
	Married St Patrick's	King of the Bretons
	sister Tigris or D'Agris*	son of Urbien

I		I
KINGS OF		Aldron (Aldroneus)
STRATHCLYDE		Married the sister of
		Germanus of Auxerre
		(according to Gardner)
		I
		Budie I
		King of the Bretons

* According to the Ancient Lives of St Patrick and Breton historians, Darerca was St Patrick's sister. According to Breton historians, Conan and Calpurnius were cousins. The ancient *Lives of St Patrick* record that St Patrick's mother, Conchessa, was St Martin's niece. If so, then Patrick and his family would have been closely related to St Martin, Conan and the Emperor, Magnus Maximus.

In this chart for the House of Wales and Brittany, members of St Patrick's family are directly recorded. This includes Eudes, Helen, Conan and Maximus as descendants of Constantine. It also presents a link to the early kings of Brittany, showing Conan as the first king. This chart records that Conan married Darerca, whom Breton historians identify as St Patrick's sister. On Gardner's chart she is named as the 'grand-niece' of St Martin of Tours, which concurs with claims found in the ancient *Lives of St Patrick*, that St Patrick's mother, Conchessa, was St Martin's niece.

The link to the kings of Strathclyde is clearly apparent. What is even more intriguing, is that it shows a line of descent for the early kings of Brittany from Conan and Darerca to Urbien and then Solomon and Aldron. Gardner's chart lists Urbien and Istrafael as the children of Conan and Darerca, as do the Breton historians. If these personal family details are reliable, then Urbien and Istrafael were St Patrick's nephew and niece.[299]

The final chart to be considered presents the line of succession for the early Kings of Brittany, according to Bertrand d'Argentré's *Abrégé de l'Histoire de Bretagne*, published in Paris in 1695. The royal status of St Patrick's family is clearly apparent from this list. The same basic claims can be found in the writings of Dom Morice and Pièrre Le Baud, amongst others.

There appears to be some discrepancy in the initial line of succession but this is understandable, considering the lack of reliable documents from the fifth century. Some Breton authors say Urbien was also called Grallon and they date his rule from 405 CE, others place it around 435–446 CE. Some accounts place Salomon's rule before that of Grallon.

When this table is compared with Gardner's chart for the House of Wales and Brittany, it suggests that members of St Patrick's family came from a significant noble lineage with an ancient Scots-Welsh pedigree that played a central part in the foundation of a monarchy in Brittany following the settlement there during the rebellion of Maximus in 385 CE.

---

[299] Ystrafael is recorded as the daughter of Conan Meriadec. She married Coel Hen Godebog of Regged, a Welsh prince born c.380 CE whose seat was at Carlisle. See Charts for the House of Wales and Brittany, Gardner, *Bloodline of the Holy Grail*, p. 342 ff.

THE EARLY KINGS OF BRITTANY

Conan (383 CE)
Married St Patrick's sister, Darerca
I
Grallon (388 CE)
Married St Patrick's sister, D'Agris or Tegreda
I
Salomon (405 CE)
Son of Grallon
I
Audren (412 CE)
Son of Salomon, 'fils aine'
I
Budic (415–487 CE)
Son of Audren
I
Hoel I 'Le Grand' (487 CE)
I
Riothem
I
Hoel II (d. 560 CE)

I	I
Rivallon	Hoel III
Married a daughter	(594 CE)
of Hoel II	Son of Hoel II

I
Alain (560–594 CE)
I
Salomon II (640 CE)
Son of Hoel III
I
Alain 'Le Long'
(660–690 CE)
Nephew of Salomon II

The dates given for all these marriages are consistent and plausible from a chronological and an historical point of view. Breton authors record that when Grallon succeeded to the throne after the death of Conan he married St Patrick's sister, Tigris.

M. Deric describes Tigris as 'the sister of Queen Darerca'.

He believed that her name confirms that she was of high noble birth and belonged to a very illustrious family. According to these authors, members of Patrick's family were senior founding members of the early Breton aristocracy.

Breton historians provide linguistic evidence to support their claims. M. Deric insists that the name 'Tigris' or 'D'Agris' confirms the high birth of her father, Calpurnius. It derives from the Gaelic name for house – *tigh* or *tig* – and king – *ri* or *ris*. D'Agris comes from *d'ag*, which means race, and *ri* or *ris*, a royal house. [300] The name of Patrick's sister may not be from the Latin *tigris* (which means a little tiger) but Gaelic, meaning 'an issue from a royal house' or 'from the House of Kings.'

A list of names for St Patrick's sisters was recorded in some of the ancient manuscripts published by Colgan in 1647. These documents include various accounts of the members of St Patrick's family, giving names for St Patrick's sisters and a brother called Senan. Darerca and Tigris are mentioned in these lists consistent with those recorded by Breton historians.

What we do not find in the *Lives of St Patrick* published by Colgan or the *Book of Armagh*, is any reference to the marriages between Conan and Darerca or Grallon and Tigris. Nor do we find any record of the alleged family ties between Calpurnius, Conan and Maximus.

These family details appear to have been recorded only in Breton sources, with one significant exception. There is one reference in the *Tripartite Life of St Patrick* that concurs with the essential substance of these accounts.

It describes how, when St Patrick came across the sea from the land of 'Bretan' (Brittany) to Ireland, he travelled with clerics who were 'sons of Conis and Darerca, St Patrick's sister, as the households of their churches say, and that is not to be denied.' This reference is intriguing in so many ways. It shows that the Irish church

---

[300] Deric, *Histoire Ecclésiastique de Bretagne*, p. 263, n. (b).

was aware of Conan's existence and his marriage to Patrick's sister, Darerca. The reference to 'the household of their churches' appears to be very archaic. It certainly pre-dates Breton historical records of the sixteenth and seventeenth centuries and it probably pre-dates Geoffrey of Monmouth, who is often accused of inventing the existence of Conan.[301]

Why did the author feel it necessary to say 'and that is not to be denied'? This is a very strange remark. Was there something about St Patrick that was known to be true, but some people in the Irish Church were denying it?

These are remarkable claims about St Patrick's family and their nobility but are they trustworthy? The origins of Brittany and its relations with the kings of France is a complex and controversial subject. It is clouded by issues which have greatly influenced the views of individual historians.

Conflicting historical accounts are linked to complex political and ecclesiastical issues concerning the so-called 'Merovingian Conspiracy' and the origins of the Kings of France, not least in terms of the relationship with Britain and Rome before and after the foundation of the Carolingian Empire.

There was obviously a battle going on for control of Brittany and the line of succession is understandably controversial.

M. Daru and other Breton authors suggest that two alternative lines of succession have survived for the early kings of Brittany. One can be traced through Conan to Salomon and Alain, and the other through Rivallon.[302] M. Deric identifies Rivallon as a child from Conan's first marriage to Ursula, not from his second marriage to St Patrick's sister, Darerca.[303]

These disputes are reflected in contradictory claims that can be found in various genealogical tables and they have significant implications in relation to understanding the truth about St Patrick. In one, St Patrick's family plays a very prominent part. In the other,

---

[301] Stokes, *Tripartite Life*, i, p. 83.

[302] M. Daru, *Histoire de Bretagne* (Paris, 1826), i, p. 94, n. 1.

[303] Deric, *Histoire Ecclésiastique de Bretagne*, p. 240–5.

they are excluded.

M. Daru says the role of Conan and Darerca in the line of succession has been erased from many historical records as a result of efforts by the Church to establish itself more securely in Brittany in the centuries which followed the collapse of the western Empire. In his opinion, the true line of succession was preserved through Conan, despite being erased in later chronicles compiled by the Church. M. Daru is convinced that the names of Conan and Salomon retain the ancient language and, therefore, an authentic lineage. The same applies to St Patrick's two sisters, Darerca and Tigris. This view is shared by a number of early Breton historians, but rejected by others, who deny the existence of Conan and his role in the foundation of a monarchy in Brittany.

The origins of such discrepancies are of great historical importance in resolving uncertainties surrounding St Patrick as they involve significant claims with regard to members of his immediate family. One of the sensitive political issues is whether the British occupied this region as refugees or conquerors. Vertot claims that the ancient Britons did not settle in Brittany until their arrival as refugees in the sixth century but his work has been criticised for distorting historical facts to show the original dependence of the Bretons on the French kings.[304] Arthur de La Borderie joined the ranks of French historians who said Conan's existence was a fable. This includes Cornette, who promulgated the view that the legend of Conan was invented to serve the political ambitions of later Dukes in Brittany who were searching for a legitimate reason to free themselves from the king of France, by claiming the Breton kings were an independent sovereign lineage. Tourault said the existence of Conan and those who descended from him was all part of a legend created by the Bretons for ideological and political motives.[305]

It is possible that the exact opposite may be true in this case.

The exclusion of Conan may have been politically motivated, to show that the Bretons were always dependent on the Franks and, therefore, held no sovereign claim to independence from France.

---

[304] O'Hanlon, *Lives of the Irish Saints* (Dublin, 1875), iii, p. 447, n. 174.

[305] Philippe Tourault, *Les Rois de Bretagne IVème–XIXème Siècle* (Paris, 2005).

Removing any clear record of Conan's identity and his position in Brittany may have helped to secure the political and ideological ambitions of France and Rome and remove any legitimate claim that he and Maximus and the British royals may have had to this particular region or to any further imperial advancement.

There is huge historical uncertainty and no shortage of political and ecclesiastical intrigue and controversy attached to this period of history.

M. Daru notes that the same authors who argue against the independence of the Bretons also question the existence of Conan and dispute claims that he was established by Maximus as the first king of Brittany, thus denying any of his successors a place within the Breton aristocracy.[306]

Most of the early Breton historians take a radically different view. They record that Maximus landed forces at the mouth of the Rance, using the Roman port of Aleth. [307] Dom Morice also claims that they landed in Brittany, as does Barbier.[308] The historical truth surrounding these events is crucial to rediscovering the truth about St Patrick and the significance of his family as founding members of the Breton aristocracy.

Many of the accounts recorded by local Breton historians who were writing before the so-called 'era of modern scholarship' are viewed as historically unreliable by some contemporary Breton and Irish scholars, who continue to wrestle with the facts concerning the origins of Brittany. Uncertainties yet to be resolved centre on a lack of reliable sources from the fifth century and complexities linked to the historical relationship between Britain and France, the claims of certain royal families and the influence of the Church.

M. André Yves Bourgès, who is a respected authority in Brittany today, advises that we should be wary of claims made by the early Breton historians concerning Conan and Maximus and the details

---

[306] 'Les auteurs qui on ecrit contra l'independence des Bretons, vont jusqu'a contester l'existence de Conan et des rois qui lui succederent'. Daru, *Histoire*, p. 42, 43, see n. 1.

[307] M. Daru, *Histoire de Bretagne*, p. 42 ff.

[308] Morice, *Histoire*, p. 6; see also Barbier, *Les Ducs de Bretagne* (Rouen, 1859), p. 16.

given about St Patrick's family. Breton authors appear to have been dependent on Geoffrey of Monmouth for information about Conan.

Likewise, he suggests that many of the details about Patrick can be found in the writings of M. Jacques Gallet, whose views influenced others. M. Gallet presents a fascinating study of the origins of Brittany in which he quotes as many ancient sources as were available to him, to document the settlement under Maximus and the role of Conan.

He includes a number of detailed claims related to members of St Patrick's family as founding members of the Breton royal family.[309] André Yves Bourgès is convinced that these claims may have arisen in the context of Breton historiography in the seventeenth, eighteenth and nineteenth centuries, when Breton authors are said to have come under pressure to provide 'evidence' to support a particular ducal ideology.

At the same time, it is important to remember that the origin of Brittany or 'proto-Bretagne' remains cloaked with uncertainty. The complex nature of historic relations between the Bretons and the Franks, not to mention the growing influence of the diocesan Church in the aftermath of the fall of Rome, suggests that the truth as to what took place in Brittany at this time may have been lost or concealed. This may have affected records concerning St Patrick and the significance of his family. This is a complex subject that relates to the so-called 'Merovingian Conspiracy' and an alliance between the Roman Church and the Franks that led to the establishment of the Carolingian Empire.

The Merovingian kings were associated with a 'Messianic' lineage, linked to the family of Jesus and Israel's King David. The Church is accused of seeking to destroy any record of this lineage, and its claim to an alternative religious authority. This is what makes the claims recorded by many of early Breton historians doubly intriguing. They are convinced that members of St Patrick's family belonged to an authentic noble lineage which was subverted by the kings of France in their efforts to be the sole inheritors of the Merovingian lineage and its Messianic legacy.[310] These claims are impossible to verify

---

[309] J. Gallet, *Dissertation sur L'Origins Des Bretons in Histoire des Ducs de Bretagne*, i (Paris, 1739).

[310] Marcus Losack, *Saint Patrick and the Bloodline of the Grail* (Annamoe, 2012).

because of the lack of trustworthy historical records. Genealogical tables cannot be taken as a reliable source for historical information.

The origins of the kings of France are especially uncertain but the detailed personal information about St Patrick's family which has been recorded in Brittany could be authentic and should not be dismissed as a legend.

The presence of so many connections in the genealogical tables is intriguing and worthy of being the subject of further enquiry by those suitably qualified for the task. The complex nature of political and ideological factors suggests that we should remain cautious. Could it be true that St Patrick belonged to a significant royal family? According to a variety of old Breton, Irish and British sources, five members of St Patrick's immediate family are recognised as having noble status. This includes Calpurnius, who is identified as a 'Scottish' prince and cousin to Conan, a close relation of the Emperor, Maximus.

St Fiacc's Hymn which is one of the earliest documents after Patrick's own writings, records that St Patrick was 'heir to his father's nobility'.[311] St Patrick's sister Darerca is said to have married Conan when he was crowned as the first king of Brittany in 383 CE. Another sister of St Patrick called 'Tigris' became an important member of this royal household when she married Grallon, who succeeded to the throne of his father and become the second king in Brittany. According to the *Tripartite Life*, a third sister called Cinnemon was remembered in Ireland as 'Royal Cinne'. Finally, there is St Patrick himself.

In his *Letter to Coroticus*, Patrick tells us that he 'sold his nobility' for the sake of others. The Latin phrase given in the earliest manuscript is '*vendidi enim nobilitatem meam*'. [312] *Vendidi* is the first person singular of the Latin verb *vendo* (to sell) written in the past tense, meaning 'I sold'. Nobilitatem comes from *nobilitas* or *nobilitatis*, which means nobility or royal pedigree. An appropriate translation of his words would be, 'I sold my nobility (my royal title) for the sake of others'. St Patrick's royal status therefore appears to be confirmed by

---

[311] St Fiacc's *Hymn*, v 2.

[312] LC:10

his own admission. His writings provide the best evidence of all to confirm that his family was of noble status.

The links we have discovered in the genealogical tables considered above reveal that Patrick belonged to a significant noble lineage linked to the Kings of Strathclyde and the House of Wales and Brittany. Members of his own immediate family such as his sisters Darerca and Tigris would never have held such high royal status without the existence of a proven pedigree.

If so, Patrick may have renounced his royal entitlements when he committed himself to the religious life and became an apostle in Ireland.

There is so much about St Patrick's life that remains uncertain.

Many claims that have been made about him are impossible to verify because of a lack of reliable historical evidence. That is what makes the study of St Patrick so challenging and exciting. There is so much about him that remains a mystery, not least because we have so little information about events taking place at the time of St Patrick in the fifth century.

St Augustine once said, 'we should not believe anything on a dubious point, lest in favour to our error we conceive a prejudice against something that truth hereafter will reveal'. If the claims recorded by the early Breton historians concerning St Patrick's royal family are true, it not only strengthens the case for locating Patrick's homeland in Brittany, it surely confirms it.

CONCLUSIONS

History is an amazing presence.
It's the place where vanished time gathers.[313]

The fifth century is known as the 'lost century', full of intrigue and mystery because so few documents have survived from the period. The truth about St Patrick's place of origins and the real identity of those who supported his mission to Ireland were lost to historical memory in the centuries after his death. Fortunately, Patrick wrote two letters which have survived from that turbulent period. Without them, we would have been left completely in the dark. These letters provide the only reliable, historical information about his life that can help solve the mystery of his true identity.

In his *Confession*, Patrick mentions five key geographical references related to his place of origin and significant events in his life. It is impossible to clearly identify these locations solely from the information given in St Patrick's own writings. Despite the uncertainties, stories about St Patrick were passed on through the centuries and in the closing decades of the seventh century the Church in Armagh commissioned a scribe called Muirchú to write the first

---

[313] John O'Donohue, *Anam Cara: Spiritual Wisdom from the Celtic World* (London, 1997).

official 'biography' of St Patrick. Muirchú's narrative was influenced by an ecclesiastical and political agenda affecting the Irish Church in general and the Church in Armagh in particular at this time.

Until then, St Patrick was historically anonymous in as much as there is no evidence to show his life was honoured by the Irish Church or that St Patrick was held in any special veneration, a fact that suggests that he may have been ostracised and almost forgotten. Thanks to the Monastery of Armagh, this situation changed dramatically. Muirchú was given responsibility for 'cleaning up the file' and providing all the necessary details so that any uncertainty that may have existed about St Patrick could be removed.

St Patrick was now elevated to a position of authority and honoured as Ireland's patron saint and founding apostle. He was presented as Ireland's champion of Catholic orthodoxy, having been sent by Rome.

In the medieval period, Irish hagiographers functioned as ecclesiastical spin doctors and were capable of masterful fabrication. St Patrick's 'resurrection' in the ecclesiastical record helped to resolve internal civil and religious conflicts, increasing Armagh's influence as the mother house of the *Patricii Paruchia* – a growing federation of monasteries claiming St Patrick as their founder.

Muirchú had access to a copy of St Patrick's *Confession* but much of what he said about Patrick was hagiographical. Muirchú's narrative was in many ways fabricated and through it the 'Legend' of St Patrick was born.

In relation to Patrick's place of origins, Muirchú made certain statements which have shaped our image and understanding of St. Patrick for more than a thousand years. He claimed to know that St Patrick came from Britain, that Patrick's homeland was in Britain and that Bannavem Tiburniae, the place from which St Patrick was taken captive, was 'without doubt' also in Britain.

Muirchú was a genius. The Church in Armagh expected him to resolve existing uncertainties. To achieve this, Muirchú created a 'map' and used descriptive geography to locate Patrick's homeland in Britain.

Muirchú appears to have been faithful to the text of St Patrick's *Confession* by retaining 'Britanniis' as the name for St Patrick's homeland but in his narrative this name was carefully and deliberately applied to the island of Britain exclusively. Muirchú may have brought order to St Patrick's story at the end of the seventh century but he achieved this by creating an illusion or 'delusion', hoping to resolve serious matters of dispute within Ireland and between Ireland, Britain and Rome. In that sense, it is not unreasonable to suggest that Muirchú 'cast a spell' around St Patrick's story.

Irish druids had been masters of the art of delusion and casting spells by magic, before they became Christians; Muirchú's narrative shows how effective Christians could be at maintaining that tradition, weaving their own special form of hagiographical 'magic', introducing ecclesiastical influences that quickly became revered, replacing older traditions.

Many of those who wrote after him accepted Muirchú's authority and built upon his account, a process which helped to develop an established tradition that St Patrick came from Britain.

The spell that was cast was so strong that it has bound the popular image and understanding of St Patrick to the present day.

Despite Muirchú's best efforts, uncertainties about St Patrick's place of origins and true identity refused to disappear. Other 'Lives of St Patrick' were compiled after the seventh century. Some of these included material that must have survived in a written or oral form and that predated Muirchú. Alternative accounts existed concerning St Patrick and various scribes over the centuries tried to make sense out of these conflicting stories.

Many of these documents emphasised St Patrick's connections with Brittany, claiming that before he was sold into slavery in Ireland, Patrick was taken captive from a region called 'Armoric Letha', which can be identified as a coastal region of Armorica, now called Brittany.

One of the ancient authors, Probus, claimed to know 'without doubt' that St Patrick's homeland was in Brittany, that he was born there and also that Bannavem Tiburniae, the place from which St Patrick was taken captive, was located 'close beside the Western Sea' on the north-east coast of Brittany which at the time Probus was writing formed part of the Frankish province of Neustria. When John Colgan published seven of these ancient *Lives of St Patrick* in 1647, this became a major resource for the study of Patrick.

Without these documents we may never have known that such alternative accounts existed. Muirchú had not been able to monopolise the material. Despite the fact that they are essentially hagiographies, these manuscripts are priceless because they have preserved some of the missing pieces in the puzzle. Although certain geographical references mentioned in these later sources are not found in St Patrick's writings, they have been of crucial importance to determine the truth about his place of origins.

We must give thanks to the scribes who faithfully transcribed these ancient names down through the centuries, despite the fact that they, like us, may not have fully understood their meaning or their precise geographical location. These scribes recognised the uncertainties about St Patrick's life held within the ancient sources and attempted to clarify them, and in so doing ensured they were passed on. Preserved within these documents are important clues that hold the keys to establishing the truth, by comparing all the ancient manuscripts in light of other historical evidence.

Much of the confusion and debate centres on the meaning of the Latin name 'Britanniis' which Patrick used to describe his homeland. Muirchú decided that it meant Britain but others suggested that St Patrick came from a region called 'Britain' on the continent. The names for 'Britain' and 'Brittany' (Bretagne) were very similar and could easily have been confused. In 1647, when John Colgan was preparing these ancient manuscripts for publication, he was aware of contradictory claims in the ancient sources. Colgan admitted that, 'because the cited authors speak in general terms, there is controversy as to which Britain or what part of Britain St Patrick was born.' [314]

This is a clear indication that Patrick's place of origins had remained uncertain despite what Muirchú had said. When Colgan published *Trias Thaumaturga* in 1647, he accepted that there was a constant tradition amongst the inhabitants of Gaul that Patrick was a native of 'Armorican Britain' and he says this was endorsed by several Irish sources.

Even though he was conscious of the contradictory accounts in the ancient sources, Colgan concluded his 'Inquiry into the Birthplace and Family of St Patrick' by stating categorically that St Patrick had

---

[314] J. Colgan, *Trias Thaumaturga*, ed. Eamonn De Burca (Dublin, 1977), app. V., p. 2.

come from Britain. The references to Brittany were discounted. Colgan ridiculed Probus, saying he was 'not sufficiently skilled in Patrician matters and the location of places'.[315]

The document attributed to Probus includes some archaic material which appears to be authentic. It can be considered as one of the ancient sources that has preserved reliable information about Patrick's place of origins. This information concurs with other references preserved in some of the ancient *Lives of St Patrick* published by Colgan that describe the place where St Patrick was taken captive as 'Armoric Letha'.

The name 'Armoric Letha' strongly suggests a connection with the Roman port city of Aleth, which was strongly fortified in the closing decades of the fourth century. The significance of Aleth as a major port and Roman military base or *tiburnia* for the Legion of Mars is well documented. It was an important base for the Roman navy before the legions in Gaul were withdrawn to protect the Empire from increasing attacks from the Barbarians. It was also an important centre for local political and military administration during the rebellion of Maximus in 383 CE. Calpurnius could have been employed here as a Decurion, supporting those soldiers who remained loyal to Maximus.

Breton historians identify the lands given to St Patrick's father, Calpurnius, within a specific region, between Aleth, Dol de Bretagne and Mont St Michel. In the Gallo-Roman period, this territory belonged to a local Celtic tribe called the Diablintes and was known to the ancient writers by various names, including Letha, Armoric Letha and Lethania Britannia. This is precisely where Château de Bonaban is located and suggests that local traditions about St Patrick could be true. Evidence gleaned from a variety of sources allows a clearer and more composite picture to emerge. This supports the case for a radical new theory of origins. All the key geographical references relating to St Patrick's place of origin that are found in his own writings can be identified within a specific geographical area on the coast of Brittany, between Aleth and Mont St Michel. Identifying them all within this region is not incompatible with the descriptions

---

[315] App. v: 'Concerning the Homeland and Family of St Patrick'. See Colgan, *Trias Thau.*, p. 220.

given by St Patrick in his own writings and nothing exists in those writings to contradict any of these proposals.

The evidence that is available to support the case for Brittany far outweighs any that can be provided for Britain. This is true to such an extent that we must now view the established tradition, that St Patrick came from Britain and that Bannavem Taburniae was also located in Britain, as unsafe and, therefore, unacceptable. Future translations of St Patrick's *Confession* may need to be revised on the basis that his use of the Latin name 'Britanniis' did not refer to the island of Britain exclusively and there is now more than sufficient evidence to suggest that it refers to Brittany. In 2015 an historic new translation of St Patrick's Letters was published. For the first time, this includes a translation of the Latin name *Britanniis* as Brittany rather than Britain, in the three places where it occurs in Patrick's *Confession*.[316]

Although the evidence to locate St Patrick's homeland in Brittany is compelling and local traditions recorded at Château de Bonaban are probably authentic and trustworthy, absolute or final verification will only be possible following a supervised archaeological excavation at the site.

There are now compelling reasons for this to be done. Celtic axes have been found in the local area and significant remains from the late Roman period are already well documented, including the network of local Gallo-Roman roads and military installations at the Roman port of Aleth (St Malo). Roman remains were discovered in the basement of the château during renovations that took place in 1859, according to a local historical study published in 1912 by Joseph Viel.[317] This author recorded details of some intriguing conversations and meetings he had with a clergyman called Rev. A. Boutlou on July 8th, 1911. Fr Boutlou was originally from the Côtes du Nord but had moved to the United States forty years previously.

Returning to Brittany to see the country where he had spent his youth, he asked Joseph Viel to be his guide in the local commune at Bonaban.

---

[316] C:23, C:32, C:43: John Luce and Marcus Losack, *The Letters of Saint Patrick* (Annamoe), 2015.

[317] Joseph Viel, *La Gouesnière et Bonaban* (1912 reprinted Livre Histoire, 2011).

Fr Boutlou informed Joseph Viel that in 1859 his (Boutlou's) father had been hired as a painter to help with restoration work that was taking place at the château. During these restorations he found several pieces of Roman mortar stuck to fragments of bricks. He believed that these remains, based on their appearance, must have been part of a Roman bathhouse or swimming pool. During the late Roman period, only the wealthiest and most privileged families had such facilities in their own homes. Could this bathhouse have once belonged to St Patrick's father, Calpurnius? Joseph Viel was convinced that excavations would reveal further remains that could easily demonstrate the antiquity of Bonaban.

Aerial photograph of Château de Bonaban. Note the lake in the foreground and the elevated nature of this ancient, walled site, which was surrounded by water until the introduction of land drainage schemes in the eighteenth century. A local tradition claims the first building on this site dated to the late Roman period and was the home of St Patrick's father, Calpurnius and the place where Patrick was taken captive.

Following M. Charles de Gerville, who had been the first to make this claim in 1848, Joseph Viel was also convinced that this was the true location of the estate owned by Calpurnius:

Calpurnius is likely to have stayed at Bonaban. Roman coins found near the château support that assumption. Celtic axes discovered on the edge of Bois Renou have proved that the site is ancient. You only need to study the topography of the area to become aware that the granite hill where many Châteaux de Bonaban, were built over the centuries, in the past was a blue chip strategic point. [318]

Examination of this ancient site in relation to the surrounding countryside had convinced him that local traditions recorded about St Patrick were true and that the description given in Patrick's *Confession* concerning his abduction by pirates relates perfectly to the local topography and proximity to the coast. Joseph Viel suggested that an archaeological excavation could reveal something of great significance and that any artefacts or other remains discovered, would substantiate the truth. He concluded his study of the local area by reflecting on the fact that the true meaning of the stories and legends attached to many of these ancient sites is to be found underground.

At the time of writing an archaeological excavation of the ancient site where Château de Bonaban is located, seems very unlikely. The whole estate of more than one hundred acres has been purchased by a private consortium and work has begun to transform the building into a luxury hotel.[319] Hopefully the local mayor, together with the new owners, will be encouraged to keep a close eye on proceedings when excavations for a new swimming pool take place, to see if any further remains from the late Roman period become visible.[320] The only way to vindicate the local tradition preserved at Bonaban would be the discovery of remains from a Roman villa of the late fourth century.

---

[318] Viel, p.118: Translated by Christophe Saint-Eloi.

[319] Château de Bonaban SAS, 35350 La Gouesnière, France. Mr. Richard Daguise, President (2013)

[320] A local association has been formed in the village, to provide information for visitors and events to honour the place where St Patrick may have once lived and been taken captive [website] https://fr-fr.facebook.com/Mémoires-Saint-Patrick/.

Where was St Patrick born?

Attempts to identify the place where St Patrick was born and establish a chronology for his life are fraught with difficulties because these matters are not easily verified. This is an important aspect of St Patrick's story that deserves to be addressed, accepting that any proposals will be tentative, as there are so many diverse and conflicting accounts.

There is an established tradition, preserved in the Scottish historical record, that St Patrick was born near Strathclyde. The author of *St Fiacc's Hymn* said he was born at Nemthor which the Scholiast identified with Strathclyde. Many early Breton historians record that St Patrick's family moved from Scotland to Brittany as part of the settlement that took place at the time of the rebellion of Magnus Maximus from 383–388 CE.

M. Daru says that as a result of the marriage between Conan and Darerca, Calpurnius inherited lands in the territory of the Diablintes, between Aleth and Dol. These lands included a coastal area covered by the Forest of Quokelunde and the higher ground where Château de Bonaban is now located. M. de Gerville, who was the first to identify Château de Bonaban with St Patrick's 'Bannavem Tiburniae', claims that Patrick was born on his father's estate in Brittany. Robidue recorded the statement that follows after his own historical enquiries and it is worth reading again, since it brings us full circle to the first time we encountered these local traditions in Brittany:

> Scottish historians hold Dumbarton to be the birthplace of St Patrick. M. de Gerville identified Bannavem Tiburniae, the geographical designation given in Latin in St Patrick's *Confession* as Bonaban *and the place of his birth.* He believed this to be so without doubt, a view shared with unanimity by all Breton historians, except Lobineau.[321]

There are intriguing similarities and differences between the Breton accounts and those preserved in the ancient *Lives of St Patrick* about the circumstances which led to St Patrick being taken into captivity.

---

[321] Bertrand Robidue, *Histoire et Panorama d'un Beau Pays* (Rennes, 1953), p. 56.

These may provide clues as to when and where St Patrick was born. If Calpurnius came from Strathclyde, as seems probable from what is recorded in Irish, Scottish and Breton historical sources, the family may have lived there for a time before they moved to Brittany during the rebellion of Maximus. From a historical point of view, it is most likely this migration took place around 383-385 CE. Once Maximus launched his rebellion and the Roman legions left Britain it would have been impossible for St Patrick's family to remain in Scotland.

The date when St Patrick was born is, therefore, relevant to the question as to where he was born. If Patrick was born between 382 and 385 CE, he could have been born in Scotland then travelled to Brittany with his family when he was an infant. He would still have grown up knowing Brittany as his homeland until the age of sixteen when he was taken captive.

On the other hand, if the family moved to Brittany sometime between 383 and 385 CE and St Patrick was born in 384 or 385 CE he may have been born in Brittany, perhaps on his father's estate at *Bannavem Tiburniae*, as M. de Gerville has proposed, or possibly with the support of his mother's side of the family at Tours, if this is the true meaning of 'Nemthor'. Without the discovery of authentic historical records, we will probably never know exactly when or where St Patrick was born.

Unfortunately, the Romans did not issue birth certificates. But it would make a very boring end to this enquiry if we sat on the fence.

A personal opinion can, therefore, be offered, not based on any reliable historical evidence, but linked to another possible clue in the secondary sources. The documents published by Colgan in 1647 contain several versions of a story which claims that St Patrick's family were only visiting their relations in Armorica, or Brittany, at the time Patrick was taken captive. None of these documents say the family had migrated from Scotland to Brittany and were resident there, as the Breton historians claim. What is common to both sources, however, is that St Patrick was taken captive from Brittany.

The differences are in some ways understandable. The earliest accounts probably emerged from oral traditions and whenever they were recorded, it is to be expected that ancient authors would explain the various stories in circulation from their own perspective and try to find ways to reconcile conflicting stories. In some accounts, the family members who made the journey from Strathclyde to Brittany are listed. Most versions identify the travellers as St Patrick, his father, Calpurnius and mother, Conchessa, five sisters including Lupait, Tigris, Liaman, Darerca and Cinnemon and a brother called Senan. Breton historians record an identical list of names (in French) and most, like M. Deric, claim the children were all born before Calpurnius left Strathclyde. In their description of the voyage, all the family members listed above travelled together to Brittany as part of the settlement under Maximus in 383–385 CE. One version of the family's migration from Scotland to Brittany includes an intriguing difference in personal detail. This concerns the list of family members who are said to have travelled with Calpurnius and Conchessa when the family boarded the ship for Brittany. The same basic story can be found in various ancient sources, but this account is unique in one significant respect. Patrick was not included by name in the list of travellers.

This version of the story appears in notes added to *St Fiacc's Hymn* by the Scholiast, as recounted by John Colgan after he had analysed and compared all the various manuscripts at Louvain in 1647. The following passage can be found in the Appendix of Colgan's *Trias Thaumaturga*, 'Concerning the Homeland and Family of St Patrick':

> In the second place, I quote from the Scholiast to St. Fiechin [*Fiacc's Hymn*, n. 5] where he says, 'This was the reason for the slavery of St Patrick. His father Calpurnius, and mother Conchessa, daughter of Ocmusius and his five sisters, Lupita, Tigris, Liemania and Darerca and the name of the fifth, Cinnemon and his brother Senan, all travelled together from Alcludensian Britain [Strathclyde] across the Iccian Sea in a southerly direction, for the sake of business, to Lethanian Armorica, alias Lethecan Britain: because in that place was a certain relative of theirs, *and because the mother of the expected offspring, that is to say, Conchessa,* was from France and a close relative of St Martin.[322]

At the beginning of this story, which we can imagine is a reflection of a very strong and ancient tradition about Patrick's family origins, the author tells us the names of those family members who travelled by

---

[322] Colgan, *Trias. Thau*, p. 220. Translated by John Luce. *Emphasis added.

ship from Strathclyde to Armoric Letha. Calpurnius and Conchessa are listed on board.

Five of St Patrick's sisters are named including Lupita, Tigris, Liaman, Darerca, Cinnemon and a brother called Senan. The one person who is not listed directly as one of the travellers is Patrick.

The passage above appears to be claiming that when the family made the journey by ship from Scotland to Brittany, Conchessa was pregnant.[323]

Could St Patrick have been the child in her womb? A possibility that St Patrick was conceived in Scotland and that when the family boarded that ship to seek their fortunes in Brittany, Conchessa carried within her womb a child that would grow to become Ireland's patron saint and founding apostle adds to the sense of adventure which eventually characterised his whole life.

This allows for a challenging but attractive and plausible conclusion to our study, that St Patrick may have been conceived in Scotland but born in Brittany. If Patrick was conceived before the family left Strathclyde let's say in late 384 CE and the family moved to Brittany early in 385 CE St Patrick could have been born in Brittany in 385 CE. In either case, whether he was born in Brittany or moved there from Scotland with his family when he was an infant, St Patrick would have grown up knowing Brittany as his homeland.

The deep sea of legend and traditions surrounding St Patrick is one in which storms of controversy have always gathered and no doubt will continue to do so. At the same time, our new theory of origins for St Patrick is very inclusive, because Scotland, Wales, Brittany and Ireland all had an important part to play in St Patrick's biography and the places and events that shaped his life and destiny.

At an earlier stage in this enquiry, we reflected on the power of maps to change and shape our world view. The same basic principle applies with regard to history. The way history has been recorded has affected our understanding not only of the past but also of ourselves, the roots of our heritage and religious identity. After the ancient

---

[323] The Latin phrase: *& mater etiam praedictae prolis, nempe Conchessa*, can be translated 'the mother of the expected offspring, namely Conchessa'. Colgan, *Trias. Thau*, p. 220. Translated by John Luce.

Britons were crushed by the Anglo-Saxons between 450 and 550 CE many fled to Ireland, Brittany and parts of Wales; the places where Celtic Christianity was strong and survived longest.

Churches in these regions were targeted by Rome for supporting the teachings of Pelagius and maintaining Jewish traditions. The years following the death of Maximus and Martin witnessed the increasing influence of Jerome and Augustine in the Church. Those associated with early Gallic, Welsh and Irish monasticism were increasingly suspect and marginalised.

Severus records that for the last sixteen years of his life, after the Priscillian controversy, St Martin avoided the company of diocesan bishops and refused to attend Church synods. This was the time of the real St Patrick, not the 'virtual' St Patrick of later legends and tradition.

Tensions and differences between the monks of St Martin and diocesan clergy continued, long after Martin's death. Martin was a very popular figure, especially among the people in Gaul and the Church recognised this when his body was interred in the cathedral at Tours and his shrine became a popular place of pilgrimage. However, this did not take place until the Council of Tours in 461 CE, more than fifty years after St Martin's death. Those intervening years were crucial, for they witnessed a dramatic increase in the authority and influence of diocesan structures and the Roman Church in Gaul.

St Germanus and Pope Celestine were key players at this stage in history, who acted to safeguard the interests of Rome. They were both very loyal supporters of the teachings of St Augustine.

If St Patrick's family had migrated to Brittany and had close family ties to Conan and Maximus and if Patrick had received spiritual formation and training at first with St Martin and then with a marginalised religious group in Brittany, then it is not surprising that St Patrick and his family may have come into conflict with these emerging diocesan authorities and their political allies. How closely St Patrick may or may not have been associated with those who were being ostracised by the Church in the fifth century has yet to be fully determined. This period is not called the Dark Ages in Europe without reason.

There are very few lights to guide us along this stretch of the highway of history. There is so much about St Patrick's story that is uncertain and will always remain a mystery but this should not prevent us from searching for the historical truth. St Patrick's life and our lives, his story and our story are inextricably intertwined and too important to be avoided or ignored.

In his *Confession*, St Patrick writes as though he had already parted company with the Church in Brittany or Gaul that may have originally supported him and some of the 'seniors' of that church had now parted company with him. His decision not to leave Ireland to defend himself further against the charges made against him suggests that he was determined to follow what he understood to be the guidance of God and his own conscience in relation to his calling and mission. St Patrick made this decision based on a deep sense of personal ethics and a spiritual calling that came to him directly from God.

He chose to remain in Ireland for the rest of his life, to continue with the ministry he believed God had entrusted to him, completely committed to those he had been called to serve.

One of the greatest unknowns about St Patrick's biography concerns the circumstances in which he died. When Patrick wrote the *Confession* he was sound of mind, but he strongly suspected that his own death was close at hand.

We will probably never know how or why he died, whether from old age and natural causes, or for some other reason.

Professor Charles Thomas presents a strong case to suggest that the influence of Palladius and the duration of his official, Papal mission to Ireland (which began in 431 CE) was far more extensive than previously acknowledged especially in Leinster and the south east of Ireland, and that the Armagh Movement in the seventh century tried to minimise his success, by whisking him off to Scotland for an untimely and sudden death amongst the Picts. Thomas is certain that 'by the eighth century, almost without exception, all and any records of Palladius had been misappropriated to St Patrick'.[324]

---

[324] Charles Thomas, 'Palladius and Patrick' in *The Island of Saint Patrick* (Dublin, 2003), p. 26.

In the fusion of records for Patrick and Palladius – *The Two Patricks* – could it be possible that in this case it happened the other way around, and that a record of St Patrick's sudden and untimely death in Scotland among the Picts has been transferred to Palladius by the Armagh hagiographers?

In the circumstances prevailing at that time, taking into account the serious nature of his conflict with Coroticus and Patrick's deep distress and concern for those female converts who had been taken captive and sold into slavery and prostitution among the Picts, it is possible that St Patrick may have gone to Scotland in one final attempt to secure their release and died a martyr's death.

It is impossible for us to imagine what life was like in the fifth century, the beginning of those so-called 'Dark Ages' in Europe, yet there is something deeply mysterious and enduring about Patrick's story, the light in his soul which captures the imagination and touches the heart.

For St Patrick, Christian faith was a real adventure that required complete commitment and total disclosure of the heart before God, with renunciation of personal glory, wealth and social status and a willingness to face great dangers in a country where the old religion was strong and violence was common.

St Patrick was the great adventurer, a pioneering apostle in Ireland, beyond the known boundaries of the civilized world. He was prepared to boldly go where none had gone before and encouraged others to follow him and risk all for the promise of salvation. Patrick holds such a special place in the hearts and minds of many people not only because he was Ireland's great apostle but because he was the last of the apostles, taking the Gospel to the ends of the earth at the very beginning of those Dark Ages when Europe was in great turmoil following the collapse of the Roman Empire.

Novelist and religious poet D.H. Lawrence catches the sense of adventure which characterised Patrick's approach to the spiritual life and was so typical of those like him who embraced Christian faith as if it was the greatest adventure of all time. His words catch something of the spirit of those days and perhaps also a part of the reality of our own times when he says:

When Rome collapsed, Europe was a dark ruin. Wolves howled in the deserted streets. Then those whose souls were still alive withdrew together and gradually built monasteries and convents, little communities of quiet labour and courage. Helpless, yet never overcome in a world flooded with devastation. These alone kept the human spirit from disintegration, from going quite dark, in the Dark Ages. These men and women made the Church, which made Europe...

The flood of barbarism rose and covered Europe from end to end. But bless your life there was Noah in the Ark with all the animals. There was young Christianity. There were the lonely, fortified monasteries, little arks floating and keeping the adventure afloat. There is no break in the great adventure in human consciousness. Throughout the howlingest deluge, a few brave souls were steering the Ark under the rainbow.

If I had lived in the year 400, pray God, I should have been one of them. I would have been a true and passionate Christian, the Adventurer. But now I live in 1934 and the Christian adventure is dead. We must all begin afresh on a new adventure towards God.[325]

Patrick's life epitomised the best of Christian discipleship, at a time when Christianity was considered to be a real adventure. Of all that we can say about St Patrick and thank him for, what cannot be denied is that he was a profoundly honest, courageous, deeply faithful and very spiritual person who sacrificed much in the service of others. During the course of his life, Patrick experienced great dangers and difficulties, but destiny now carried him to the threshold of Heaven. St Patrick is one of the greatest of saints and deserves to be remembered for who he really was. Whatever trauma he may have carried from the past, Patrick had found peace in his own heart and with God.

As the days of his mortal life drew to a close, St Patrick knew he was moving inexorably closer to the paradise he so strongly believed in and deeply longed for, clearly sensing God's presence, anticipating glory and fully prepared for death. His faith was so complete that he knew in his heart the adventure would continue. St Patrick strongly believed that death was not the end; it was just the beginning of an even greater adventure and more mysterious journey.

---

[325] D. H. Lawrence, *Letters*, 1934.

When he chose those final words that end his *Confession*, Patrick knew he was entering that mystic, sacred place, the proverbial 'thin place' where earth and heaven seem to meet and there is a sense that God is not far away. He could sense he was standing on the edge of a glory that is not of this world. However much he might have wanted to hold on, St Patrick understood the time had come to let go. And even though there is so much more of St Patrick's story that remains to be told, the time has come for us to let go too.

May the Blessing of God and St Patrick always be with you.

A POSSIBLE CHRONOLOGY

FOR SAINT PATRICK

384:	Patrick's family move from Scotland to Brittany.
385:	Patrick is born in Brittany (possibly at Tours *(Nemthor / Naem-Tour)* or on the Family estate at Bannavem Tiburniae.
401:	Patrick is taken captive from Brittany.
407:	Patrick escapes from slavery in Ireland.
407-411:	Patrick is trained at St Martin's Monastery.
411-420:	Patrick undertakes religious and spiritual formation with 'barefoot hermits' in the Isles of the Tyrrhene Sea, near Mont St Michel.
420-427:	Patrick continues formation on these islands.
428:	Patrick is ordained by St Senior on Mont St Michel and commissioned for the Mission to Ireland.
428:	Patrick returns to Ireland as an Apostle.
429:	St Germanus sent to Britain by Pope Celestine.
431:	Palladius sent to Ireland by Pope Celestine as part of the first official mission from Rome (Prosper's Chronicle).
432:	Traditional date given in the Irish annals for the beginning of Patrick's mission in Ireland.
460:	Patrick writes his Letter to Coroticus.
460-461:	Patrick writes The Confession.
461:	Traditional date for St Patrick's death.

HISTORICAL BACKGROUND

307	Constantine Chlorus becomes Emperor in Britain.
314	Constantine the Great, son of Constantine Chlorus, becomes Emperor of Rome.
323	Birth of St Martin.
336	Athanasius, exiled in Gaul, founds monastery at Trier.
357	Publication of St Athanasius' *Life of Antony*.
360	Hilary helps Martin (aged 37) found monastery at Liguge.
380	Maximus invited to marry Helen or Ellen, daughter of Eudes (Eudav Hen) a king of the ancient Britons.
383	Maximus declared 'king' and Emperor by the Roman Legions in Britain under his command.
383	Rebellion of Magnus Maximus. British Legions cross to Gaul landing at Aleth (St Malo) and the mouth of the Rhine, attacking on two fronts. Maximus takes over the imperial palace at Trier as a centre for his command. Valentinian flees, Gratian killed in Paris.
383	Maximus becomes Emperor of the West, in a treaty with Theodosius, Emperor of the East and is recognised by Sulpitius Severus as 'king'. Martin lobbies Maximus in support of the Priscillians.
384	Calpurnius leaves Strathclyde in Northern Britain and follows Conan to Brittany as part of the settlement under the new Emperor.
385	Birth of St Patrick (?)
385	Queen Helen (Ellen) wife of Magnus Maximus meets St Martin and becomes a devoted servant.
385	St Augustine converts to Christianity.
385	Conan made king of Bretagne, Duke of Armorican Tract.

388	Martin warns Maximus that Valentinian is plotting to kill him.
388	In Brittany, Conan marries St Patrick's sister, Darerca.
393	Paulinas of Nola and his wife take vow of continence.
393	Conversion of Sulpitius Severus to asceticism.
393	Sulpitius Severus visits Martin (aged 70) at Marmoutier.
393	St Augustine writes the '*Confessions*'. Severus writes a *Life of Martin*.
397	Death of St Martin, 11th November.
397	Irish King Niall of the Nine Hostages raids Brittany.
400	Patrick, aged 16, taken captive from Bannavem Tiburniae.
402	Alternative date given for St Martin's death. Also 405.
405	Pelagius travels to Rome and North Africa to challenge St Augustine.
405	Roman legions leave Britain, enter Gaul to defend Rome. On 31st December the River Rhine freezes again at Mainz in Germany. Barbarians cross in vast numbers and rampage through Gaul. Thousands killed. Parts of Gaul become a 'wasteland'. Patrick escapes from Ireland, returns by ship to Brittany.
407	Patrick joins St Martin's community at Marmoutier for four years and is trained and tonsured there.
410	August 29th, Alaric enters the Salesian Gates in Rome.
410	Patrick leaves St Martin's monastery. Joins a community of 'barefoot hermits' in the 'Isles of the Tyrrhene Sea' located off the coast of north-east Brittany. Undertakes spiritual formation there for nine years.
411	Augustine and Jerome write and campaign strongly against the 'heresies' of Pelagius and Priscillian.
420	Death of Conan in Brittany. Pelagius is condemned and disappears.
421	Patrick 'sells his nobility' for the sake of others and is commissioned by St Senior on Mont St Michel. Returns to Ireland as an Apostle?

423   Darerca (Conan's widow) goes to Ireland to help her brother.

423   Grallon appointed king in Brittany. Marries Patrick's sister, Tigris.

429   St Germanus sent by Pope Celestine to Britain to combat 'the Pelagian Heresy'.

431   Palladius sent to Ireland by Pope Celestine as 'the first bishop to the Irish believing in Christ' (Prosper).

432   Traditional date given for St Patrick's arrival in Ireland.

459?   St Patrick writes his *Letter to Coroticus* of Strathclyde.

460?   St Patrick writes the '*Confession*'.

461   Traditional date given for St Patrick's death. Patrick disappears from all known historical and ecclesiastical records for the next two hundred years.

664   The Synod of Whitby. Wilfrid acts as spokesperson for Rome. The Kingdom of Northumbria accepts the authority of the Roman Church, regarding tonsure and the Easter cycle.

672   Wilfrid arranges for Dagobert II to marry Gizeles, Comptes de Razés. With Wilfrid's support, Dagobert is restored to the Merovingian throne in Gaul.

678   Dagobert's assassination. Wilfrid's God-daughter marries Gizeles de Razés (according to Lobineau's genealogy).

680   Anglo-Saxons take the Kingdom of Strathclyde and pose a real military threat to Ireland.

680   Muirchú writes a 'biography' of St Patrick. Civil war in Ireland between Romani and Hibernensi.

695   'The Donation of Constantine' is published in Rome.

697   Synod of Birr in Ireland. Roman Reforms accepted.

697   St Patrick is accepted as patron saint of all Ireland, founder of the Church in Armagh and is now officially recognised as Ireland's apostle.

720   King Nechtan of the Picts evicts Irish monks and then declares his kingdom-to be conformed with Rome.

780	Welsh Church conforms to Rome.
795	Vikings attack Ireland and Scotland.
800	Charlemagne crowned in Rome as the new Emperor.
1066	Battle of Hastings, the Normans takeover Britain.
1156	Norman Invasion of Ireland. The 'Romanisation' of Western Christendom is secured until the Reformation.

BIBLIOGRAPHY

d'Argentré, Bertrand, *Histoire de Bretagne* (Paris, 1618).

— *Abrégé de l'Histoire de Bretagne* (Paris, 1695).

Barbour, Philippe, *Cadogan Guide to Brittany* (London, 2008).

Le Baud, Pierre, *Histoire de Bretagne* (Paris, 1638).

Bede, *History of the English Church and People*, trans. Leo Sherley-Price (USA, 1980).

Bieler, Ludwig, *The Patrician Texts in the Book of Armagh* (Dublin, 2004).

— ed., *Four Latin Lives of St Patrick* (Dublin, 1971).

— *The Life and Legend of St Patrick* (Dublin, 1949).

— *The Works of St Patrick* (New York, 1952).

— 'The Problem of Silva Focluti', *Irish Historical Studies*, 3/12 (1943).

— *Clavis Patricii II: Libri Epistolarum Sancti Patricii Episcopi* (Dublin, 1993).

Binchy, D. A., 'Patrick and his Biographers', *Studia Hibernica*, 2 (1962).

Bizeul, *Memoire sur les Origins du Mont-St-Michel* (Paris, 1844).

Blanchet, A. 'Fouille du mur de l'ancienne ville Alet', *Bulletin Archéologique du Comité des travaux historique et scientifiques*, 25 (1908).

Blondel, Louis, *Notice Historique du Mont-St-Michel, de Tombelaine et d'Avrenches* (Avrenches, 1823).

Bonner, Gerald, *St Augustine of Hippo: Life and Controversies* (2002).

Brenot, C., 'Les monnaies romaines des fouille d'Alet', *Les Dossiers du centre regional d'archeologie d'Alet*, 2 (1974).

— 'Monnaies d'Alet', *Annales de Bretagne*, 76/1 (1969).

Bury, J. B., *The Life of St Patrick, His Place in History* (London, 1905).

Cahill, Thomas, *How the Irish Saved Civilization* (New York, 1995).

Camden, *Britannica* (Abridged, London, 1701).

Carew, Mairead, *Tara and the Ark of the Covenant* (Dublin, 2003).

Carney, James, *Studies in Irish Literature and History* (Dublin, 1979).

de Paor, Liam, *St Patrick's World* (Dublin, 1993).

de Paor, Marie, *Patrick: The Pilgrim Apostle of Ireland* (Dublin, 1998).

McCarthy, Dan, *The Irish Annals: Their Genesis and History* (Dublin, 2008).

McCarthy, Pádraig, trans., *My Name is Patrick* (Dublin, 2011).

Chadwick, Nora, *Age of the Saints in the Celtic Church* (Durham, 1960; facs. edn, Llanerch, 2006).

Charles-Edwards, T. M., *Early Christian Ireland* (Cambridge, 2000).

Chèvremont, Alexandre, *Les Mouvements du Sol sur les Côtes Occidentales de la France,* ed. E. Leroux (Paris, 1882).

Colgan, John, *Trias Thaumaturga*, ed. Eamonn De Burca (Dublin, 1977).

Commission Histoire de Skol Vreizh, *L'Histoire de la Bretagne et des Payes Celtique* (Morlaix, 1966).

Conneely, Daniel, *The Letters of St Patrick* (Maynooth, 1993).

Cope, Julian, *The Megalithic European* (London, 2004).

Cosgrave, B., ed., *The Life of Bishop Wilfrid by Eddius Stephanus* (Cambridge, 1985).

Ó Cróinín, Dáibhí, ed., *A New History of Ireland* (Oxford, 2005).

Cunningham, Bernadette, *The Annals of the Four Masters: Irish history, kingship and society in the early seventeenth century* (Dublin, 2010)

Cusack, M. F., *Life of St Patrick, Apostle of Ireland* (London, 1877).

Daru, P. A., *Histoire de Bretagne*, i (Paris, 1826).

Davies, Oliver, ed., *Celtic Spirituality* (New York, 1999).

Deric, Gilles, *Histoire Ecclésiastique de Bretagne*, ii (Paris, 1778).

— *Memoires Relatifs a L'Histoire de France* (Paris, 1835).

Desfontaines, Pierre François Guyot, *Histoire des Ducs de Bretagne,* i (Paris, 1739).

Desroches, Jean-Jacques, *Histoire du Mont St Michel*, i (Caen, 1838).

Doremet, Jacques, *L'Antiquité d'Aleth* (La Cane de Montfort, 1628).

— *De Antiquité de la Ville et cité d'Aleth, ou Quidalet*, ed. Thomas de Querci (St Malo, 1894; Slatkine Reprints, 1971).

Errman, Bart D., *Misquoting Jesus: The Story Behind Who Changed the Bible and Why* (New York, 2005).

Flemming, William, *Boulogne-Sur-Mer* (London, 1907).

Anon., trans., 'St Fiacc's Hymn', *Ecclesiastical Record* (1868), O'Curry MS, Catholic University.

Geoffrey of Monmouth, 'History of the Kings of Britain', in *Six Old English Chronicles*, trans. J.A. Giles and Aaron Thompson, (1848).

de Gerville, Charles, *Lettres sur la communication entre les Deux Bretagnes* (Valognes, 1844).

Gibbon, Edward, *Decline and Fall of the Roman Empire*, 8 vols (London, 1862).

Giles, J. A., *Six Old English Chronicles* (London, 1868).

Gregory of Tours, *History of the Franks*, trans. Lewis Thorpe (London, 1974).

Hanson, R. P. C., *St Patrick His Origins and Career* (Oxford, 1997).

Heather, Peter, *The Fall of the Roman Empire* (London, 2005).

Henry, René, *Au Péril de la Mer* (Paris, 2006).

Howlett, David, *Muirchú Moccu Mactheni's 'Vita Sancti Patricii'* (Dublin, 2006).

— *The Book of Letters of Saint Patrick the Bishop* (Dublin,1994).

— *Four Latin Lives of St Patrick,* (Dublin,1971)

Kenney, James, *The Sources for the Early History of Ireland: Ecclesiastical* (Dublin, 1997).

Langouet, L., 'La Forêt du Scissy et La marée de 709, Légende ou Réalité?' *Dossiers du Centre Régional d'Archéologie d'Alet*, 24 (1996).

— *Alet Ville Ancienne* (Rennes, 1973).

— 'L'Histoire d'Alet', *Dossiers du Centre Régional d'Archéologie d'Alet*, 2 (1974).

Lanigan, John, *Ecclesiastical History of Ireland*, 4 vols (Dublin, 1822; 2nd edn, Dublin, 1829).

Lappenberg, Johann Martin, *A History of England under the Anglo-Saxon Kings*, i, trans. Benjamin Thorpe (London, 1865).

Lobineau, G. A., *Histoire de Bretagne*, 2 vols (Paris, 1707).

MacDari, Conor, *The Bible: An Irish Book* (London, 2005).

Macnab, Duncan, *Archaeological Dissertation on the Birthplace of St Patrick* (Dublin, 1865).

MacNeill, Eoin, *Saint Patrick, Apostle of Ireland* (London, 1934).

— 'Silua Focluti', *Proceedings of the Royal Irish Academy, Section C: Archaeology, Celtic Studies, History, Linguistics, Literature*, 36 (1923).

Manet, Gilles, *De L'etat Ancien et De L'etat Actuel dans La Baie de Mont Saint Michel* (St Malo, 1829).

— 'Memoires Sur Les Origins du Mont St Michel', *Memoires de la Societé Royale des Antiq. De France*, 17 (1844).

Maury, Alfred, 'Observations sur Les Origins du Mont St Michel et en particulier sur l'existence de la Forêt de Scissy', *Memoires de la Societe Royale des Antiq. De France,* 17 (1844).

Milne, Kenneth, *Christ Church Cathedral: A History* (Dublin, 2000).

Mitchell, Dugald, *History of the Highlands and Gaelic Scotland* (Paisley, 1900).

Mohrman, Christine, *The Latin of St Patrick* (Dublin, 1961).

Molloy, Dara, *The Globalisation of God* (Inismor, 2009).

Moore, Thomas, *History of Ireland* (New York, 1835).

Morice, P. H., *Histoire de Bretagne*, 2 vols (Paris, 1742–6).

— *Memoires Pour Server de Preuves a L'Histoire de Bretagne*, 3 vols (Paris 1742–6).

Murphy, John, *The Life of St Patrick Apostle of Ireland* (Baltimore, 1853).

Nennius, 'History of the Britons: Historia Brittonum' in *Six Old English Chronicles*, ed. J. A. Giles (London, 1858).

O'Donnell, James, *The Ruin of the Roman Empire* (US, 2009).

O'Flaherty, Roderic, *Oxygia* (Dublin, 1775).

O'Hanlon, John, *Lives of the Irish Saints* (Dublin, 1875).

O'Leary, James, ed., *Ancient Lives of Saint Patrick* (New York, 1880), *Project Gutenberg* [ebook] <http://www.gutenberg.org/files/18482/18482-h/18482-h.htm> published online 1 June 2006.

O'Loughlin, Thomas, *Discovering St Patrick* (London, 2005). — *St Patrick: The Man and His Works* (London, 1999).

O'Neill, Patrick, 'The Identification of Foclut', *Journal of the Galway Archaeological and Historical Society*, 22/4 (1947).

O'Rahilly, Thomas, *The Two Patricks* (Dublin, 1942; repr. 1981).

Origine Gallo-Romaine de l'Eveche d'Alet, *Annals de la Societe d'Histoire et Archéologie de Saint Malo* 95, 1974.

Palgrave, Francis, *History of Normandy and Britain* (London, 1861).

Anon., *Life of St Patrick*, (Paris, 1870).

Poslan, M., *Cambridge Economic History of Europe* (Cambridge, 1966).

Pfister, J. G., 'Stray Leaves from the Journey of a Traveller in Search of Ancient Coins', *The Numismatic Chronicle and Journal of the Numismatic Society*, xix (London, 1857).

Probus, 'Life of St Patrick: Vita Auctore Probo' in *Four Latin Lives of St Patrick*, trans. Ludwig Bieler (Dublin, 1971).

'Histoire de Bretagne', *Foreign Quarterly Review*, xii, London, 1827.

Reeves, William, *The Culdees of the British Islands* (Dublin, 1864). Facsimile reprinted by Llanerch Publishers, Somerset, 1994.

Rio, Joseph, *Myths Fondateurs de la Bretagne, Aux Origins de la Celtomania* (Rennes, 2000).

Robidue, Bertrand, *Histoire et Panorama d'un Beau Pays* (Rennes, 1953).

De Roujoux, P. G. *Histoire des Rois et des Ducs de Bretagne* (Paris, 1828).

Rouze, Michel, *La Forêt de Quokelunde* (Paris, 1953).

Ruault, L'Abbé, *Abrégé de l'Histoire des Solitaires de Scissy* (St Malo, 1734). de Saint-Pair, Guillaume, *Le Roman du Mont-Saint-Michel* (Caen, 1856).

Sulpitius Severus, 'Life of St Martin' in *The Nicene and Post Nicene*

Fathers, xi, eds Philip Schaff and Henry Wace (New York, 1894).

— 'Dialogues' in *The Nicene and Post Nicene Fathers*, xi, eds Philip Schaff and

Henry Wace (New York, 1894).

Skene, W. F., *Celtic Scotland* (Edinburgh, 1886).

Stephanus, Eddius, *Life of Wilfrid*, trans. J. F. Webb (London, 1986).

Stokes, Whitley, *Tripartite Life of St Patrick* (London, 1887).

— Anon., *Anecdota Oxoniensia* (Oxford, 1890), facs. edn trans. Whitley Stokes, as *Lives of the Saints from the Book of Lismore* (Somerset, 1990).

Sullivan, William, *Historical Causes and Effects from the Fall of the Roman Empire 476 to the Reformation 1517* (Boston, 1838).

Taylor, Jeremy, *Dreamwork* (New York, 1983).

Thierry, Augustin, *History of the Norman Conquest* (London, 1847).

Thomas, Charles, *Christianity in Roman Britain to AD 500* (Berkeley and Los Angeles, 1981).

Thompson, E.A., 'Procopius on Brittia and Britannia', *The Classical Quarterly*, New Series, 30/2 (1980).

Todd, J. H., *St Patrick, Apostle of Ireland* (Dublin, 1864).

Tourault, Philippe, *Les Rois de Bretagne IVème–XIXème Siècle* (Paris, 2005).

de Saint-Luc, P. Toussaint, 'Histoire de Conan' in *Dissertation Historique sur L'Origins des Bretons*, i (Paris, 1739).

de Saint-Pair, Guillaume, *Le Roman du Mont-Saint-Michel* (Caen, 1856).

Trébutien, Guillaume-Stanislas, *Le Mont St Michel au Peril de la Mer* (Caen, 1841).

Tukner, J.H., 'An Inquiry as to the Birthplace of St Patrick', *Archaeologica Scottica*, v (1890).

Turner, Sharon, *The History of the Anglo-Saxons* (London, 1852).

Ussher, James, *A Discourse on the Religion Anciently Professed by the Irish and the British* (London, 1631).

Viel, Joseph, *La Gouesnière et Bonaban (*Livre Histoire, 2011)

Villemarque, *La Legende Celtique* (Paris, 1864).

Wallace, J. M., *Chronicle of Fredegar* (Oxford, 1960).

Wenzler, Claude, *Genealogies of the Kings of France* (Rennes, 2010).

William of Malmesbury, *The Kings before the Norman Conquest*, trans. Joseph Stevenson (Somerset, 1989).

— *The Antiquities of Glastonbury*, trans. Frank Lomax (Somerset, 1992).

Williams, Hugh, trans., *Two Lives of Gildas by a monk of Ruys and Caradoc of Llancarfan* (Cymmrodorion Series, 1899; facs. edn Llanerch, 1990).

Kaiser, Ward and Denis Wood, *Seeing through Maps: the Power of Images to Shape our World View* (Massachusetts, 2001).

Woods, Richard, *The Spirituality of the Celtic Saints* (New York, 2000).

White, N. J., *Translation of the Latin Writings of St Patrick* (London, 1918).

Wylie, J. A., *History of the Scottish Nation* (London, 1887).

Zimmer, Heinrich, *The Celtic Church in Britain and Ireland* (London, 1902).

CHARTS AND ANNALS

Chart of Roman Roads, *Statistique Monumentale du Department du pas De Calais* (Commission des Antiquities, 1840).

Annals of Ulster (AU), trans. Sean Mac Airt and Gearoid Mac Niocaill, Dublin Institute for Advanced Studies (Dublin,1983)

Annals of Tigernach, trans. Whitley Stokes, i, *Revue Celtique* 16 (1895); facsimile edition published by Llanerch, 1993.

Annals of Ireland by the Four Masters, 7 vols, de Burca (Dublin, 1990).

Annals of Inisfallen, trans. Sean Mac Airt (Dublin 1944 [1951]).

Celt: The Corpus of Electronic Texts (UCC)

[website]   http://www.ucc.ie/celt/published/T100004/index.html.

ABOUT THE AUTHOR

MARCUS LOSACK is a graduate in Theology from Christ's College, Cambridge and the Irish School of Ecumenics, Trinity College, Dublin and served in parishes in the U.K., Ireland, North Africa and Sicily. As Senior Lecturer and Course Director at St George's College in Jerusalem, he arranged visits to the ancient desert monasteries of Egypt and Sinai and other sacred and historical sites in the Holy Land. As Executive Director of Ceile De, an ecumenical organisation in Ireland that specialised in Pilgrimage and Study programs in Celtic Spirituality, he has arranged visits for adult and youth groups to ancient and sacred sites associated with the Celtic Tradition in Ireland, Britain and Brittany. Marcus has written three books on St Patrick. As an engaging and truly inspirational teacher and educationalist, he is deeply passionate about his subject. Marcus welcomes invitations to speak as a visiting lecturer or guest speaker for retreats, seminars and international conferences.

Other publications include: *St Patrick and the Bloodline of the Grail – the Untold Story of St Patrick's Royal Family* (Ireland, 2012); *The Letters of St Patrick* – An Historic New Translation (co-authored with John Luce (Ireland, 2013) and *Glendalough – A Celtic Pilgrimage*, co-authored with Fr Michael Rodgers (Columba Press, Dublin, 2011).

For further information and enquiries
please contact marcuslosack@gmail.com

Printed in Poland
by Amazon Fulfillment
Poland Sp. z o.o., Wrocław